May-20 '44 Lincoln Chri

M. A. Simonsen.

I WAS MADE A MINISTER

THE AUTHOR
Aged 72

I WAS MADE
A MINISTER

AN AUTOBIOGRAPHY

EDWIN   HOLT   HUGHES
A Bishop of The Methodist Church

A B I N G D O N
C O K E S B U R Y
New York • Nashville

SET UP, PRINTED, AND BOUND BY THE
PARTHENON PRESS AT NASHVILLE, TEN-
NESSEE, UNITED STATES OF AMERICA

To

MY TWO GRANDMOTHERS
ABIGAIL BENNETT HOLT
PHOEBE JONES HUGHES

CONTENTS

❧

INTRODUCTION

THE TITLE OF THIS VOLUME, "I WAS MADE A MINISTER," IS taken from Paul. The Church has given it a place in one of its rituals of ordination. I have therefore read it many times, and have heard it more times as the Epistle was given in the ordaining hour. From the beginning of my episcopal work the five words charmed and thrilled me. They seemed to be written in larger type. Though not printed in italics, they insisted on a peculiar emphasis. They were a part of a longer sentence, yet my tendency was to halt after the word "minister," as if there were a period there, or even a space that marked a paragraph. I had to be on guard lest the listeners in the service should think that my voice had failed, or that I had dropped into a forgetful abstraction. In more intense moments I imagined that I saw the Great Apostle looking up from his manuscript, and that I could hear him say, "I was made a minister."

The words took me captive because they touched the deeper places of my nature. If the proprieties had permitted, I could have said, "I am now doing my part in making a minister." Then I would have added, "I was made one myself." All my life bore in that ministerial direction. I had the experiences of a parsonage in childhood so that I might bear them forward into other years. Forced changes from one college to another meant that I was being carried onward to a clerical career. This was

1

not all of my own choosing. There were a few years in which the thought of the ministry was almost a torture. Yet the actual decades have given me a commentary on the way in which hate can change to love. While I do not sympathize with the overdone counsel, "Do not enter the ministry if you can help it," I still declare that I have had no religious experience more definite than my call to preach. I put this statement into no Calvinistic form. God does not cancel free agency in a summons to the ministry any more than he cancels it in the summons to salvation. Though not irresistible, my ministerial life has never ceased to be a "calling."

I may add the further statement that I have been only the "minister" that "I was made." All my life has run in that sacred groove. Nothing else has tempted me. Meager starts towards magazine writing, with generous fees, frightened me, lest I should be diverted. I have had no desire to follow the example of clerical acquaintances who have allowed literature to crowd out sermonizing. I have avoided luring sidetracks as if they would lead me away from the City of Life. Such lectures as I have delivered had homiletical origins. If I have not always followed John Wesley's advice about being "a man of one book," I have certainly been a man of one work. If I had tried to relate in these pages only the nonministerial things in my experiences, the resulting manuscript would have been a slender thing. The justification of this book is, "I was made a minister," and I have not been made anything else. I have seen days when I mourned over the imperfections of my work, Sunday evenings when I would scarcely have been surprised if my office-bearers had told me that I was an unfruitful servant. But I have never known an hour when I would not say in solemn joy, "I was made a minister."

This is the apology for the title. What is the apology

for the book itself? Autobiographies call for an explanation. Their Introductions usually contain paragraphs of
justification. There is the fear that people may think
that the book is an effort of the man to give himself an
encore. A further fear is that the author may be deemed
the chief applauder among those who demand a literary
reappearance. It is customary to explain an autobiography by affirming that many persons have demanded its
writing. Sometimes this excuse is given in such terms
as to create the impression that a clamor overcame reluctance and made the record of one's own life a case of
conscience.

The stimulus of this book is not so vigorous as that. Yet
those who have said that my memory should command my
pen have been men of such judgment as would conquer
minor hesitations. So far, also, as my Church has had an
official voice, authorized to call for the making of books,
that solo counsel has led the chorus of persuasion. If,
then, this volume is not written in response to a clamor,
it is still true that it is written out of respect for influential
advisers.

My own reluctance has had several causes, the first
being that I have recently read autobiographies which did
not exalt the recorded careers. This may have been due
to the fear of self-glorification, or to hasty writing; or because the lives, while successful in their general trend,
had not secured a vigorous relation to great issues. I
recall one such volume that I put aside with the distinct
regret that it had been written.

There was a greater reluctance. The question was: Is the
career worthy of printed record? Does the man who feels
that his own life demands a book have a right to be classed
among the meek? Several current autobiographies gave
the impression that their authors were the heirs of all the
ages in the foremost files of time. When a man indicates

that he is determined not to leave himself unsuggested, or appears about as humble as the Washington Monument, he assumes risks. It is precarious to take one's own history as a text and one's own self as one's own hero. Yet friendly persuaders have convinced me that my life in its providential breadth, so far as geography was concerned; in its providential meaning, so far as causes were involved; and in its providential significance, so far as Methodist Union has been realized, called for what might be designated as the personal minutes of my soul's meetings.

This volume is not correctional. An example of this type of self-analysis is H. G. Wells's *Experiment in Autobiography*. It contains an advertisement of a revised life— a statement of withdrawal from the Fabian groups of Socialism; a self-accusing rejection of his confirmation in the Church of England; and a denial of the touches of faith that appeared in *Mr. Britling Sees It Through* and *God, the Invisible King*. The Britling book confessed a glimmering belief in God to which an imaginary character had been driven by the sorrows of war. The Invisible King volume presented a considerably reduced Deity and indicated an attempt to ungod the Lord! A witty English paragrapher put it,

> The new theology by Wells is stated,
> God is, but has been greatly exaggerated.

But the Autobiography banishes even the attenuated Less-than-Almighty. On completing the story one feels that Mr. Wells has pushed some things out of the door and thrown other things out of the window, and that the rooms of his life appear to the author to be still plentifully furnished only because the house has shrunk.

This volume is not one of retraction, or a confession that the main centers of life have been shifted. The years

4

have confirmed the things which an early dedication espoused. A break with the Christian faith and with the Christian ministry would be the final insincerity. I can humbly adopt Paul's statement, "I am persuaded." Indeed, as I review my own reasons and emotions, I find in myself what I have found in other men—that a reputation for conservatism comes not because advanced positions have been abandoned, but because the emphases have been moved to the essentials. I cannot think of any progressive ideas, adopted in my earlier days, that I have repudiated. But I no longer think it necessary to defend the evolutionary theory, or to prove that there are two Isaiahs, or to discuss before weary audiences the more vital theory of Biblical inspiration. Holding still to the so-called critical views of an ongoing Classroom, I have prepared my lessons for the Pulpit. I still believe in the documentary theory of the Pentateuch; but I believe, too, that God has appointed me as one of his modern Redactors!

This means, of course, that the ambition of preaching has changed. So-called liberals confess that this process has been theirs. The earlier achievements were satisfying; the latter achievements were more so. To me, at least, they have been so unexpected as to make life a surprise. Such Napoleonic dreams as I, being a normal boy, may have had, moved into a different realm when I was converted. If the ambition of Christ for a redeemed world captures a man, the minor visions are caught up into its meaning.

There are, also, other surprises. I recall how startled I was when, as a preparatory student, I entered a declamation contest and received "honorable mention." When, in my first pastorate on Iowa's prairies, I had a considerable ingathering of souls, I found it hard to credit the spiritual drama unfolding before my eyes. When I won oratorical contests in my senior year in college, I was fearful that a mistake had been made in the grading. When I went from the seminary to my beautiful suburban church, I wondered whether the bishop would not recall the appointment. When, four years later, I was assigned to the pastorate of a great church in New England, it required months for me to realize that the experience was real. When I was elected president of DePauw University, the word reached me at 2:00 A.M. on April 1. I queried whether someone was not victimizing me by the type of joke customary on that date! I do not overstate when I declare that my years have brought me a procession of surprises. Often I have been compelled to say to God, "Thy mercies are new every morning, and fresh every evening."

It was thus with my call to the episcopacy. When, in 1907, some prophesied that the next General Conference would elect me, I smiled at such anticipations. I did not believe that the Church would break a precedent held for sixty years and choose so young a man. When the election came, I was dazed. As dear and splendid Bishop McDowell went suddenly out of this life, I was startled by the statement of a colleague that God was calling me to special leadership in Methodist reunion. The kindly tributes given on my retirement from official duties were the most surprising. Even the demand of thoughtful men for this autobiography was unexpected. Bishops have had journals—as Asbury had. Bishops have had biographers—as Bishop Simpson had in Dr. Crooks, and Bishop Quayle had in Dr. Rice. But an episcopal autobiography! In my knowledge of Methodist history there has been no such thing. Why should I be so bold as to be the pioneer?

I presume, however, that an autobiography is no more an evidence of conceit than a journal is. Allan Nevins, doubtless as successful a biographer as the present period has, declares that the ideal sources are diaries—and the current files of newspapers. On this twofold basis my biographer would be helpless. There are no diaries. The patience of the personal chronicle has not been mine. Nor would the newspapers give much assistance. Where a man has prided himself, rightly or wrongly, on dealing with eternal themes rather than with current events, the public press does not give him large space.

Once letter writing offered source material—as Theodore Roosevelt's letters to his children, Phillips Brooks's letters to his friends and relatives, and Henry Adams' letters to his limited intellectual circle would indicate. But literary letter writing is no longer abundant. Even the formal ending, "Your most obedient and humble servant," has been condensed into "Yours truly"—often with the pronoun abbreviated. The investigation of plenteous files of correspondence, when retirement comes, shows how few letters have claim to preservation. Months of toil are disposed of in moments of clearance. The rubbish piles become the only archives.

It follows that the material for a described life is often so personal and portable as to compel autobiography. This gives another subtle suggestion. Some say that the success of the biographer depends upon his likeness to his subject. Boswell had many of the characteristics of Johnson—his attractive vanity, and his desire for association with renowned persons. If this general principle has some warrant, then an argument appears for autobiography. A man is more like himself than any other person is like the man. The offset is that one is so near oneself that one cannot see oneself. The eyes cannot behold each other save by a reflection. We can see only small parts of our own faces—and the slight looks are not reassuring. The biographer depends upon direct vision; the autobiographer is compelled to depend upon the looking

7

glass. He may go away and straightway forget what man-ner of man he is.

The protection comes from a deliberate training in the art of abstracting one's self from oneself. If there is a split personality that is perilous, there is also a split per-sonality that is beneficial. The seventh of Romans passes into the eighth of Romans because Paul becomes ac-quainted with Paul and sees the need for a Unifier of life. The Psalmist's prayer, "Cleanse thou me from secret faults," shows his faith that he has found One who can reveal secret faults even to the secretor. The truth of an autobiography will much depend upon a writer's power to interview himself impartially and accurately.

There is a social side to an autobiography. It must have a lonely author, but the record is not worth writing if he has been lonely in his living. He has had companions. Thackeray makes Esmond say concerning his own journal that, if certain matters had been recorded in the propor-tions they had held in actual life, the resulting autobiog-raphy would have been "such a diary of folly and driveling, raptures and rage, as no man of ordinary vanity would like to leave behind him." One recent autobiography is brutally frank. Old friends, no longer on earth, were either maligned or so slightly praised as to be put at a discount. John Quincy Adams' journal won the dreadful title, "a treasury of damnations." An autobiography pub-lished while its author still lives may be lured toward a kindness which forbids the tearing down of other men's pedestals in order that the man may secure doubtful ma-terials for his own. At any rate this autobiographer is venturing to dwell on the earth with his own book, for a season. Let me add that the law of brevity has often made it necessary to apply a relative clause to a man who de-serves a page.

So the reason of this volume may be extracted from the

above paragraphs. I have no faint hope that I am writing an immortal record. Yet, believing that as an immortal person I have been allied to eternal causes, I shall write with a frank simplicity that avoids on the one side delusions of grandeur and on the other side delusions of insignificance. Caesar's *pars quorum eram* comes into the pages—yet so as to emphasize the *pars* and the *quorum* and to omit, as the great commentator did, the word *ego*. In a recent amazing volume about the members of a wonderful family who often lived in the palace of the scornful and who, partly because of this, frequently missed affection and met defeat, the author explains many failures by saying that the able men never learned how to pass from "I" to "We." I think that I partly mastered that lesson; and I trust that these pages may give loving salutations to my colaborers, and, most of all, to that Master who once said that severed from him we could do nothing.

As to the *ego* side of the case, another word might be written. George Bernard Shaw, in the lengthy Introduction to the republishing of one of his earliest books, *The Irrational Knot,* jocularly stated that he disclaimed responsibility because there remained no physical atom that his body possessed when the pages had been penned. He declared that if the physiologists were right in their scientific insistence that the body changes wholly in approximately eight years, there had been a series of utterly different Shaws in the decades. How could the present one be given credit for the excellencies or given debit for the defects of that distant literary output? Under this theory, which Shaw himself could not have held seriously, the writer of this autobiography has had more than "nine lives," the usual number for another species! Yet there abides a sense of unity—a feeling that an identity, however changing, has presided over the stream of consciousness and over the series of events. The older man and the younger man have been bound together in an inexorable unity. The different tenements have seen the dweller change, but they have not made him another. In the assurance that the person is one and so has gathered the years to himself until they are one, he now records them as offered to Christ the Unifier. This review is itself sent forth in the trust that he who has blessed the child, the youth, the man may now bless the book which tells the story as a prelude to entries in the Book of Life.

CHAPTER I

FAMILY

THE EXPERT IN GENEALOGY REMAINS WITH US. HE HAS A wide domestic range. As each person has two parents, four grandparents, eight great-grandparents, and sixteen great-great-grandparents, and the number doubles for each further generation, the options are many. Persecuted in one person, he may flee to another. A fee paid for diligent research may produce a family tree loaded with the fruit of pride.

I

My own boasting covers a short history. The knowledge of ancestry halts with the third generation. My great-grandfather on the paternal side was Robert Hughes. He is a dim figure for us all. A part of the Welsh tide of immigration held up among the Blue Ridge Mountains, he spent his days as a hillside farmer. My own father had a faint memory of him, but my boyish questioning elicited slight information. There is a tradition that Elizabeth Hughes, my great-grandmother, was one of Francis Asbury's first converts in western Virginia. If this is true, she must have had a sturdy independence that shrank not from relations with a religious group then ridiculed and frequently ostracized.

II

My grandfather, Francis Tincher Hughes, I recall distinctly. He was a bearded and severe person who did not seem to know that he had drawn a prize in the second

11

generation. My tiny attempts at intimacy availed nothing. I returned from each visit with the feeling that he did not care much for me. He made no profession of religion and joined no church. My one fierce remembrance resulted from his forbidding me to make a dam across a slender stream near the rural home. He feared that I might flood the hillsides. So he stopped the young beaver decisively. When I think of what the Croton and Roosevelt reservoirs have meant for our native land, I wonder whether my forebear was justified in nipping the bud of a promising engineering career. My tender remembrance came at the close of my last visit, when my father besought him to come to the Saviour, while my grandfather wept pitifully but seemed unable to cross the line of confession.

III

My grandmother, Phoebe Jones Hughes, was different. I can still see her extended arms, hear her quaint mountain phrases as she invited affection, catch the tunes of the hymns that she sang so devoutly, see the glowing pride that she had in her splendid preacher-son. When she died amid her hills, my father was informed by a delayed letter. I can see him sitting in the parsonage as he carried the tokens of tearful sorrow. I slipped into his room several times each day, but I knew not how to give him comfort. I had long seen that he had canonized his mother and had given her the loftiest place in his gallery of saints.

IV

Of the Holt ancestry my knowledge is scarcely larger. The record stops with John Holt, my great-grandfather. He was a soldier in the Revolutionary War, coming from Norfolk, Virginia. There is still a street in that city named for the family. When independence had been won, and John Holt had returned to his regular pursuits, he was called out with his company by George Washington and sent to help in putting down the Whisky Rebellion. His descendants have frequently engaged in similar crusades. He settled with a kindly family near Uniontown, Pennsylvania, spending his life there, while several sons moved into western Virginia. He was an earnest Methodist. He often taught school. His only letter that I have seen was sent to one of his children—being mainly an answer to an inquiry about a complicated problem in algebra. He works it out to the correct solution. This leads me to doubt whether I am his descendant.

V

My grandfather was Matthew Holt, one of several sons of the Colonial soldier. He died in the year of my birth. My mother adored her father and, perhaps in daughterly preference, insisted that I resembled him. A painting of him shows a noble head and a strong and stern face. The family declared that he carried authority with him so that he seldom used verbal commands. Knowing his will, his children acknowledged his unspoken calls. My father affirmed that in his knowledge of Methodist doctrine, law, ritual, history, Matthew Holt was the best-versed layman he had ever met. A letter written by him when the antislavery debate was rending the Church shows remarkable sagacity. Until the War of 1861-65 wrought its dreadful effects along the border, Matthew Holt was supposed to be wealthy. But the devastations of the strife and family lawsuits that came after the war depreciated the estate toward zero. The widow and children were left in the village of Glenville, West Virginia, practically without patrimony.

13

VI

The Holts are a vigorous group. One of them, the
Hon. Homer A. Holt, a second cousin of my mother, was
recently governor of West Virginia. The one son of
Matthew Holt who survived for a full life, Dr. Matt S.
Holt, who practiced medicine at my mother's birthplace,
Weston, West Virginia, for more than sixty years, was
an intense radical, beginning his rebellion against all
standing orders when he was five years old. An agnostic
in religion, a socialist in politics, and a candidate for both
governorship and senatorship in his native state, he
created a debating society on street corners and by fire-
sides. His son, the Hon. Rush Dew Holt, was elected to
the United States Senate ere he was thirty years of age.
I record my affectionate admiration for my uncle, and
my faith in the political honesty of his distinguished son.

VII

Grandmother Holt belonged to the Bennett family—
people of much force and often of considerable wealth.
Her brother, the Hon. Jonathan Bennett, was related to
the Confederate Treasury and was for a time a member of
the national House of Representatives. He gave to Stonewall Jackson one of the letters that secured entrance for
the military genius to West Point. One of his sons, the
Hon. Lewis Bennett, my mother's first cousin, was once
a candidate for the governorship of West Virginia, while
a grandson who died in the World War has a memorial
window in Westminster Abbey. A letter from my great-
grandfather Bennett to my grandmother indicates she was
regarded one of the reigning "beauties" of the period.

VIII

My grandmother, Abigail Bennett Holt, was deeply
religious. Her singing moved my young heart with the
14

sense of spiritual melody. I thought her a beautiful woman, and a more beautiful character. Her love never failed me; and my visits with her were events of affection. After she went away to heaven, her place was taken by her two daughters—Aunt Laura Holt Doyle, early widowed; and Aunt Margaret Holt, a domestic saint who became partial mother to all the nieces and nephews, especially to the orphaned children of her lovely sister, Rebecca Holt Wiant. My grandmother's death brought my first poignant sorrow. When the word reached me, I, who had been a stranger to grief, discovered the meaning of the pillow bedewed with tears. All night long I wept without restraint. Now, after more than fifty years, whenever I read Paul's tribute to Lois, the grandmother of Timothy, my heart travels to the village where my grandmother dwelt. I hear again her kindly voice. I see again the lovely wrinkles of her face. I rest again in her unfailing affection.

IX

Such were the backgrounds of my parents. My father, Thomas Bayless Hughes, was born in 1836 in a log cabin in Fayette County, then in Virginia. Those hill regions offered little opportunity for education. Three months per year were fairly long school terms. Youth lived, and fished and hunted in the free air of the mountains. Emphasis was laid upon the prowess of bodily strength. My father was tall, agile, red-headed, accurate of finger upon the gun's trigger, and swift of foot. He was the champion short-distance runner of two counties, never defeated in the hundred-yard dash. He had little more technical schooling than Abraham Lincoln received. He was seventeen ere he saw the miracle of a railway train.

Like Lincoln, he pursued informal education. At nineteen he came to definite religious experience. For a

15

time he was a member of a Baptist church. But in the theological debate that was then intense he was not satisfied with the Calvinistic God, nor could he sanction a fence builded around the altar of Holy Communion. Following these convictions, for many months he walked seven miles to a Methodist church set amid the hills. When in 1855 his purpose was fixed toward the Christian ministry, he joined another candidate in renting a cabin; proceeded to keep house, cook, and study for two years; dug ginseng root for the medical market; and in 1857 passed the examinations and was received on trial in what later became the West Virginia Conference.

The two years had been spent with solid books, in company with grammar and dictionary. He learned something of Hebrew and Greek. He pored over the standards of his church, perused Butler's *Analogy,* read Wesley's *Sermons,* studied Adam Clarke's *Commentary,* relished Watson's *Institutes,* and devoured Fletcher's *Checks to Antinomianism.* He was a purist in speech. I cannot recall that I ever heard him mispronounce a word or misconstruct a sentence in an address or sermon. His home became a school. When company was not present no blunder in language was permitted to go without correction. It was a boresome process, grievous at times, but afterward bringing forth the good fruit of precision. He preached as pastor and presiding elder for more than fifty years. I yield to no mere filial partiality when I say that he never failed in any assigned task. Whether in the West Virginia Conference or in the Iowa—now the Iowa–Des Moines—he not only wore, through fifty active years and nearly ten years of retirement, the flower of a blameless life, but carried the banner of a holy crusade.

He had the combination of mind and heart that made him an evangelist. He was logical, without coldness; earnest, without fanaticism; direct, without cheapness; appealing, without artificiality. When I say that he received thousands of people into the Church, I mean precisely that. In his earlier ministry his revival services sometimes swept whole communities into the confession of Christ. His iron constitution endured the strain of very "protracted meetings." All down the way of my own long ministry I have met in many states the men and women who found the altar of grace through my father's ministry.

If I were to estimate his preaching, I would say that one lack was the sense of humor. He was a hearty laugher, but he did not originate humor because he made no study of the laws of exaggeration and incongruity. He did not cultivate imagination. He was not a reader of novels, and he seldom indulged in poetry. I can recall but two pieces of fiction that he read—*Uncle Tom's Cabin* and, in later years, Sheldon's *In His Steps*. Both of these were in reality tracts. Harriet Beecher Stowe's novel, *The Minister's Wooing*, scandalized him. He would have regarded the reading of *Robert Elsmere*, or *John Ward, Preacher*, as worse than wasted time, but he read devotional books by the hour. While I watched him his lips would move in prayer. Often when I burst into his study I would find him on his knees. Then I would quietly close the door, go down the stairway softly, and move into the outdoors as a refuge against soberness.

He had an amazing independence. Though he had great respect for the Baptists, and for their service to the nation, yet to satisfy his theological conscience he regretfully left their fold. His parents were convinced advocates of secession and slavery, but he abandoned their views and became an ardent promoter of union and freedom. His father once declared that he had begotten a son who would have become a great man if the Abolitionists had not ruined him. The family tradition is that Francis Hughes

17

always put an adjective before the word "Abolitionists."

The great changes that my father experienced culturally, denominationally, spiritually, politically, might suggest a morbid conscience. But his decisions were not dramatically made. He moved without noisy proclamation from one moral region to another. His judgments were never violent. He maintained a kindly attitude toward the camps from which he departed, keeping an affectionate admiration for Dr. Broadus, the great Baptist preacher of the South, and for Alexander Campbell, the human founder of the Disciples. He placed Robert E. Lee and Stonewall Jackson in his personal Hall of Fame— and Love. I never heard him speak even critically of his co-workers in other denominational fields. When men talk as if fifty years ago the different churches were trying to get at rival throats, I wonder what kind of sectarian parents gave them their training.

I recall a humorous illustration of his tolerance. On the streets I had engaged in dispute with a Presbyterian playmate. Our debate related not to doctrine or polity, but to posture in public prayer. The Presbyterian preacher stood, and the Methodist preacher knelt. Family devotions and required church attendance had made me familiar with the Bible. So I went to the Scripture for my forensics, quoting such words as "kneel before the Lord our maker," and Daniel "kneeled upon his knees"; then I swept into the New Testament to point out that "the Pharisee *stood* and prayed." I won the debate against my juvenile opponent, left him confused, and went homeward to recount a victory. My father disappointed me. He came dangerously near to becoming a Presbyterian. He said gravely that the posture of the heart was the one thing the good God desired. I doubted my parent's loyalty to his church. I saw that I still had missionary work to do in my own family circle.

18

My father had one contest of which he was scarcely conscious. When I became old enough to "psychoanalyze" him, it made an interesting study. He was an aristocrat in his instincts, but a democrat in his principles! Far more than he knew, these opposing things made a battleground of his heart. Some of the Welsh Hugheses have claimed that they were lineal descendants of the Plantagenet kings. Indeed, the most distinguished representative of the clan in America has told me that "Hu" meant king, and that the added "s" signified "son of a king." I am not assured either of the genealogy or of the philology, but I do know that my father had a royal air. Never detecting in him the slightest sign of conceit, I still never knew him to surrender a regal dignity. His appearance compelled people to look at him. This quality worked into his social carriage. Someone said of him that he was made of silk. The doubtful things had no place with him. Vulgarity kept at a distance. Long before he perused a book of etiquette he was a gentleman, because he carried good manners in his nature.

He had a sensitive body. Pain for him was very painful. Yet in the prosecution of his work he seemed unconscious of hardships. His first annual salary was $100; his second, third, and fourth, the same amount; while in the fifth year, when the war in 1861 swept the men in western Virginia into the armies, his income from his circuit was $17.50. There were only slender supplements of missionary money. Yet he never spoke of the wolf that prowled at the parsonage door; and never in later years of modest comfort did he talk of his past in the mournful notes of self-heroism.

I write thus because he was a living link between our day and a pathetically sacrificial past. When he was born the pioneers were still surviving. Francis Asbury lay in his rude coffin only twenty years before my father was placed in a rude cradle. My grandparents probably saw "the prophet of the long road," the intrepid itinerant of the mountain and the swamp. Father was forty-seven years old ere he lived in a house that had a bathroom, or electric lights, or a hydrant. When he became presiding elder, his district boasted four miles of railway. He traveled on horseback or by the old-fashioned buckboard. My memory frequently sees him returning from the muddy itinerary. At the edge of the village I would sit on the rail fence, waiting until the lone rider would come over the hill. Then I would climb upon the horse and sit behind the preacher-parent as the steed splashed his homeward way. Often the picture secures a beautiful reversal. I find myself thinking that near the borders of a celestial land the father now waits to welcome the son; and that, as one homely poet declares, he will know me from afar and return the greetings of the long-gone earthly days.

He lived into his eighty-second year and became a figure, revered in Iowa and California. His last testimony on earth kept the dignity of the divine household. His splendid frame was shrinking and his marvelous voice failing, yet he repeated his confidence—

> Which of the monarchs of the earth
> Can boast a guard like ours,
> Encircled from our second birth
> By all the heavenly powers?

Though his illness prophesied dreadful pain, he largely escaped it by the mercy of God. One day he closed his eyes on earthly scenes, as he himself breathed the name of Christ, and awoke in the land of pure delight. He was ready for its climate. When he came to his eightieth birthday I wrote "with mine own hand" lines by Ralph M. Thompson, and sent them as my filial celebration—

20

Could I forsake these rugged ways,
  The paths where now I walk with men,
And hie me back to childhood's days
  To be in body born again!

From out this soul I call my own,
  From out my heart forever free,
You are the father, you alone,
  I should ask God to give to me.

X

My mother, Louisa Holt Hughes, was born in 1838. She was a tiny thing, never weighing one hundred pounds until she passed her sixtieth year. If all true marriages are made in heaven, the angel of our home was wise in his selection of its founders. The word "match" is exactly right. The qualities of my mother supplemented the qualities of my father. He lived in the spiritual dreamlands; she was acquainted with that region, but still dwelt in the area of practicalities. My father was not a businessman. He thought he was, yet I can recall no slight investment on his part that turned out successfully. The original sum decreased and usually disappeared. His horror of debt protected him, and he never disgraced his calling by insisting that merchants and coal-dealers should pay his current expenses. Neither did he ever say that, since he was giving his life, men ought not to expect him to give dollars.

But my mother had commercial genius. Father used to say that if she were placed in prison for life she would find a cavity in the cell and endow it with savings. She exercised pathetic economies. She put impossible things away, saying that "they might come in handy sometime." She was a great believer in the "rainy day," and she was always preparing her umbrella or roof. When the fall season for college came, and my father was perplexed

21

about meeting expenses for travel and tuition, she would wait for him to "husband" his resources, and would then appear with her favorite bank—a stocking. The day following my father's death she went on a secret errand, and reappeared from a trust company with sufficient funds to pay all expenses of the funeral and of the long journey to the family grave plot in Iowa.

She was an expert in the managing of holidays. Never understanding why we celebrated All Saints' Eve by doing destruction to windows and gates, she arranged for a domestic taffy pull and kept us at home by kindly guile. When Easter came she showed ingenuity in finding vegetables that would color the eggs and save the cost of purchasing the dyes. She glorified Christmas stockings by the use of tissue paper—wrapped around the apple, the cooky, the toy, the nickel that climaxed the toe of the magic footwear. By her planning, my father had his three sons in the West Virginia University when his salary was twelve hundred dollars per year, and the house. I recall it all so well because I then graduated from "blue jeans"—the more disliked because of their tough longevity. If the six children did not receive a college education, it was not because the domestic treasury failed, but because other prices were not placed over the educational counter.

When I was born—on December 7, 1866, at Moundsville, West Virginia—my father's salary amounted to only five hundred dollars per year. I was the third child. The inflated after-war prices still prevailed. But my own review of experiences does not give me gloomy thoughts. Often people say to me, "You must have had very hard times." Well, if we did, we did not know it; so what difference did it make? I recall no hungers, save those that belong to a growing boy when he is a silo. Garret beds did not prevent slumber. Mush and milk on Sunday evenings excited no joy, and yet routed starva-

tion. Hand-me-down clothes were no humiliation, because my brother Matt's garments looked so well on him
that they seemed to assure my own elegance. My sense of
deprivation lay almost wholly at one point; I could not
do certain things because I was "the preacher's son."
When Robinson's Circus came to Buckhannon, West Virginia, and I saw only the street parade, I had honest doubt
as to the value of the ministry and the Church. I still
believe that some official member should have taken me
in all the tents as an excuse for his own adult longing.

My mother had a gift of humor. Her manner added
to the quaintness of her sayings. When the Confederate
troops, or guerilla bands, swept into the village, the young
preacher and his wife swept out of it—at the other end of
town. The parsonage was destroyed by fire. The refugees
fled on horseback over the mountain roads, refused hospitality everywhere because the dwellers were suspicious.
At one cabin door a slouchy and ignorant woman appeared
in the light of her kerosene lamp. She said that there was
no possible room in her house, yet still declared that she
was related to "the Hugheses." Far beyond midnight my
mother's call halted my father in the steep path. As the
horses stood head to head, she expressed the pious conviction that the difficult experience was providential. To
my father's inquiry about the reason for her faith she
replied that if they had not been compelled to flee they
would never have discovered "the Hughes relatives"!
Thus she scattered her sallies and smiles along life's ways.
Even as I write this, I hear her merry laughter and become
aware of how her joyful spirit lifted my father's soberness out of the ditches of despondency.

This humor was the token of her courage. I never
saw her flinch from a hard situation. Only once did I
see her shed tears amid any physical trials. In moving
from one church to another field, we had a twenty-eight

23

mile stage journey over the rutty roads of April. The parents had with them the five children, the oldest twelve, the youngest six weeks of age. For thirteen hours the stage jolted its way forward. When darkness fell on the hills, I saw by the dim light of the stage lanterns the tears of sheer weariness falling upon my mother's shawl.

She lived for almost ninety years, and kept the relish of life and an accurate memory. Her last delirium was maternal. When her mind responded no longer to the usual calls, she slipped back into the past. She was a young mother again, and God was giving her the joys and problems of the old dear life. She had me in her arms once more, was using the fond mispronunciations of childhood, was speaking my given name in the diminutive, was declaring that I had always been "such a good baby" and that she knew that I would not cry unless I had ———, and she named one of the homely complaints of childhood. Thus, crowned with parenthood, she went into the nearer presence of the Greatest of Parents. When he pointed invitingly to one of the heavenly mansions where her preacher-husband awaited her coming, she may have shown modest reluctance as she remembered the little parsonages scattered along the earthly itinerancy. Then she smiled into the face of God and with trustful courage moved into the opening portal. Within, the companion of the earthly years greeted her in the rapture of reunion. She had never called him by his first name. Having the old-fashioned idea of ministerial dignity, she invariably spoke of him and to him as "Mr. Hughes." Even after he received the degree of Doctor of Divinity, her habit of address did not change. I have imagined, however, that when she met him at the door of a celestial home and glanced around to see that there were no eavesdropping angels, she called him Thomas with the rising accent of love.

24

CHAPTER II

SCHOOLING

I<small>T IS NOT ACCIDENTAL THAT IN THE EARLY CHAPTERS</small> OF every biography the instructor is introduced. Dr. George A. Gordon called his own life story *My Education and Religion* and gave the impression of those two forces as working together in his career. In the current period the old classic, *Tom Brown's School Days*, has had a revival; while the new classic, *Good-bye, Mr. Chips*, has received an affectionate welcome. When we consider that often one third of the whole life period is spent in the company of teachers, we find reason for exalting the educational process.

I

Strangely enough, I have no remembrance of my earliest teachers. I can recall the buildings and the playgrounds, but the persons who placed the First Reader in my hand are gone beyond recall. I fear that the first principal that I remember impressed me because he was a cripple who managed a crutch most dexterously, and who managed me with equal but gentle dexterity when I had a modest part in a fist fight. He sent me out of the room of discipline—unpunished but not unrepentant. I have not the slightest recollection of my teachers in my father's first three appointments. This may have been due to the itinerancy. Where a time limit moves a pastor every three years, the panorama of education does not halt long enough for deep personal impressions. The one-year pastorate at Cameron, West Virginia, was memorable, not because a teacher enthralled me, but because our striking family physician, Dr. Samuel B. Stidger, started us into three generations of intimacy. My youngest brother was named for the son LeRoy, a noble man, and father of Dr. William L. Stidger, well-known preacher and writer, and now professor in my theological alma mater.

II

I was never a student in a high school. I went from the grades into the preparatory department of West Virginia University. Many of our higher institutions then carried provision for subfreshmen students. The system gave an opportunity to belated people too old to enter a high school, and yet young enough to wish an educational start. My two years at Morgantown were fruitful. Perhaps because I was with him frequently, Adam Lawrence, principal of the preparatory department and teacher of Latin, did me incalculable good. He gave me a solid grounding in the classics, taught me to watch English words with a view to tracing their derivation, and opened windows toward ancient literatures that have always given me joy. My visits to Morgantown are never complete until I make a pilgrimage to the place where Adam Lawrence dwelt. My imagination sees him walking the streets accompanied by a Negro manservant whom we called "Topsy" and whose lisping affectations gave the town great delight.

III

I would gladly have continued at West Virginia University. My father, being removed to First Church, Parkersburg, West Virginia, insisted that I transfer to Ohio Wesleyan University. To my objection that Ohio Wesleyan was "too religious," he made the chuckling reply

26

that this was the very reason why he intended to enroll me at Delaware, Ohio. So to the Buckeye State I went in the fall of 1883—to be met at the railroad station by a group of young West Virginians. Even before I had found a room these students took me to the famous sulphur spring. As I had been ignorant of that flowing fountain, I ascribed its odor to collegiate tricksters who had treated it with the eggs usually tossed at politicians. That bubbling spring became dear to all Ohio Wesleyan men. Bishop McDowell used to say that he wished to be buried in his alma mater's hood and gown, so that St. Peter would know whence he hailed; but that if he were assigned to the other place where his tongue needed cooling, he would insist on an application of sulphur water.

Dr. Charles Henry Payne was president. He was a native of New England—a poor boy who moved through hardships to an education; a graduate of Wesleyan, at Middletown, Connecticut; a user of Yankee English, immensely amusing to his students when he told them in chapel that he had visited "Torontor, Canadar"; a strict Puritan in all his "idears" of life; a disciplinarian whose decisions, slowly reached, were no more altered than were the laws of the Medes and Persians; a wonderful preacher who could attract larger audiences than any famous outsider; a pulpiteer with mannerisms easy to imitate, but with a piercing conviction and a choice of pungent words that triumphed over a peculiar delivery; and, withal, a man of such reverent devotion that his prayers were events. I cannot recall that the chapel exercises were ever boresome. They were not only the daily bulletins of college life; they were the headquarters of Christian idealism, and spiritual resting places between recitations.

In later years it was interesting to observe the changing attitudes toward President Payne. I do him no injustice when I say that among the students he was popular only with the distinctly serious and religious groups. He discouraged intercollegiate athletics, forbade dancing and theatergoing, and regulated under strict chaperonage the coeducational life. Yet one of the evidences of the President's power was that he influenced for good, and often to a complete change of life, young men who did not like him. He was the greatest evangelist that I have ever known—not a splendid wandering comet, but a fixed star that illuminated one campus through many years. On the day when I myself "stood for prayers," after his balanced intellectual and spiritual appeal, I was one of fifty-two young men and women who gave response. My recollection of "Dr. Payne's revivals" holds no impression of fanaticism. Our country and our Church have been made immeasurably richer by his evangelistic zeal which combined clearness of mind with fervor of heart.

One later result was that students who moved on to character became his increasing devotees. He "lost caste" with me in my freshman year by compelling an apology for my participation in "destructive class spirit," and by exacting a written promise that I would thereafter refrain from pouring ice water down sophomore backs. Yet he became a wonderful influence on my life. When years later I read the press dispatches that told of his death in New York City, my eyes knew tears. When I reach the Better Land I shall make an early call on Charles Henry Payne, to assure him of a gratitude that grew to ever larger measure. They buried his dust at Taunton, Massachusetts. I have always felt that he should have had sepulcher at Delaware, Ohio, in the vicinity of "Professors' Row," where so many of his teaching comrades wait for the call of God.

My professors at Ohio Wesleyan were men of marked personality. To John Henry Grove my debt is large—for awakening my mind, and for a quickening friendship.

28

Professor Thomas C. Trueblood tamed my vigorous speech and cured me somewhat of a needless vociferousness—just as he has been doing for many years at the University of Michigan, until his disciples are found in both houses of Congress. Drs. McCabe, Williams, Whitlock, Perkins, Semans, Parsons, Nelson were made on big patterns. Some of them doubtless would not, in critical review, stand the tests of modern pedagogy. They did, however, communicate size and power to open-minded students. No one of them was a failure. Professor Clara Conklin was a drillmistress in literature. She gave her scholars insight, and an exactitude in composition whose value has been unfailing. I had but one course under Professor Cyrus B. Austin, one being enough to convince him that I was not destined to be a famous mathematician and astronomer. What a friend he was! And how devoted to those Puritan ideals that he maintained without fanatical sourness!

I record with eager gratitude my obligation to my alma mater. Every foot of her campus is dear to me. While I have never been disillusioned in regard to my profession, I have occasionally wished that I might have had a more remunerative career, so that I could have given to my college a financial aid commensurate with the help that she gave to me. I never read these lines, written by Matthew Arnold in "Stanzas from the Grande Chartreuse," without thankful remembrance:

> For rigorous teachers seized my youth,
>   And purged its faith, and trimmed its fire,
> Showed me the high white star of truth,
>   There bade me gaze, and there aspire.

IV

The larger part of my sophomore year was spent at Grinnell College, in Iowa. My father had been transferred from the West Virginia to the Iowa Conference, and had been assigned to Grinnell. As the financial burden of my parents would be lessened if I lived at home, I took two terms of work at Grinnell. The college was an excellent one. But my years at Ohio Wesleyan had given me some wonderful associations. I was especially enamored of my college fraternity, Delta Tau Delta, of which later I was to be editor and national president. That tie prevailed with me; and my real homesickness sent me back to Delaware, even though I felt obliged to drop out of college temporarily in order to make money for my further education.

I have always regretted that my bonds to Grinnell College were not closer. The teacher who most influenced me there was the late Professor John M. Crowe. Often he dragged himself to his recitations, in spite of weakness and pain. But he knew so well the Logos—transferred by another John from the beloved Greek language into our Christian vocabulary—that he endured as seeing Him who is invisible. I made at Grinnell, also, friendships with "the Palmer boys," Almond Ellsworth and Frank E., and with the late Eugene E. Stacy, long secretary of the Young Men's Christian Association of Indiana, that have given me warm fraternity in all these years.

V

Graduating from Ohio Wesleyan in 1889, I matriculated at Boston University School of Theology. Two wonderful benefactors made it possible for me to complete my preparation for the ministry. The Hon. Morris Sharp was a trustee of Ohio Wesleyan, and a successful banker at Washington Court House, Ohio. His wife was Madeline Baker Sharp—later Mrs. William W. Davies, her second husband being my beloved teacher at Delaware. Mr. and Mrs. Sharp were strictest Puritans. At one time

Mr. Sharp was a candidate for governor on the Prohibition ticket in Ohio, while his gentle wife had been one of the women crusaders who knelt upon the sawdust floors of saloons and prayed men out of their destructive business. These good friends, having no children, became spiritual parents of nieces and nephews, and of others of us beyond their own domestic circle. In May, 1889, I won, as Ohio Wesleyan's representative, the Interstate Oratorical Contest, held, oddly enough, at Grinnell, Iowa, where I had been a student, and where my parents still dwelt. Mr. Sharp wired me, wanting to "pay the expenses of my theological education at any school" I selected. So the hindrance of my college debt was overcome. My roommate, the late George W. Allen, and my very close friend, the late Henry B. Brownell, one of the noblest men I have ever known, had brought me into the circle of Mr. and Mrs. Sharp's love. Within six months I was self-supporting. But though Mr. Sharp's outgo for me was not large, my debt was beyond calculation. I had my room at his home, just as I had my room at my parents' home. I am often a pilgrim to Washington Court House, where I make grateful visits to graves that lie beneath a marble mausoleum. Those two good souls came to love me truly as a son, and they felt that their kindly investments brought a filial income that gave them happiness.

VI

Boston in 1889 was a treasure place for theological students. Phillips Brooks, Edward Everett Hale, George A. Gordon, A. J. Gordon, David Gregg, Samuel E. Herrick were in local pulpits. In Cambridge, Alexander McKenzie was still powerful; while across in Chelsea, Charles E. Jefferson was beginning his career. At Harvard University each Sunday some well-known preacher could be

31

heard. In Tremont Temple, Joseph Cook was delivering his Monday Lectures; and though his sonorous utterances were losing their charm and he seemed like a burned-out Vesuvius, he still served as a foil against extreme liberalisms. The Lowell Lectures were having their vogue. Boston itself was a curriculum. Theological students had to be on guard lest the outside courses should divert them from the inside courses. The education of the city could well interfere with the education of the school.

My coming to Boston was near the end of New England's literary "flowering." I met Samuel Longfellow. Papini and others have scorned the better-known brother, Henry Wadsworth Longfellow. But you cannot readily cancel certain passages from "Evangeline," or "The Children's Hour." I attended James Russell Lowell's funeral service in Harvard Chapel, where the ritual, read by Phillips Brooks, suggested neither poet nor ambassador but committed an "uneulogized" soul to the keeping of God. On December 6, 1889, I walked boldly along Beacon Street to Oliver Wendell Holmes's residence. I left with the servant a copy of *The Autocrat of the Breakfast Table,* and a note saying that a theological student would be made happy if Dr. Holmes would write the last verse of "The Chambered Nautilus" on the flyleaf, and that the next day, December 7, my twenty-third birthday anniversary, would be a good date for the kindly penmanship. I returned on December 8 and found that my audacity had been rewarded. That volume is still on my safest shelf and awaits a decision among greedy literary heirs. Later I heard Holmes read "The Last Leaf"—in a voice made tremulous by age, and in a manner that made the poem a personal parable.

I met Edwin Arnold and heard him deliver a dreadfully prosy lecture at Harvard. What he said would scarcely have been likened to a candle in a garret—so far from suggesting "The Light of Asia." Yet in closing he declared one unforgettable thing—"Gentlemen of Harvard, in 1776 and 1812 you conquered your fathers. In the years from 1861 to 1865 you conquered your brothers. Will you permit a Briton to say that your next victory must be over yourselves?" The brilliance saved the words from impudence.

The faculty at 72 Mount Vernon Street was small— only seven members. Theological education had not reached complexity. The first year I had Olin A. Curtis in what we called dogmatic theology. He was a sensitive person, with a fund of genuine inspiration. I knew well that the "liberal atmosphere" of the institution troubled him, and I could have prophesied that his perhaps needless irritations would ere long lead him to seek a position elsewhere. He did his students real service, not only by his classroom lectures, but also by remarkable addresses and sermons.

Professor Henry C. Sheldon had church history. He made a transition to the department of "dogmatics." He fitted the period in an amazing way. The extreme conservatives and the extreme liberals doubtless criticized him. Yet a review of the nineties and of the following decades would show that, with the exception of William Newton Clarke, who wrote *The Outline of Christian Theology*, no seminary teacher so surely held to a good past or directed to a good future.

Dr. Luther T. Townsend was the professor of homiletics and pastoral work. He was an incisive preacher. He invariably used a manuscript, but he made the pages glow with sacred fire. His sermon on "Fixity of Character," based on the words, "He which is filthy, let him be filthy still: he that is holy, let him be holy still," was thrillingly memorable. His counsels with reference to pastoral life and work were valuable. Students found

33

that often in their labor he came back to them in surprising advices.

Professor Marcus D. Buell taught the New Testament and acted as our dean, while his wife, Edith Buell, was our motherly counselor. Dr. Buell's students were kept busy—so much so that at one time they offered a respectful protest against heavy assignments, and were met by their teacher's reasonable adjustments. He paid great heed to the connectives in the original Greek and in the translation. We became familiar with his questions—"What does 'then' refer to?" "What does 'therefore' do in this passage?" "What does 'for' sustain and why?" His nickname became the two Greek words *Kai gar*—to celebrate his fashion of pouncing down on helpless conjunctions and equally helpless scholars. In their future work, however, the "boys" were to discover that many sermons grew out of Professor Buell's exegetical method. When he died there was no one to whom we could send a letter of sympathy. "Aunt Edith" had passed beyond the reach of earth's postal system. No little child had come to his arms. No close relatives remained in the inner circle of his heart. His "boys" were his mourners. In the loving tributes leadership was naturally taken by two of his students who themselves became Bible teachers—Professor Rollin Hough Walker, of Ohio Wesleyan, and Professor Arthur D. Enyart, of Rollins College.

Dr. William Fairfield Warren was president of Boston University. In spite of heavy administrative duties, he taught the course in comparative religions. It was the finest instruction of this sort then offered in the United States. One of his lectures on "The Quest of a Perfect Religion" was a thrilling fancy, mingled with profound thought. It shook our circle of students from rim to rim and sent us back to our rooms in the upper dormitories as if we carried a new credential of our faith. Dr. Warren had mystical hold on his old students. We never outgrew him. Years after I graduated, I was for almost twelve months his partial successor, serving as acting president of Boston University. For the commencement exercises President Emeritus William Edwards Huntington, a matchless character, offered the prayer. Dr. Warren, then in the advanced eighties of his life, gave the benediction. He came to Symphony Hall only for the moments of the apostolic blessing. Two men assisted him to mount the platform. He moved slowly to its center, lifted his aging hands, and in pathetic tremulousness pronounced "The peace of God" benediction. I found myself tearful and wondered whether the strain of the immense commencement had broken my self-control. Yet as, without irreverence, I glanced over the throng, I saw the old students of the venerable man passing through their baptism of tears. It was his final word to us. Ere many months passed he went from earthly scenes to repeat in heavenly ecstasy the Gloria "to the Father, the Son, and the Holy Spirit." This had become for those who loved him his favorite form of greeting.

Our professor of Old Testament literature was Hinckley G. Mitchell, who became a storm center of theological controversy. We all called him "The Rabbi." He looked the part. Short in stature, scraggily bearded, nervous in his gait and speech, direct and smiling in his social approaches, he lived near the school and was, with Dean Buell, the teacher with whom the students had closest fellowship. When one of us was ill, he would breeze into the room, make cheerful suggestions, and go away—to return soon with gifts of medicines or fruits. Though he was ordained, I never heard him preach. The school was his sole field of labor, and the classroom his only forum.

His department was then most controversial. *The Andover Review* and *The Methodist Review* were quiver-

35

ing with debate. Andover Seminary had become a battle-ground. Its splendid history, with the memories of teachers like Austin Phelps, could not save it from the shock that paralyzed it into weakness. An intelligent liberal once pointed to its buildings taken over by Phillips-Andover Academy and said that the institution had died from a "surplus of intellect and a deficit of heart."

Dr. Mitchell had no deficit of heart. Not only did he love his students, but he could go with them to any gospel mission and work at the "mourner's bench" with the drunken derelicts of the North End of Boston. As I estimate the events that led to his leaving the school, several factors played their part. He was a good writer, but a poor speaker. When he attempted to extemporize answers to abstruse questions, he was not always skillful. Occasionally, too, he set so-called orthodoxy at a disadvantage by contrasting its representatives with carefully selected examples from the heretical groups. In addition, it was difficult for an Old Testament teacher, in that sensitive time, to avoid the appearance of pointing out, with something like the delight of skill, the limitations of the ancient records. The Methodist Episcopal Church was conservative, though it prided itself on its catholicity. The bishops were given a veto on the election of professors in the Boston University School of Theology—which power they had not sought and which later they were glad to surrender. By a narrow margin they had endorsed Dr. Mitchell for a period of service. Soon thereafter he published his book *The World Before Abraham*. Some of the bishops regarded the volume as a challenge, and for the next period of service they refused endorsement. An intense debate followed.

To those who loved Professor Mitchell the situation was harassing. Our "little Rabbi" became a pathetic and heroic figure. The students themselves were feverish. A few of them, good men with "fundamental" proclivities, joined in the attack on their teacher. One of these ere long presented definite charges of heresy. Dr. Mitchell was defended by Francis J. McConnell, a young preacher then rapidly winning the recognition that later made him a college president and a bishop, and an ecclesiastical figure for the world. The "attorney for the Church" was a strangely conscientious man who combined with some peculiar streaks of ability an obsession for presenting charges. Dr. Mitchell's Conference, the Central New York, finally passed a resolution with this gist: that while it regarded some of Professor Mitchell's teachings as contrary to the Holy Scriptures and to the doctrinal standards of Methodism, it did not think it wise to proceed to a trial. This extraordinary decision was not then contested by Dr. McConnell, who knew well that it could not possibly be approved by the Committee on Judiciary, or by the General Conference. The presiding bishop who did not declare out of order the plainly illegal action by which a Conference condemned a minister for heresy and in the same sentence refused him a trial wisely admitted that he was wrong and stated that he was sorry. The transfer of Dr. Mitchell to the New England Conference changed the theological waters from the Atlantic to the Pacific. The waves ceased to roar and be troubled.

Hinckley Mitchell is slowly receiving a vindication. Certain facts confused the situation. He became professor in the Universalist Theological School of Tufts College. His devoted wife had been a frankly confessed Unitarian. His funeral services were held in King's Chapel, the Unitarian church in central Boston. The brilliant teacher who edited Dr. Mitchell's modest autobiography, *For the Benefit of My Creditors,* gave to some readers the impression that his views represented his old professor's views. In the essentials Hinckley G. Mitchell was distinctly orthodox. Today his Biblical instruction would scarcely make a ripple, not to speak of a tidal wave.

The tragic happenings brought their compensations. After our "little Rabbi" had gone beyond the reach of all accusations, the New England Conference nobly set aside technical hindrances to the care of his invalid widow. The most important legacy that he himself left "for the benefit of creditors" was a Christlike spirit that did not fail through trying years. He carried love into the other world. As the men who had pressed the battle against him followed him thither he greeted each with a smile. Those who knew him well cannot think of him as being anywhere save in the companionship of his Messiah. If his old students do not at once find him, it will be because in the orthodoxy of Love he has a place higher than their own. He will summon them to the heights and will himself be unconscious of his own preferred rank.

In his autobiography he told of the witty remark made by a shrewd uncle. Informed that his nephew would enter the Methodist ministry, and knowing that the youngster was often tardy, the old man said that Hinckley would always have to be sent "to a charge that had only an afternoon appointment." But Professor Mitchell did not delay at the Gates of Pearl. He was promptly welcomed into the best of Tabernacles.

My debt to the School of Theology is incalculable. The first six months in Boston were distinctly disappointing—solely because my preconceptions were wrong. My thought of the purpose of a theological education was incorrect. I had anticipated that the courses would give more specific teaching, and especially that they would furnish material for preaching. I conceived that homiletical pigeonholes in the brain would receive ideas and illustrations for future use. In season I grasped the better thought—that the aim was to make us big enough to do our own

work. If my first year was discouraging, my last two
were joyful. At Ohio Wesleyan I had experienced semes-
ters of delight. I was in all the campus activities. I did
not always allow my studies to interfere with my education. But at Boston I was only a student. Social life
was taboo. By day and by night I toiled. Seventy-two
Mount Vernon Street became for me a monastery.

In one respect the courses were deficient. We did not
receive adequate instruction in the art of speech. Teachers in "elocution" were not always taken seriously. Professors in some Eastern colleges despised proper expression, apparently thinking that their wonderful ideas
needed no outer skills. I have seen many ministers with
high ideals and fine preparation failing, relatively, because they did not learn how to deliver their messages. If
a man halts in pronouncing the definite article when its
use is inevitable, he halts his service also. There are today preachers whose usefulness would be immeasurably
increased if some instructor were to teach them how to
make the voice an efficient servant.

In this respect of appreciation I had been fortunate. I
have already referred to my teacher, Professor Trueblood.
In my second preparatory year at West Virginia I auda-
ciously entered into a declamation contest. Doubtless some
people slyly laughed at me. But I told them earnestly how
Regulus became very saucy to the Carthaginians, and I
made "the rivers run crimson to the sea." Though only
fifteen, I won honorable mention, and the self-discovery
that I might be able to speak in public with fair efficiency.

My participation in the old-fashioned oratorical contests
at Ohio Wesleyan was most valuable. Senator La Follette,
Senator Beveridge, President James A. Blaisdell, Dr.
Howard H. Russell, Dr. Charles E. Jefferson, Dr. Olin A.
Curtis, Judge James H. Wilkerson, President John L. Hill-
man, Bishop Francis J. McConnell, and many others re-

39

ceived the benefits of these tests. At the time we over-estimated the honor involved. I can still hear the cheers of my fellow students from Ohio Wesleyan when in 1889 the decision of the judges gave me the final recognition. I cannot forget, also, how I was greeted with a parade when I returned to Delaware after my victory. But the real triumph was in the lesson that I could accomplish things by hard work. Young as I was, I mastered that point thoroughly—so that the after-rewards of speaking experience were greater than the immediate rewards.

In my "student appointment" I was highly favored. My first year was devoted to studies. Evidently the courses were prepared under the idea that they would command full time. My nearness to the seminaries, Boston and Garrett, in the years of my episcopacy and my long supervision of theological student preachers gave me abundant chance for observing effects. Phillips Brooks once said to several of us that student appointments were always mistakes. He felt that they mixed the periods of life. Every stage of calendar living should, he felt, be kept true to itself. A child who of necessity wore a man's clothes was a sad object. A student who was a regular preacher took the bloom from both fields of living. He argued the case convincingly, and he lived up to his argument. His years at the Alexandria Seminary were wholly scholastic. Then he burst with grand suddenness upon his first congregation. This plan was doubtless followed because Brooks as a student had no financial problem.

In my second year at Boston I became pastor of Hope Chapel—a virtual mission. It was only seven minutes' walk from the school. There was no Sunday morning service. I was under contract to conduct the prayer meeting on Thursday evening, to attend the church school on Sunday afternoon, and to preach each Sunday night. As the seminary classes ceased at four o'clock on Friday, I had the

THOMAS BAYLESS AND LOUISA HOLT HUGHES
Golden Wedding Photograph

evening of that day, all of Saturday, and all of Sunday
morning, with portions of Sunday afternoon, to devote
quite largely to the preparation of my one sermon. Hope
Chapel was under the auspices of the Old South Congregational Church. Dr. George A. Gordon was its eminent
pastor. My stipend was generous. Ere I graduated I had
paid all my debts, and had saved funds for my marriage.
My strict purpose had been not to wed until I had fully
completed my theological course. I have been accustomed
to say to students that I not only held to that plan, but
that even after graduation I waited a full week! In June,
1892, I received my diploma. I was appointed by the
faculty to give one of the "orations" at the commencement
exercises. My first companion in this recognition was the
late Franklin Hamilton, afterward my colleague in the
Board of Bishops. He declined the honor; and Rollin
Hough Walker, who was substituted, gave a most excellent
address, showing the promise that he has abundantly fulfilled. He remains my dear and intimate friend. In that
fond circle that still surrounds me on earth stand Edwin
C. Dixon, schoolmate but not classmate, a most honored
figure in Wisconsin; Edward H. Todd, president of the
College of Puget Sound, who with holy persistence helped
to save two worthy colleges; Herbert F. Quimby, a faithful
worker in the New Hampshire Conference; Henry S.
Powell, of the North-East Ohio Conference, who, whether
as pastor or district superintendent, met the best ideals
of his profession; Olaf R. and Rennetts C. Miller, earnest
in reforms, as in friendship; Henry L. Wriston, who saved
a great ministerial insurance company from collapse; Otho
F. Bartholow, but recently retired after an amazingly successful pastorate at Mount Vernon, New York; George H.
Murphy, a fine character and worker in the Indiana Conference—with them I walked with solemn joy toward the
appointed work of my life.

VII

There is yet another period to be described. Having my pastoral assignment near Boston, I could still pursue postgraduate work. I had special lectures under Dr. Rishell. I took such courses under Dr. Sheldon as I had not taken prior to my graduation. All these proved steadying supplements to the thrilling studies under Dr. Curtis. I have always been grateful that I was able, amid pastoral duties, to add thus to theological preparations.

But my chief postgraduate experience was under Dr. Borden Parker Bowne. He was an immense figure in educational life, with a repute that was more than national. Though he was not regularly on the faculty of the School of Theology, we students were permitted, under conditions, to take his course. He often made fun of the theologues, calling us the sons of "the dragon's teeth," while really knowing that his main products were to come from our ranks. Practically every student who was to carry his personalistic philosophy to chairs in other colleges entered his classes from 72 Mount Vernon Street.

Dr. Bowne knew that I was not naturally fitted to be one of his specialists. Although his courtesy would avoid comparisons that were odious, he used to say that if anybody were to ask who had been his best student, he would reply, "The student, than whom I have had no better, was Francis J. McConnell." That remark meant more than the words said. But Bowne's praise of me was always in realms other than philosophy. He came to my inauguration at DePauw University and made me happier by commending my address—as indeed he had given me joy by ascribing merit to my funeral tribute to the late Hon. Alden Speare. But he was philosopher enough to know that I would never be a philosopher.

I knew that the prophecy of my future looked toward a pulpit rather than toward a classroom. So far from being

42

sensitive about this, I was gratified. Looking over my old papers I am convinced that I chose my lifework wisely. My review of John Caird's *Introduction to the Philosophy of Religion* and my dissertation on Janet's *Final Causes* did not fill me with shame, but both were proofs that God did not call me to be a second Plato. Dr. Bowne's volumes on psychology and metaphysics puzzled me greatly. On the other hand, I regarded his *Introduction to Theism* as one of the most wonderful discussions I had ever read. I perused carefully Francis J. McConnell's book *Is God Limited?* Yet in the end I was utterly convinced that one reader was distinctly limited. I have several times read with care Augustine's *Confessions,* doubtless the most remarkable treatise of the kind ever written. The earlier chapters gave me rapture. The chapters on Time and Space bewildered me utterly. The two mysteries were wholly beyond me—and I had doubts about Augustine.

Yet Dr. Bowne invited me into his regular classes—all of them. I took every one of his prescribed courses. He surprised me by asking me to take his special courses in both Kant and Spencer. This I did, in fellowship with Albert C. Knudson, later dean of the Boston University School of Theology. These postgraduate studies were pursued while I was pastor of a large church. Professor Bowne had the gift of wit. I was occasionally detained from his hours by funerals. The fourth time I gave this mournful excuse he remarked that evidently my "ministry was being attended by a rather remarkable mortality." Yet I never knew him to wound the heart of a student. The smile on the teacher's face was so kindly as to cushion the shaft.

He had, as well, the gift of sympathy. When, shortly after the birth of my second son I was anxious about the health of my wife, he held me after class one day, inquired solicitously about her welfare, and then asked if I would do him a favor. After I replied, "Anything in the world,

Dr. Bowne," he requested that when I returned to my parsonage I would on his behalf kiss the cheek of my "little boy." So I carried that token to the parsonage cradle, feeling that I was acting vicariously for one of the greatest men I had ever known.

Once I said semipublicly to Dr. Bowne that while his important service lay in the preparation of teachers who did like "to retain God in their knowledge," I still wanted him to recognize the service he was rendering to men like myself—tyros in the philosophic realm. He put something into the backgrounds for us. When in later periods the world was woefully shaken, his students kept the faith. They did not flee to the gospels of despair, nor fall back upon the overdone sovereignty of Barth's God. Holding to a doctrine of personalism that included man as well as God, they walked the earth in confidence because they lived under the sky of a real faith.

I never read Fitzgerald Flournoy's tribute to one of his teachers without feeling like sending it over the wireless ways to the place where Dr. Bowne now dwells:

> I cannot count the things you did for me.
> You wakened me and led me forth to find
> Immortal company, and made me see
> My path in the republic of the mind.[1]

My own place in that realm has not been broad or high, and the light that I gave to it has been in no sense brilliant. Yet the way has not been closed, nor has the gentle beam failed on cloudy days. When in the hush of a darkening evening I have found myself in reverent remembrance consulting my old teacher, I have found it easier to pursue my journey into Another's Presence and to say to him, "Rabbi, we know that thou art a teacher come from God."

[1] From "To a College Professor," II. Used by permission of Dr. Flournoy.

CHAPTER III

PASTORATES

MY PASTORATES RAN THE GAMUT OF TYPES—A RURAL church, a mission church, a suburban church, a city church—while a village church, a town church, and a large county-seat church came in as summer extras. The one thing lacking was the circuit, which comprised two or more country or small community churches placed under the care of one minister. Yet, as the actual experience began with the faithful horse and the traditional saddle-bags, the mere number could add only the Sunday travel and the open-air meditation of the highways.

There is, of course, a peculiar romance about "first" things. Lake Itasca's glory lies not in its size, but in its character as the source of the Mississippi River. Starting places may be as renowned as goals. Therefore I give much space to my initial pastorate. Once, by request, I prepared the story for an Annual Conference. Later it was revised for the semicentennial of my reception on trial in the Iowa Conference, now the Iowa–Des Moines. The session was held at Newton, lying within Jasper County in which I had preached my first sermon, had been granted my first license, and had been received on probation. There I celebrated the twenty-fifth anniversary of my Conference membership in 1912, and the fiftieth anniversary in 1937. In this later session three members were present who had been in the Conference when I was admitted. Only one of my classmates survives—the Rev. John Wesley Potter, D.D., now retired. With him I have had a rewarding friendship. One other classmate, the late Thomas S. Poole, was my unfailing friend; but he had gone to heaven before our Golden Anniversary. When I was received on trial, though I had served a year as a supply pastor, I was only twenty years of age; "Tom" came in at the age of forty-one. My reception was opposed because I was so young; his because he was so old. But the votes were for us, and we walked into membership hand in hand. In all the decades the hands were never unclasped!

If the story of my first church appears intimate, this feature is explained by the fact that there were present about fifty of the children and grandchildren of my old officials and other parishioners. They were in the front pews of a crowded Conference—its guests, and the guests of my own heart. I shall carry the picture always in this world—and then into whatsoever God may bid me enter.

I

The summer of 1886 was to me a time of problem. I had finished my sophomore year. I was in debt. In the earlier summer I had tried to sell books, but after two weeks of discouraging efforts I was convinced that I had not been divinely called to be a book agent. Many times since I have wished that other men might find out the like fact.

God often leads men to their proper work by allowing them to fail in something else. We are saved by our satisfactory failures. It was so with me. I had long carried secretly the knowledge that I ought to preach; but I was young, and so timid about speaking in public that I had never spoken three consecutive minutes without either memorizing or reading. My father must have known through experience of my dilemma. He began with gentle urgings to help me take my first steps. A stranger in the prayer meeting one evening had spoken on the passage:

46

"Be strong in the Lord, and in the power of his might." He not only suggested to me a line of thought, but he made me feel that in the strength of the Lord I might preach at least one sermon. So I began to prepare my first message. For weeks I struggled with my theme— "Spiritual Strength." I would never have been able to do anything with it if I had not had my father's help. In due time I had written what I hoped would occupy thirty minutes of speaking. I felt that to speak less than that would be a confession of inability. Since then I have discovered that it may be an evidence of genius to preach less than half an hour.

It was arranged that I should make my first attempt at a little rural church called Bethel. I went with a good friend, a circuit rider. On Saturday evening we were received into a farmer's home. Within sight on a hill stood the white meetinghouse.

Sunday morning, August 15, 1886, I arose early according to the farm custom, had breakfast, and then went out alone into the fields, while trying to get the manuscript thoroughly into my mind. My audience was one cow who did not seem to think much of the sermon. If I could have avoided the horns of my own dilemma I should have been willing to risk the close company of hers through the length of that Sabbath. A sense of humor came to my aid. I had read of a little girl who had written this essay on the cow: "The cow is the greatest animal on earth." One day the preacher called and the fond mother asked the child to read her essay. Feeling that something was due to the reverend visitor, the wee girl changed her page and the new edition appeared as follows: "The cow is the greatest animal on earth—except religion." I realized that the child's exception was correct, and that I must leave that great animal and seek a more critical audience in the service of religion. The church made me tremble

47

whenever I caught a glimpse of its whiteness. My feelings were contradictory. I wanted the hour for the service to come, and I was afraid to have it come. I took my place in the pulpit with the pastor. I would have been glad if everybody had stayed at home save the sexton and the preacher. The pastor wisely had me offer the opening prayer. This served to educate me into confidence. I had never before tried to lead pulpit devotions. The Lord helped me to forget myself and to carry the audience in an intercessory way before the Throne of Grace. I preached my sermon word for word. The congregation listened respectfully. However, I discovered in that first audience a difference in hearers. One man listened with a look of intelligent sympathy that heartened me greatly; another looked sour and bored, and made me wish that he had stayed at home. There are good preachers; and there are also good hearers. What the people in general thought of the sermon I never discovered. I heard but one comment. As I walked across the fields one man called out to another, "The young fellow did very well, didn't he?" The compliment was not strong, but seldom have I caught any word that was more musical. In the afternoon the pastor assured me that I had made a hopeful beginning. When I returned home the next morning to meet the nervous inquiries of my parents, I honestly reported that I had gone beyond my expectations. Later my father told me that when the time drew near for the morning service he had found my mother weeping as if her heart would break. She was passing with me through the trial in the little church ten miles away. It may be that her prayers kept my tongue steady and my heart strong.

Four weeks from that Sunday I began my work with my first church. The Conference session was held a goodly distance from my home. I concluded not to attend for reasons "pecuniary to myself." I met my father on his return and said to him, "Where am I appointed?" He replied, "To Madison." Where and what Madison was I did not know. It was a township nine miles from the nearest store, depot, town, or post office; eighteen miles from my own home. It was necessary that I have a horse. My father bought me a little "Black-hawk Morgan," worn out in the service of a country doctor. His name was Billy. He was a wonderful saddle horse, with a peculiar movement somewhere between a walk and a pacing that covered the ground at a remarkable rate. Often I rode the eighteen miles in three hours. An old West Virginia preacher friend had loaned me a pair of saddlebags, and I thus began in the orthodox way.

I had learned how to reach the home of the superintendent of the Sunday school, George D. Wilkinson. In the evening I arrived in front of his spacious farmhouse. I was nineteen years of age. My manner of dressing did not make me look older. I found visitors at the home— six or eight people—all connected with the church. With outward boldness I dismounted and informed the group that I was their new pastor. They looked surprised; they had not before heard from Conference. The visiting man was blunt and asked me some plain questions: "Have you ever done any preaching?" I replied meekly, "A little, not very much." "Are you married?" I laughed and replied, "No." "Well," said my questioner, "you can't tell anything about what boys will do in these days." The visitors, on the road home, met a lady member of the church and informed her that they had a new preacher. "What is he like?" she asked. The farmer pointed to her boy, five years of age, and said, "He'll do to play with Bertie there all next summer."

I found difficulties. The good woman of the house told me kindly about some discouraging features: how disappointed the people would be that Dr. Busby had not come back; how two of the best people would leave the next week for Kansas; how the class leader had got mad on politics and had left the church; and how I must not expect that I could do very much at first, though in season all would be well. I went to my rest with a troubled heart—relieved by the thought of the sweet-faced woman who had said, ere she drove away, "I am always a good friend to the pastor; I want to help you all I can. Come and stop with us often."

For Billy, my horse, I grew to have a real affection. I always tried my sermons on him before I gave them to my people. When I mentioned this fact once, one of my hearers asked if I wore spurs. I replied, "No." Then he asked, "How did you keep him awake?" But Billy as a traveler had no tendency to sleepiness, neither was he sleepy as a hearer. He was a model audience. His ears were ever pricked up and open. He always moved when I preached. He made progress. He never criticized. He was "hoofbound," but he was not hidebound. In the summer, being hitched outside the window, he would hear again the sermon that he had heard the day before; but he never told anyone. As a good Methodist horse, he would sometimes respond with an earnest whinny. The people knew his gait, and as far away as they could see him on prairie or hilltop they could say:

> We know you by your daily walk,
> There's a meetin' here tonight.

He was a worthy member of that company of itinerant horses that carried the Methodist preachers over stream, beyond plain, across mountain. When the artist finally paints the typical face of him who yearned over the souls of men in log houses or in dugouts, his brush, if at all just, must not neglect the faithful horse. The equestrian

50

statue of Asbury in Washington is genuine history wrought into bronze.

Early the next morning I inquired the way to the church. I saddled my horse and took my way to the altar. Making my memory critical, I recall that the house was in dire need of painting, seated with badly worn chairs, paper dangling in shreds from the ceiling. But for me the place was transfigured. It has been my privilege to visit some of the finest churches in the world. I have never seen any that so impressed me with grandeur as did that little country sanctuary. To my heart it was a cathedral. I stood in the pulpit; I was stirred with pride. This was my church. I was to preach in this pulpit. I glimpsed the majesty of Bunyan's Palace Beautiful.

On Sunday I preached one of my only two sermons. The people had heard of the young preacher and were present in goodly numbers. I do not know the impression I made. I heard sundry murmurings about the failure of the Conference to send Dr. Busby back; but to all these I replied that it was not my fault, that I had been sent to them, and that I could do nothing else than to go on and do my work as well as I could. Within a few days my elder came to hold my Quarterly Conference. He had heard that there was disappointment and hoped to quiet the people. He was an Irishman, Dennis Murphy by name, an enormous man in size, somewhat an imperialist in make-up, and a bit unpopular with some of the members. He preached on Sunday morning, taking as his text, "Let no man despise thy youth." What effect the sermon had on the people I do not know. I remember my first elder gratefully; he was a good friend, and I loved him.

I found a discouraged church. An effort had been made each winter to hold special meetings, but when results did not come then, they did not come at all. It was not expected that people would be converted at other times. Seven years previously a revival had swept over the community, and on the strength of it the church had lived. Only one young person belonged to the membership. She had joined on what was supposed to be her deathbed. It must be confessed, then, that there was ground for discouragement. An appropriate text would have been, "Fear not, little flock; for it is your Father's good pleasure to give you the kingdom." If I conquer my tendency to idealize, I must confess that the voice of the croaker was in that land. Michelangelo said that he always "criticized by creation." That is the only Christian way to criticize. The creating critic says, "Things are not as they should be; let us pray and work." The rabid critic says, "Things are dead; we cannot accomplish anything." The first finds his courage strengthened and his spirit sweetened; the second looks at the clouds and does not sow, regards the winds and does not reap. He shakes his fist at the skies and strikes at the passing breezes. It is his own field that he does not plant, his own harvest that he does not gather. A church, like a man, is "saved by hope." Despair has no motive. It is lying down with no intention of getting up again. But this critical mood does not rest content with inaction. It says that the divine chariot cannot move, and it blocks the wheels and tears up the road. Its victim must do something; so he criticizes the rest of the church.

I loved the people—loved them all. A review of my feelings discovers no other attitude, though often I feel that I failed in all things else. As for the sermonic side, I wrote my earliest sermons and committed them verbally to memory. An experience at Haven Church, where Bishop Stuntz began his ministry, proved to me that I could speak extempore. This was bad in some ways. Directly I returned to the diligent use of the pen.

I visited industriously. The people were not many, but

visiting took time. The best I could do was to make three calls a day; two was the usual number. Unless a meal was eaten in the home the call was rated as a failure. I went to one home, took dinner, then on to another and took supper; then—if allowed to go on—I might go to another and remain all night and eat breakfast. This I did until I knew all my people intimately; every child and every hired man I could call by name.

I felt ere long that the hearts of the people were with me. So on November 14 I began my meetings. I preached every evening including Saturday and Sunday. For two weeks I worked without apparent result. Then my father came to my aid. On Saturday, when I went home with him, he advised me to discontinue the special effort. But I could not stand it to close the services without having reached some of the young people. The road back to Madison was an Itinerant Gethsemane. I saw the autumn fields with misty eyes. I repeated, "The harvest is past, the summer is ended."

The parish was divided by a creek which trailed its slow way through the meadow. My prayers selected the leader of the young people north of the creek and the leader south of the creek. I felt that if I could secure them, there would be a general turning to Christ and his Church. In my extremity God gave me my desire; one night the two for whom I had longed arose and took their stand for the Master. From that time on the meeting ran conqueringly. It mattered little how I preached. The tide was set toward God and it came to the flood. At the end of seven weeks there remained few young people in that community who had not come out on the Lord's side. Of those received on probation all but two were taken into full membership. When the day came for their reception, not being myself ordained and therefore not entitled to administer baptism, I sent for the old pastor, Dr. Busby,

53

whom they so much loved. He preached and baptized my converts. How happy were the parents! How glad were the older people to see the salvation of God! And how grateful was the pastor to come to victory out of such discouragement, and to see his people united in the joy of the Lord! We began the year with thirty-seven members and we ended it with ninety-two. I could not return for a second year, for I was to go on to college again. But in September I carried a petition to the bishop signed by nearly all the people and all the little children who could either write or make a mark; it asked that I might be returned for another year. Somewhere among my treasures I have that petition still.

It is not easy in this day to visualize the old rural conditions. There were no automobiles or telephones. The horse was the dependence for traveling as well as for plowing. To go from the center of Madison Township to Brooklyn, the nearest considerable town, and return, required approximately five hours. When parents anxiously waited for the birth of a child, the doctor's arrival required from six to ten hours. The rural free delivery was still a dream and post-office boxes did not mark the roads. Often mail was received only on Saturdays when the farmers "went to town" for shopping. There were no bathrooms in Madison Township—though the people were as cleanly as in any fine farming community in the West. There were no "movies" to distract the young people from work in the fields. No radio boomed its disturbance into the farmers' homes.

Life was simple and uncomplicated. The church was the conspicuous building. It lifted itself in steepled beauty above the prairies. It was, moreover, the social center. To it the people resorted for the closer exchanges of fellowship. Courting usually made its modest beginning when the young man "saw the girl home," or came with his freshly washed buggy to "carry" her to the Sunday evening service. The preacher was relatively without competition—his foe not being the jerky hero or heroine of the modern film, but the indifference of his natural constituency. That simple form of life had its advantages. We had time for thinking, and for those fine intimacies often lacking in the crowded life of the city.

The financial outcome of the year was interesting. My salary was $300. I boarded either at home or among my people. I began the year with a good suit of clothes. In the winter and spring there came an epidemic of matrimony. I was overpaid by the extent of an extra collection taken on my last Sunday. I received honoraria for some evangelistic work. The result was that I had in bank when Conference came $392. It was enough when increased by what I made by working in college, and by prize money received in my senior year, and by $200 borrowed with no security save continued life and honor, to put me through the remaining two years in college. I went to Conference also with every benevolence more than met, and with all funds raised for repairing the church.

There are some events that ask for special attention. How well I remember the Christmas that I spent there— my first Christmas away from home! My meetings, still in progress, had kept me at Madison. Toward evening, as I sat in one of the homes of my people, I heard a sly step behind my chair. Turning, I saw the farmer's youngest child running away. Into my lap she had tossed a handkerchief. It was not of value on a money basis, but what care I took of it! I must have kept that kerchief for five years. It was the one memento of the first Christmas spent away from home. I held it as it grew thinner and thinner until at last it was translated.

The year had its dramatic happenings. One of these was connected with my first experience in marrying people.

Father had said, "It will scare you more than it will when you get married yourself." And he was right. The groom was twenty, the bride twenty, and I had just reached my twentieth birthday. On a Sunday afternoon at 2:30 I married them. Four weeks from that day, at precisely 2:30, the bride passed away. Hers was the first marriage I ever performed, her funeral the first I ever attended. It was the custom for all funerals to be held at the church and for the pastor to preach a sermon. This I did one bitter day in January, preaching to a packed house—many people having been drawn together by the peculiar occurrences. In the case of one other young man I used every part of our church ritual that relates to individuals. I received him on probation, helped to baptize him, received him in full, married him, and two years later cared for his obsequies. His only child bears my name.

That small congregation was a miniature world. Every audience has its man who cannot keep awake. One such was in my first church. With him drowsiness was unconquerable. He had been known to go to sleep while milking a cow. He would awake in his wagon and find that his horses had caught the soporific contagion and were dozing in the fence corner. But this sleeper had some excellent qualities. He never blamed the preacher for his slumber. Nor did he ever say that while he often closed his eyes in the service he never really ceased to hear. Perhaps he felt that confession of irresistible sleepiness was to be preferred above the confession of the discourtesy of closed eyes. I used to hope that at the end he might not be so drowsy as to miss Gabriel's trumpet.

The serving saint was in evidence—an aging woman whose deepening wrinkles never could conceal the face and smile of an angel. She talked ill of nobody. She had that Pauline love that thinketh no evil, hopeth all things, endureth all things. The Pope had never heard of her;

56

LOUISA HOLT HUGHES
Aged 82

but the people canonized her. They did not call her Saint; they called her "Aunt Ellen." She was one of those rare souls that attract people, make them feel like claiming relationship. Was there sickness? She was sure to come. She had presided at half the births in the township. She had no diploma and no becoming white cap or apron or cuffs. But she was a trained nurse all the same—a worthy successor of Florence Nightingale. Her credentials were writ with the finger of God himself. A long while ago she graduated from that wide country hospital and went into the region where there is no sickness. What she will do in the country of everlasting health, who can tell? But for her there will be no idle eternity.

The children were like the children of the town and city—the same blueness of eyes, the same sweetness of voice, the same infant frailties. There I got my early lessons in the theology of childhood. I was the intimate friend of every boy and girl. In the winter, when the snow sloped itself into white furrows, and when no horse could tunnel a way through the roads, I had opportunity to get acquainted with the little people. I discovered then how easy it was to give a child the idea that religion was scarcely natural, that it was something to be added as a kind of an appendix to mature life; that the little people could be baptized and could pray and would be saved if they died, while they were not technically saved if they lived; and that the orthodox way was for them not to consider themselves Christians until they had gone a certain distance in the wrong direction, in order that some day they might rush back into God's Kingdom. Two instances I remember that illustrate my meaning. One was in the life of a boy being reared in a home whose air was Christian; the other was in the life of a boy whose home was only nominally a Christian home. The first boy came to regard his religion as food; the second to regard his reli-

57

gion as medicine. A child feels an atmosphere long before it defines a situation.

There were some characters in my church whom I need not treat anonymously:

There was Gavin Lang—a Scotchman, brought up a strict Presbyterian, a man of fine character, generous and painstaking. He was not a member of the church, though a Christian man, and he was overjoyed when all of his "childer" came within the fold. John L. Reams, my only class leader, was hasty and generous, full of fun, cracking his jokes, sometimes forgetting that he had perpetrated them before. One joke he had on me which he ever loved to tell. I fear it was not original. One night we were being entertained at a home. When the time came to retire, we were put in the same room. He asked me, "Which side of the bed do you want?" I said, "Oh, I am not at all particular." Then he said, 'You can take the under side and I will take the upper side." When I dropped off to sleep Uncle John was still shaking the bed with his chuckles. If I were to see him tomorrow he would have his laugh again.

Joshua Leonard was one of the prosperous farmers in the section. He was abrupt and outspoken. He did not seem to me at the first to have a pleasant face. I was his pastor many weeks before I knew him. Then I found that he had a warm heart. With him I had a friendship that will be renewed on the other side. It was he who asked me the questions on the day of my arrival—his wife who gave me the warm welcome.

Perhaps the most noticeable character was Gordy Smith. After my first service he shook hands and said: "My name's Smith; this is my wife; her name's Smith, too. I don't see why they had to remove Dr. Busby. I wish we could have kept him always. I live one-half mile north of the church. Come and see me; but don't do what some preachers have done—stay too long." His wife was one of the finest women I have ever known, and also the largest in size. But she was not openly sensitive. I used to say to her: "Don't stay away from church. When you are absent it makes such a difference in the size of my congregation." She would laugh and promise to be ever on hand. Their home being convenient to the church, I often stayed there. Frequently the thermometer would go below zero. Gordy Smith would put his head in my door and say, "Brother Hughes, have you got enough kiver?" I cannot forget the time I was to go into Brooklyn to preach. The church there was deemed a large one, and it was quite an event to be invited to preach in its pulpit. My people were anxious to have me do well. When I mounted my horse and was ready to start, Gordy Smith looked at me in his queer way and said, "Now see here, Brother Hughes, I want you to do tonight what the turkey did when she sat on a hundred eggs." "And what was that?" I asked at once. "Why, she spread herself," was the reply. Whether I followed the example of the aforesaid turkey I know not to this day.

One of our saints was known as "Mother" Jones. She was aged and was getting blind. She too had been canonized by the people. In her younger days a good singer, the melody still lingered in her quavering voice. I have often been stirred by song but never more so than when Mother Jones sang the hymn which begins:

> If you cannot on the ocean
> Sail among the swiftest fleet.

I can hear her feeble voice singing:

> If you are too weak to journey
> Up the mountain, steep and high,
> You can stand within the valley
> While the multitudes go by;

59

You can chant in happy measure
As they slowly pass along;
Though they may forget the singer,
They will not forget the song.

Neither the singer nor the song has been forgotten. Long ago Mother Jones had her voice renewed and is joining in the songs of the redeemed in heaven.

Two years after leaving this church I came by a strange coincidence to represent the colleges of Ohio in an oratorical contest at Grinnell, Iowa. My first church was eighteen miles distant. It cost one dollar to gain admission. Yet numbers of my people came across the country in their carriages, and stopped overnight at the hotels—to hear their old pastor speak for just ten minutes. The judges gave me the prize! In that vast audience I still see the anxious faces of my farmer-parishioners. After my college mates had cheered and tossed their hats, these friends took my hands and said, "We knew they couldn't any of them beat you." It is worth while to have lived to be able to count such loyal hearts among your friends. After I had been gone from them several years, they planned to drive over the nine miles to the town and have their group pictures taken to send me. Fifty-three of them did that very thing. The picture groups were three: the older married folks in one, the younger married folks in another, and the young folks in the third. Those pictures I have treasured through the years. They revive as tender memories as can well be entertained. They show, also, faces betraying that sturdy character on which the future of church and nation so much depends.

The most of my first parishioners have passed into the heavenlies. One of the delights of my own future, if I am permitted to enter the Holy City, will be to see again the people who were so patient with my mistakes and inexperience, who sent me forth with tears and regrets, and

who rejoiced in succeeding years to know of any success
or gladness that came to me or mine. I look into the faces
in my pictures and I find myself repeating:

> Our old friends, our true friends—
> We'll cherish them forever;
> Our hearts from our old friends
> No changes shall dissever.

Often my railway journeys carry me through Brooklyn,
Iowa, in whose cemetery the dust of many of my first people reposes. Always, by the clairvoyance of love, I am
awakened from slumber. If I am on the proper side of the
Pullman I push up the window shades and look upon
God's Half Acre where the white moonshine falls on
the white tombstones. I am tempted to sing and am hindered only by the proprieties or by the possible wrath of
comrades in alleged sleep. Those other sleepers in that
cemetery awaken me to memories of lasting friendships;
to the renewal of early ministerial vows lest I forget my
first and ardent love of the work of God; to gratitude that
my life was cast with them in its initial ministry, and that
it has been cast with their successors in my several pastorates; and to the immortal hope of a renewed fellowship
with them when the cities of the dead answer to the upward gravitation of God's power and "plenish" the everlasting City of Light and Love.

Thus do I review a chapter whose print is blurred by
the misty tears of affection. My people were very patient
and good to me when I was so young and so inexperienced.
Often I have the affectionate vision of them all. I see
them lifting toward me their "white shields of expectation"; hear them calling to me words of cheer and of anticipating welcome to heaven. Then over the borderland
between the sweet fields of Iowa and the sweeter fields of
Eden I tell them in the name of God that their minister

61

of more than fifty years ago is still on the way to meet them in the Better Land.

II

Much could be written about brief summer pastorates as apprentice periods. Two of these had marked influence. In 1889 I filled out two months of a Conference year for the church at Marengo, Iowa. Full pastoral work was impossible for so short a time. It was understood that visiting should care only for emergencies. So I gave the weeks largely to reading and sermon preparation. I occasionally still find notes and manuscripts that were produced in that quiet period. Several members of the church made lasting impressions on me—Charles Baumer, a native of Germany, who combined in himself the catechetical tradition of Lutheranism and the earnestness of Methodism; "Father" Lyon, a gentle soul whom the community had loved under that paternal inscription; and "Aunt" Judy Groff, a wonderful character with whom all claimed kinship. This list indicates that the memorable persons for a pastor's heart are not necessarily the holders of wealth or of social position.

Aunt Judy Groff's husband was known as "Dickey" Groff. He was a Harvard College graduate. His finely trained intellect had never been able to subdue certain peculiarities. He was a pseudo merchant, maintaining a medley store whose dusty and unclassified contents deserved the name "Old Curiosity Shop." He preached for a minor denomination; and his quaint sayings made for county jollity. He would ask the children what kind of trees were in the wood. Given answer in terms of oak, or chestnut, or birch, he would reply: "No! Round trees!" "What kind of stones are in the creek?" To replies in terms of sandstones or limestones, he would say: "No! Wet stones!" Yet occasionally in the midst of these peculiar remarks there would flash a scintillation that told of fine philosophies and put life in the idiom of brilliance.

The other summer pastorate came at St. Paul's Church, Tiffin, Ohio. William Fraser McDowell, being but thirty-two years of age, had been elected chancellor of Denver University. He went to Colorado to lift a state's ideals higher than her Rocky Mountains! The panic of 1892-93 drove the money men into shivers and reduced the university's attendance until in 1895 the College of Liberal Arts had but one graduate. The new alumnus humorously met the situation by giving the Class Yell—

> Sakes alive! Sakes alive!
> I am the Class of Ninety-Five!

That summer pastorate brought me bonds of intimacy with Doctor, afterward Bishop, McDowell—bonds never broken by any unseemly force.

His goods, including library and manuscripts, were not moved until the fall. So I had plenteous reading matter. Even his written sermons remained, but could not be plagiarized, since the people had already heard them! Yet they were a constant reminder that I had succeeded a master of assemblies. My recourse was hard work. As Carlyle would say, I "toiled terribly" and laid foundations that have remained firm through the years.

One event made, perhaps, an undue impression on me. A child was to be baptized. I was not yet ordained. So I sought the reverent service of two neighbor clergymen— only to make a discovery of that High-Church theory which shocked me distinctly and which still stands as a barrier against church union. So stringent were the conditions laid down by my alleged colleagues that I determined to wait for my own ordination as deacon in September, ere the rite was administered to the child. It was my first experience with the superstition which de-

mands the unity of Christ's people, and still denies it by
narrow conduct. I thanked God then for membership
in a Church that in no degree disfranchises faithful souls
because of a sacramentarian doctrine or an exclusive ministry. Ritualistic walls as a religious prison have never
impressed me as adorning the faith of Christ our Saviour.
Had he himself commanded them, he could certainly have
given the prescription in terms that would not cause
agelong debates or become themselves the occasions of
condescension.

III

My first year in the Boston University School of Theology was given wholly to my studies. Social life was
eschewed. I had no desire for a student appointment.
My intent was to keep the student period true to itself.
As recounted in a preceding chapter, Phillips Brooks had
declared vigorously that the stages of life should not be
mixed. This advice had a bearing on another problem
that was then emerging. Theological students, unlike
students in law and medicine, were occasionally being
married and were bringing their brides to Boston to be
touched by its "culture." Often the touches were received
in rather pathetic quarters that forbade parenthood, while
distance from the dormitory prevented participation in
the School's fellowship. My observation convinced me
that in normal cases marriages of the students were not
wise. Some of my friends were disappointed later in my
semipublic statement that my aid for quarters on a campus
for husbands and wives would be reluctant. I am not
enthusiastic about connubial dormitories. Nor do I regret that I lived up to my theory—not to be married until
I was graduated from the seminary.

Hope Chapel, whose pastorate I accepted in my second
year, was the mission adjunct of the Old South Congrega-

tional Church. The services were held in a Lutheran church. Thus I was working in the sanctuary of one denomination, being supported by the funds of another, and administering the sacraments under the ordination of a third. I was leading a triple life. I have always thanked God for the joyful training that I had in that wider fellowship. My appointment was ideal. I escaped one of the perils of a student pastorate—that of careless preparation for the pulpit. My two years in that mission chapel were of immense benefit to me. I wish that I could feel that they were of corresponding benefit to my needy parishioners.

One valid argument can be given for pastoral service in the seminary years. It tends to break the dominion of cold theorizing. The utter autocracy of the intellect is not good. Seminarians tend to the critical mood. Often the men who pay their own expenses in order that, by addresses, they may help the students are mercilessly criticized by them. Ministerial success may be readily achieved in imagination. It is not so easily achieved when one deals with stubborn material that refuses to give a quick response in Christ's name. Perhaps a measure of youthful pharisaism is inevitable. Later we reach the gentler charity toward ministerial comrades. Spurgeon used to say that he could address the Parliament with less trepidation than he felt in speaking to seminary students.

In my mission district I found one condition that I have not encountered since. The community was a mixture of whites and Negroes. There were several intermarriages—invariably that of a white woman to a Negro man. These couples were compelled to make their own social life, being more or less ostracized by both races. Such knowledge as I gained in succeeding years as to the children of these mixed marriages was not reassuring. My heart ached for the people who dwelt in a social no man's

65

land. The definite choice involved in the marriages apparently increased the social handicaps, and the resulting homes did not have the spontaneous joy that was manifest in the more normal circles.

My chief in this pastorate was the late George A. Gordon. He allowed me complete freedom. His officials assigned me a regular pew in the Old South Church; and often on Sunday mornings I heard the majestic messages of the Scotch immigrant who, coming as a penniless boy to America, won a conspicuous place in our church life. Dr. Gordon laid emphasis upon an intellectual ministry. Harvard had filled him with Plato. He himself did not fully recognize that the Apostle Paul in him frequently outdid the philosopher. Occasionally his pulpit utterances were grandly emotional. When a campaign for the destruction of the English sparrows was on in Boston, his sermon on "God and the Sparrow" touched the city. The tiny birds, with their pluck and pugnacity, might well have discovered that the spirit of Francis of Assisi brooded in the heart of a modern pulpiteer.

When I left the pastorate at Hope Chapel Dr. Gordon and his people gave me gifts of gold and books. The generous salary had cleared away my college debts and crowded my shelves with volumes purchased under wise counsel. One thing was noticeable in this mission work. It gloriously defeated itself. The young people, lifted by the Gospel to nobler life, moved ere long to the so-called better sections. I have found them and their descendants, meeting the demands of high citizenship, and dwelling in the suburbs of earthly cities as they moved onward to a New Jerusalem.

IV

In April, 1892, two months before my graduation, I was appointed pastor of the Methodist Episcopal church at

Newton Centre, Massachusetts. The edifice of worship, a well-located wooden structure, had been erected in the seventies, when the theory prevailed that the church building was to grow with the growth of the membership, rather than that the expensive architecture must come first. The membership was approximately one hundred and twenty. But what a personnel! The list held the names of a former vice-president of the Atchison Railroad; a former treasurer of the same line; the president and the secretary of the Boston Chamber of Commerce; two professors of Boston University; a future president of the same institution; and Dr. and Mrs. William Butler, missionary founders in India and Mexico. Thus, two months before my proud hand reached for my diploma, I was instructing this select group on Sunday mornings! My people were earnest, but not fanatical. A review reveals the fact that forty-one of them could take a modest part in speech or prayer in the social meetings. My immediate predecessor was the late William R. Clark, a recognized saint of New England Methodism. For five years he had steadily developed his membership in substantial character and service.

Graduating on June 1, 1892, I was married on June 8 to Miss Isabel Baker Ebbert, daughter of Dr. and Mrs. Jonathan B. Ebbert, of Atlanta, Georgia. Of my wife a portrayal is given in another chapter. Reared a Southern Presbyterian, she found the Newton Centre church ideal for her transition to Methodism. The parsonage became the joyful center of our people—even as she made it the ideal working and resting place for her preacher-husband. Although the Newton population was high-class, it was not wrongly complacent. If congregations did not make vocal response to earnest preaching, they did give facial Amens. My own people were loyal to the church, harmonious, and generous toward every crusade that represented the Redeemer. In my second year they gave to missions an average of more than ten dollars per capita, and found gladness in the World Dream of Christ. They supported an evangelistic endeavor that covered the nights of an entire month, resulting in conversions that increased the membership by more than 25 per cent. The years passed in fellowship that was radiant and in service that was glad.

The morning of joy was ere long overshadowed by sorrow. The first child, wee Margaret, dwelt in our kingdom for only four months and twenty-one days and then was transferred to God's nearer Kingdom. At the time I recall reading Phillips Brooks's sermon on "The Consolations of God." I was touched and helped as well by Lowell's poem entitled "On the Death of a Friend's Child." I can still repeat some of its lines:

> Children are God's apostles, day by day
> Sent forth to preach of love, and hope, and peace;
> Nor hath thy babe his mission left undone.
> To me, at least, his going hence hath given
> Serener thoughts and nearer to the skies,
> And opened a new fountain in my heart
> For thee, my friend, and all. . . . .

I wonder still if these early experiences of grief are not parts of our preparation. A wise lady-saint among my people said to me then, "You will better know someday what this little child has done for you." It did not require long years for that revelation. So many of God's ministers lose their first child. Tiny hands lead them into consoling ways. The glad days are interrupted by sadness, so that our young and rosy hopes may be accompanied by the minor requiems. We go more knowingly with our people into the vale of sorrows. God changes the name from Joses to Barnabas, and makes each of us the lieutenant comforter of his people.

In my Newton Centre days I came into intimacy with Samuel Francis Smith. He was a quaint old Baptist clergyman whose drawling speech would not have suggested the poet. The first time I delivered an address on patriotism, Dr. Smith introduced me—being himself felicitously presented to the audience by William Edwards Huntington as "Samuel Francis Smith, of America"! His hymn has not been banished by the "Star-Spangled Banner" or by Mrs. Bates's "O Beautiful for Spacious Skies." Oliver Wendell Holmes's humorous line about the failure of fate to conceal his classmate "by naming him Smith" still stands good. I have rejoiced because the man who wrote "My Country, 'Tis of Thee," wrote also "The Morning Light Is Breaking"—giving a lesson much needed in our day, that the American and the missionary, the nationalist and the internationalist, may dwell peacefully in one heart.

At Newton Centre, also, I often met Elizabeth Stuart Phelps, daughter of Austin Phelps. She had married Herbert Ward, a man much younger than she was—so that she was often referred to as "The Youth's Companion." Her *Gates Ajar* had comforted many people, while her *Singular Life,* having, it is said, a Methodist preacher as its hero, added to her repute. I had a special reason for giving her admiration. I was ready to conduct the funeral services of Mrs. William Hahn, a pious German immigrant whose husband had done his heroic part in the Civil War. Mrs. Ward slipped into my hands a poetic tribute to the faithful soul of her neighbor. So far as I know, the lines have never before appeared in any book. I enter them here as a testimony to their author, as they are witness to a saintly woman.

69

Long was the march, but strong the step
    That trod the loneliness of life.
We give thee proudly to thy rest,
    A soldier's wife.

Sweet was the soul, and brave the lips
    That quivering uttered no complaints.
We give thee to our Father's heart,
    Thou Christian saint.

While in my Newton Centre pastorate I was much influenced by the Rev. John Watson, of Scotland, who became quickly famous as the author of dialect stories representing the hill people of his nativity. Under the pseudonym of Ian Maclaren he published *Beside the Bonnie Brier Bush* and *The Days of Auld Lang Syne*. Like other European authors, he came to the United States on lecture tours. I heard him as he spoke in Tremont Temple, Boston. A typical clergyman, he made a favorable impression, while in the speedy handshakings in the formal line he showed no wrong reserve. A biography of a few years ago treated him with a minimum of courtesy and declared that his sermonic output was cheapened by a descent to the Chautauqua Tent style. But the truth was that Dr. Watson kept his own personal equation true. He had never aspired to be a Platonian pulpiteer.

Three of his stories stand out in tender conspicuousness—"A Doctor of the Old School," "Domsie Jamison," and "His Mother's Sermon." The first relates to a Highland doctor, the second to a schoolteacher, the third to a young preacher who, as I myself was then tempted to do, noticeably displayed the progressive label. He found a gentle antidote against overdone criticism in the remembrance of his mother's counsel that he is "always to speak a gude word for Christ." The frequency of these worn volumes in the second-hand bookstores shows what wide

70

currency they once had. Many copies have I bought for younger ministers—that these successors may be saved from a false pride and may learn how to make their hearts companions of their minds.

That Newton Centre church of mine had a vigorous personnel. I cannot fully list its distinctive spirits. It seemed as if the Lord had gathered the cream from a dozen ordinary congregations and had placed it in my ecclesiastical cup! We all gave an emphatic premiership to the late Hon. Alden Speare—a Vermont boy who came from his native hills to Boston and began his modest commerce by tithing his income for Christ's work. Among the rich men that I have known, I still class him with the two most generous. He literally knew the meaning of Christ's saying—not found in the Gospels, but recovered by the Spirit in the Acts—"It is more blessed to give than to receive." He reveled in benevolence, being most anxious that his church and his children should know that form of the Lord's joy. With impulsive affection he took me to his heart and kept me "in the round-tower" to the end, as if I were another son in company with his boys, Lewis R. and E. Ray. Scores of times, when I have thought of Alden Speare, I have involuntarily repeated Paul's word, "I thank my God upon every remembrance of you."

William Edwards Huntington, Mr. Speare's son-in-law, was then dean of the Boston University College of Liberal Arts. He quickly reversed the role and became pastor to me and to my family. He baptized all our children. I teased him more than once by saying that he would not have established the expensive precedent of a five-dollar-gold-piece gift to each christened child if he had known how many more would call for the touch of his baptismal hands! As dean, and later as president of Boston University, he served his generation by the will of God, and

71

by the love of God in his own heart won the love of multitudes.

How can I make record of the others! I recall affectionately Edwin M. Fowle, whose kindly cheer never failed him amid hardships; William M. Flanders, with a genius for fellowship, a gift of wit, and a loyalty that wavered not when aid was needed by his friends; Avery L. Rand, who made a specialty of crisp statement and became the town's skilled parliamentarian; Sarah Wood Rand, his wife, one who could read a superior book propped on a near-by chair, while she made her seven children ready for school; William P. Cooke, one of the outstanding dental doctors of New England, a layman splendidly informed in Methodist history and polity; George F. Richardson, who had the grace of the skilled usher, and who never failed his pastors in loving hospitality; Moses W. Merrill, whose utter deafness never persuaded him to discontinue the public worship of God, and who rendered me a service because I felt that I must have my sermon manuscript ready for him to read as he sat in the silence of his own soul's sanctuary; Henry D. Degen, a statuesque gentleman preferred in the city's politics, and a member of a General Conference, who reverently walked the aisles of God's house and carried its meaning on all the streets of life; Alexander Montgomery, born on the banks of the Penobscot River, and therefore a rejector of Columbia River salmon. A man who, being beyond middle age and too modest to approach the altar with confidence, still gave his humble confession of Christ; made ready to meet his only child, Alice, in the heaven where she long preceded him, and shared his beautiful grave plot and memorial stone with his young pastor's family—so that today the dust of our children sleeps in comradeship.

What friends they all were! Could a better transition place have been found for my beautiful bride as she passed from the South to the North, and from Presbyterianism to Methodism! Over nearly half a century my memory carries the Christmas scene when on the morn of the blessed Day our members' kindnesses caused our parsonage to look as if a hundred helpers of Santa Claus had made its rooms a specialty. So do my wonderful people come trooping back into my grateful heart.

I did not dare to preach to them without careful preparation. They were my pressure—not because they were critical or demanding, but because they were sympathetic and knowing. Someone has said that a proper congregation gives back to a preacher in showers what he gives to them in mist. There is truth in this spiritual weather report. Without doubt our ministry is always ministering to ourselves. Our "works follow with" us! I could not tell my old Newton Centre people how much they did for me. They continued my education. Through half a century there have been returning the benedictions which my young lips pronounced on their lives.

V

Five men appeared one Sunday morning in the Newton Centre congregation. They had the self-conscious air of an investigating committee. Even if their efforts to hide themselves had not revealed them, one of my officials caught the intent of a pastoral theft. The result was that in April, 1896, the desire that I should be appointed to Centre Church, Malden, Massachusetts, was confirmed by the bishop.

The city had an interesting history. If its political records had not been as significant as those of some other civic neighbors, its ecclesiastical records made up for the lack. In my pastorate the town celebrated the two hundred and fiftieth anniversary of its settlement. A Westerner could scarcely conceive of that length of time.

Michael Wigglesworth had been pastor there for almost fifty years, the village's physician as well as its minister. There he had written his poem "The Day of Doom," with its appalling descriptions of the Judgment. Its verses definitely condemned the nonelect children to "the easiest room in hell" and gave Arminian debaters poetic proof whenever a Calvinist denied that his intellectual forebears had ever explicitly assigned the little people to perdition. In the poem the condemnation of the toddlers is given in God's own words!

Yet in the town where Wigglesworth sleeps beneath the epitaph written by Cotton Mather, Adoniram Judson was born in the Congregational parsonage. Judson did not specialize in technical theology, but so escaped from the doctrine of decrees as to feel overwhelming responsibility for the world's salvation. The stormy career whose escapades give material for a movie film began in Malden and ended with a sepulcher in the ocean—as if no other tomb could be appropriate for so abundant a life.

Still later, another man-child arrived in Malden—Gilbert Haven. As Judson refused to make election apply to continents, so Haven refused to apply it to races. The modern champion, amid the antislavery debates, hotly repudiated reprobation as applied to the Negro people. A study of these three men suggests a progressive revelation—too meaningful for partisan use, and yet so significant as to claim more than a paragraph of religious history.

The Methodist annals in Malden were noteworthy. Centre Church's human founder was a glass-blower from Cambridge, Joseph Marsh, a local preacher who on weekdays skillfully fashioned tubes into desired forms, and on Sundays put the silver trumpet of the Gospel to his lips. Ere many years the little society received strong recruits. Probably in 1822, the Minutes of the First Congregational Church showed this record: "The Pastor stayed the Church

74

after communion and presented the request of Bro. G. Haven for a letter of dismissal that he might unite with the Methodists." A committee was appointed to confer with "Bro. Haven." Evidently the conference was not a success. Shortly thereafter the people were again "stayed," and the letter was duly given. Two years later the like request was made by "Sister Hannah Haven." The issue was political. The elder Haven had been deeply offended by a strong Federalist sermon delivered by the pastor.

The record was simple, but the results were many and great. Intermarriage with the Havens brought into Methodism the powerful Cox family. As the mother of the Haven home remained with the First Congregational Church for two years after the birth of Gilbert Haven, Jr., it is even likely that the child was baptized at the altar where Wigglesworth had officiated, and where the wee Judson had been lifted to receive the touch of the sacred waters. But the denominational change of the Haven family meant that leading influences moved into the Methodist line; that the consecrated Cox wealth passed into the Wesleyan treasury; that two bishops, Gilbert Haven and Erastus O. Haven, the latter a virtual founder of the University of Michigan and of Syracuse University, were to be consecrated; and that in the succeeding generation the late William Ingraham Haven was to enter the New England Conference, and to become an efficient secretary of the American Bible Society. Could a pastor in 1824 have fully evaluated that day or had a vision of the long-run effects?

When in 1906 I came to this church the fruitful years had crowned its work with power. The Haven Homestead did not long abide next to the sanctuary; but the Haven influence, unlike the residence, could not be removed. I remember my first approach to the church doors. Having been appointed on Monday, I came the next Sunday, to view my name neatly painted as "Pastor" on the fine Bulletin. That quick thoughtfulness gave me what the moderns would call a thrill. The prompt change had been made by Peter Graffam—as efficient a trustee of church property as I have ever known. The congregation, in its size and quality, astonished me. I was so young; but here I was—minister of one of the strongest Methodist churches in New England. Only the sense of responsibility could have pushed my pride into its proper place. I began with the right text: "We preach not ourselves, but Christ Jesus the Lord; and ourselves your servants for Jesus' sake." I think God opened to me at once the hearts of my new parishioners.

A decision previously made in two instances seemed to be vindicated by the Malden opportunity. I had gone to the Newton Centre church at a salary of $1,200 and house, when I was being solicited to consider $3,500 and house by a Congregational church. I was not much tempted. My attitude was not sectarian. The Methodist Church had spent thousands of dollars on my education; had been the chief influence in developing the character and usefulness of my parents; had led me to a confession of Christ; and had never failed me in any way. I came soon to a conclusion that departure from one's spiritual nativity was a serious thing. If I had been doctrinally at variance with my Church, or utterly restless under its government, or wholly doubtful of its leadership, I might have had a different feeling. William Robertson Nicoll declared that only the call of conscience should lead to a denominational change; and he intimated that even then conscience should have close scrutiny. I had no quarrel with the men who had left Methodism to take up ministry in another church. Indeed, in some cases I would have advised such a course. But with myself the situation kept returning to a simple test in the form of a question: Would you

76

make this proposed transition if the salaries offered were somewhat lower than those proposed in your own denomination? I had no preference for the auction-block theory of the ministry. I could find no deep reason for leaving the Church that had nurtured me. A review of that decision has never given me momentary regret. Yet my relations with other churches and ministers have always been friendly and affectionate. I have been happy to be a loving comrade of all groups that witness to Christ and promote his Kingdom. When one thinks of the Christian populations on a merely arithmetical basis, it would be dreadful to believe that any one Church had been given a monopoly on the road to heaven.

The interdenominational relations in Malden scarcely suggested rivalry. Those who speak as if half a century ago the different churches dwelt in hostile camps misrepresent the situation. The difficulties in association were mostly made by those who laid stress upon the need of union—and this often without any apparent idea that if an ecclesiastical doctrine prevented a courteous attitude and common endeavor, it was sure to make a later barrier against complete brotherhood. If any of our denominations wishes to call itself a "bridge church" over which our several groups may walk to unification, other parties have a right to ask what there is on the farther bank of the stream. Does the road on the proximate end of the bridge lead to the place where you will have to build a span over the Tiber?

My closest friend among the ministers of Malden was the late James F. Albion, pastor of the First Parish Universalist. He was endowed with gifts and graces for the pastoral life—a fine and smiling presence, an eager and practical sympathy, an appealing and human speech. Though himself a frank confessor of the doctrines of both Murray and Channing, he never seemed to question the

77

sincerity of an evangelical conscience. He felt a bit disturbed occasionally because so many of his funerals were those of people with a "doubtful destination." He gained a sober amusement from the fact that their families felt that the deceased were safe only in the hands of a Universalist minister.

One peculiarity in the city's religious life helped to lower fences until they became only lines. Several large denominations had no local churches—as, for example, the Christians so numerous in the West and South; and the Presbyterians, whose compact with the Congregationalists had prevented wide organization in New England. Yet the members of the Christian Church came occasionally to New England, while Presbyterians from the West, and from Nova Scotia, New Brunswick, and Newfoundland, were constantly arriving. A consequence was that the inside of our church came to have so many outsiders. On one Sunday I received into membership the representatives of eight different denominations, and at the same communion received on probation a former Roman Catholic and a former Unitarian. In this way the tribes of the Lord came to the testimony of a common Israel. For the majority of the Christian people in Malden exclusive ecclesiastical claims would have been regarded with an indulgent derision.

Julia Ward Howe, who lived in Melrose near at hand, I came to know quite well, having the privilege of speaking on the same platform with her several times. As an aging woman she was striking and attractive. One felt the invisible companionship of her splendid father, whose wealth did not spoil his daughter; and of her husband, Dr. Samuel G. Howe, glorified by splendid service for the education of the blind. Her popular fame rests on verses that were born of the travail of war. In Washington a party of Bostonians forgot their reserve and marched along the streets singing "John Brown's Body." In the dawn of the next morning Mrs. Howe wrote to the tune "The Battle Hymn of the Republic," giving form to "the long lines of verse swinging through her brain." "The stump of pencil" moving swiftly in the semidarkness became a pen of fire and storm. Soon Chaplain McCabe, afterward a Methodist bishop, sang the lines with his silver voice and started the hymn on its turbulent vogue. Its memorable vigor should not be allowed to hide her other compositions or to push the story of her work for freedom and for woman suffrage into forgetfulness.

One argument that Mrs. Howe used for votes for women was unique. Declaring that national life was domestic life enlarged, she observed that when Matthew Vassar submitted his plans for the dormitory of the college that was to honor his name, he omitted provision for clothes closets in the rooms of the lady students. The application lies on the surface of the illustration.

Edward Everett Hale I met on many occasions. To me he was not an attractive speaker, nor was he as broad in spirit as he conceived himself to be. Each time I encountered him closely he was distinctly critical of the evangelical groups, especially of the Presbyterians, who were not numerous in the region where he had spent his ministry. His fame on the practical side rested largely on his "Lend a Hand" slogan, while on the literary side his name was glorified by his authorship of *The Man Without a Country*. One of his stories, *My Double and How He Undid Me*, still has a vogue as a piece of humor. Dr. Hale could not have had a double. He was so unmistakably himself. With his long hair, his gray whiskers, his whirling cape, his wide hat, he was a Boston institution. When the twentieth century came in he was chosen to offer the prayer at the Watch-Night Service. The vast crowds stretched away into acres of darkness on Boston

79

Common. When the venerable figure appeared on the platform beneath the Golden Dome and began his petition with the Psalmist's words, "Lord, thou hast been our dwelling place in all generations. Before the mountains were brought forth, or ever thou hadst formed the earth and the world, even from everlasting to everlasting, thou art God," a wave of reverence swept over the throng and brought to the people the sense of eternity.

The industrial situation in Malden was most happy. The great Converse Rubber Works had as a leader the late Elisha S. Converse, known by his church title as "Deacon." A fair-minded and kindly employer, he made the vast factory adopt his mood. All our charities became his beneficiaries. He never kept his purse by claiming that he was keeping his head. Nor did he ever excuse the millionaire's caution by borrowing the garb of the widow with the two mites. As long as the spirit of this great man ruled the industry of the city, strikes were unknown. I cannot recall that in eight years the industrial pulse moved above the normal and caused the gathering of feverish agitators.

One of my office-bearers was a splendid magnate. The late Roswell R. Robinson traced his ancestry back to the *Mayflower* along several different lines. He could have adopted Paul's pride of lineage: "If any other man thinketh that he hath whereof he might trust in the flesh, I more." He was the head of the Robinson Brothers' Indexical Soap Company, which manufactured all the Cuticura soap through more than twenty-five years. A man slight in stature, with white hair and ruddy cheeks, he specialized in silence. But he was garrulous with his checkbook. It was not necessary to ask him for money. He was a genius in anticipating the ministerial agent. In the last year of his life he gave me unsolicited so many thousands of dollars for the causes of Christ that I hesi-

80

tate to mention the sum. I count it a day's work of vast value that, when another man was proposed as a trustee of Boston University, I insisted dogmatically that Roswell R. Robinson was the premier among all possibilities. I had my way, with the result that the university received many thousands of dollars; the lovely Robinson Chapel for the theologues; and, at last, the endowment of an annual dinner at the Boston Methodist Social Union for the theological students and their wives. I never attend that annual banquet without feeling that I am the grandfather of the occasion.

When Roswell R. Robinson came to his deathbed, his delirium took the form of generous giving. He was writing checks for the Saviour's work, being particularly anxious that "the Bishop come, and cash the check for the mortgage of $22,000 on the Louisburg Square dormitory of the School of Theology." This dream his loyal daughter, Mrs. Helen Robinson Richards, fulfilled after her father's death. I think of this shy philanthropist whenever I read the less awkward translation of the American Revised Version: "Make to yourselves friends by means of the mammon of unrighteousness; that, when it shall fail, they may receive you into the eternal tabernacles." Mr. Robinson gave his attitude to the industrial life of his city, and labor and capital kept peace. At the gates prophesied by the Saviour throngs must have greeted this gentle pilgrim who on his upward journey sanctified earth's market places.

As I went from Malden into educational work, the Centre Church pastorate was my last. I was blessed in its official personnel. For more than seven years the evening congregation was maintained with as large numbers as the morning, because this vesper meeting was not made secondary by scrappy preparation following absorption in the earlier meeting, and because my official members gave

81

wholehearted loyalty to the evening service, which by definite agreement never continued more than an hour. How can I single out their names without discrimination!

Joseph Stevens and Lyman H. Richards, both ex-captains of sea vessels who allowed none of the preacher's nautical metaphors to go astray.

Wilbur H. Sargeant, LeRoy S. Johnson, and John G. Chandler, faithful trustees, who kept the House of God as the place of his excellent glory.

Charles N. Peabody, the assiduous Sunday-school superintendent, a comrade in service with whom I shall take up renewed fellowship in another School by and by.

Charles L. Dean, twice state Senator, and thrice Mayor of the city, whose remembrance of calendar dates and whose prolific handshaking received jocular attention, but became political capital.

Charles Raisbeck Magee, finally my brother-in-law by his marriage to my wife's sister. A really majestic person in appearance, with a splendid head and with eyes that were windows for a big soul. The best-informed Methodist layman in New England and a real lover of the Church. A dear and wonderful friend whose staunch loyalty made him a counselor without irritation, and a leader without jealousy. A personal evangelist when his duty so called him, and my chief aid in bringing his intimate, William F. Chester, to a confession of Christ.

Charles Edward Mann, the church historian, an adept in local records relating to the Christian life, and in the wider knowledge of the Wesleyan movement.

Joseph C. Robinson, freight trainmaster of the Boston and Maine Railroad, a man whom I led to Christ when he was seventy-eight years of age, and who on the night of his death sent word to his old pastor that he would wait for him beyond the veil.

All these that I have mentioned are now in heaven.

Within the present church the remainders of my pastorate are not many. Three of the Hawley sisters are still there. Mrs. Bessie T. Hawley, their mother, was the best Sunday-school teacher I have had in my ministry. M. Louise Small, official secretary, will be surprised by the entries that the Recording Angel has made about her on the Books of Life. Mr. and Mrs. William M. Bailey became neighbors in residence and in heart. Mr. and Mrs. Willard Welsh, unfailing friends with whom I have walked along ways of joy and sorrow, have had a door of hospitality that ever swung on glad hinges for my coming.

All these came then, or later, into the official life of Centre Church. If I went beyond that list, where would my pen find a stopping place? One other must have mention, the daughter of my long-time friend and trustee, John G. Chandler. I stood with Josephine Chandler when she was married to a noble and kindly man, Andrew Pierce. "In love with life and raptured with the world," she still came early to the sorrow of widowhood. Later her spirit which craved the eager ways of gladness and service summoned its heroism for the endurance of frailty. I trust that she may not resent the fact that the pastor of her young girlhood and the friend of the intervening years gives her a gentle place in this pastoral record.

CHAPTER IV

EDUCATION

I CANNOT RECALL THAT IN MY SCHOLASTIC PREPARATION, or in my earlier ministry, I had even the slightest ambition for an educational career. Still the drift in that direction soon came. For years I was secretary and treasurer of the Alpha Chapter of Boston University, composed of the graduates of the School of Theology. After I began the pastoral ministry invitations for school commencements began to reach me. On the tenth anniversary of my graduation from Ohio Wesleyan I was called upon to give the address to the Class of 1899. Later I was solicited to take the headship of a school whose type of work did not at all appeal to me, but which did offer to the right man a worthy opportunity. Even then I had, so far as I can recall, no plan for educational service. I remember my surprise when Bishop James Whitford Bashford told me that in due season the Church would insist on my taking a college presidency. Since this Bishop had frequently shown an uncanny power of prophecy in these personal affairs, I found myself for the first time pondering the matter in my heart.

In March, 1903, a committee from the Board of Trustees of DePauw University at Greencastle, Indiana, appeared in my congregation at Centre Church, Malden, Massachusetts. I learned afterward that, while the two men were not displeased with the sermon, they were distinctly impressed by the pastor's aptness in taking an offering for some important cause! They well knew that their institution was in need of a promoter, and they were cheered to find one in embryo! The committeemen were the late Deloss M. Wood, of the Northwest Indiana Conference, and the late Charles E. Bacon, of the Indiana Conference. With the late William D. Parr and the late George W. Switzer they had made a ministerial quartet that gave faithful service to DePauw University. All being graduates of the institution, they carried in their hearts the tradition of their alma mater's glory, and in her darkest years they never failed in filial loyalty. In truth, their wise endeavors had quite as much to do with saving the college for posterity as did the financial gifts of their lay comrades.

In my first negotiations, which implied no committals on their part or my own, I had meager leanings toward the suggested presidency. I was most happy in my pastorate. I did not see, as I later saw clearly, that for the management of a church college the pastoral instinct is not only good but necessary. My remembrance of my dealings with these men makes me wonder why they did not at once look elsewhere. Perhaps they would have done so if Dr. Francis J. McConnell had not given them a transcript of my uncertain attitude—far more accurately than I myself could have done. On the night of March 31, 1903, I was aroused from a hotel bed at Brockton, Massachusetts, and informed by newspaper reporters that I had been elected president of DePauw University. I was quite sure that the report was a mistake. Never had I known of an election to such a position without an iota of consent on the part of the noncandidate. But early the next day telegrams confirmed the rumors, and I was faced with the necessity of making a decision.

DePauw University in 1903 was still on the edge of collegiate bankruptcy. Her name had been changed from Indiana Asbury—not at all at the request of Mr. Wash-

85

ington C. DePauw, her chief benefactor. The change of name had not been pleasing to many graduates. The finding of plentiful supplies of natural gas in northern Indiana had made it difficult for Mr. DePauw's southern Indiana factories to compete with their rivals. His philanthropies were generous, but not so large as to support the widening program of the institution. In addition, a kindly treasurer, who was as honest as sunlight, made loans on the basis of friendship rather than financial security, while the one-treasury system allowed the unsafe mingling of current expenses and endowments. Deficits had become appalling. All this made for a loss of financial confidence. The prophets of despair were many.

But there were decided reassurances. Dr. William H. Hickman, as chancellor, had improved the finances and had secured Minshall Laboratory for the scientific departments. Dr. Hillary Asbury Gobin had been chosen as acting president, following the administration of Dr. John Price Durbin John, one of the ablest educators of the period. Though never formally inaugurated, he continued as president for years. Gifted with a genial Irish wit which pleased but never wounded, endowed with an accomplished mind that was concealed by a saintly character, having an administrative skill that came from kindly motive and an active faithfulness, he led the university through its years of famine. The moral confidence that the alumni, the church leaders, and the citizens of Indiana had in Dr. Gobin was steadily transferred to the college itself. I was fortunate in having him for my predecessor, even as I was fortunate in having him as vice-president. He was always a generous asset, and I came to revere him as an elder brother in the DePauw family.

The University had a remarkable social endowment in its alumni. Its first president was Matthew Simpson, afterward editor and bishop—and through the war period the friend and counselor of Lincoln. Though the institution had less than two thousand male graduates, it had furnished seven United States senators, five governors, and over fifty college presidents. It was much as if Matthew Simpson's genius had passed into the college and continued to bring forth its own kind. The debt of $22,000 and the deficit of $6,000 were more than offset by a wonderful tradition and by an assured repute—that few institutions in the world were such amazing producers.

I came to Greencastle on an unwilling visit. Courtesy bade me take the journey. When I stood on the platform of Meharry Hall and looked at the student body, I quickly discovered God's will for myself. The institution attracted splendid young life. Indiana had a peculiarly American quality. She had a reputation as the homeland of authors: Charles Major, Lew Wallace, James Whitcomb Riley, Meredith Nicholson, George Barr McCutcheon, George Ade, Booth Tarkington gave varied credentials in this respect. An alert humor was in the atmosphere and it breezed each year to the DePauw campus. I heard ere I went to the presidency that the student body was a chief factor in the higher education given in the charming county seat.

So on May 2, 1903, I wrote my formal acceptance and began to plan the transfer of my duties. I had no misconception that the main business of the head of an institution of Christian learning was to walk to his office looking Socratic, or come to chapel in the guise of Plato, or maintain a forum like Cicero. I knew that bitterly hard work awaited me. So far from having a large circle of friends in Indiana, I had scarcely a group of acquaintances. I did have one strong staff on which to lean. Martin V. Bieger, new president of the Board of Trustees, and a growingly prosperous manufacturer, had been on the committee that allured me. He had promised me that, as he had no children, he would make DePauw University his child and would give generous support. Yet when I reached the railroad station at Greencastle and stood there with my family clustered around me, there was placed in my hand a telegram announcing the fatal illness of Mr. Bieger. My first public duty in the state was to speak at his funeral services. His loss was a staggering blow indeed, but as I backward stepped I felt that I touched solid ground in the eternity of God's love. The withdrawal of the earthly help sent me in more prayerful search to the heavenly resources.

My new constituency did not know my tremors. It was a time of doleful prophecies concerning denominational colleges. All the despairing things that are being said now were being uttered then. The professional colleges would dovetail downward and consume the junior and senior years. The high schools would dovetail upward and devour the freshman and sophomore years. The figure of the upper and nether millstones was a rather mild one at that time. State appropriations were to become more immense. What chance had DePauw to compete with such colossal treasuries? These and other doubts were rife. Yet the years that have passed since that period have seen the erection of very few educational tombstones, but have witnessed an almost unbelievable growth in Christian institutions that did not betray their ideals by religious indifference or their programs by irreligious deficits.

It is not easy for one to make record of one's own accomplishments. Though I must have failed in many things, I did not fail in work. I declined to accept any more salary than I had been receiving as a pastor. For two years I turned into the treasury of the University remuneration that I received from outside sources. I labored madly, day and night, on the campus and over the state. I put shameful burdens on my body. Coming

88

to the University in September weighing 151 pounds, I staggered up the stairway of my home after the commencement exercises in 1904 weighing 120 pounds. I marvel that I survived. The progressively better health of the third of a century past has never wholly overcome the effects of those first arduous months. But from the couch on which I fell on that day I said in confidence to my comrade, "If the Lord will give me a few years more, we will put Old DePauw on solid foundations." When in these near years I have gone over her campuses, through her halls, into her accounts, I have thanked God that he gave me a modest part in strengthening her wonderful life.

The constituencies served by a church college are so related to the institution as to give them differing estimates. They are:

The trustees, who think constantly of the financial side of the enterprise.

The professors, who regard the school from the standpoints of their own specialties, and support.

The students, who think of the halls and campus as the area of an enlarging liberty.

The alumni, who estimate the institution and are occasionally tempted to think of its administration from the artificial angle of athletic repute.

The preachers, whose interest is largely religious, and who, though they themselves may send to the institution students, and even children, who are not saintly, insist on a standard of life for the college higher than they can secure for their churches.

The teachers in the public schools, who consider the college as the next stage of life for their pupils, and who may have prejudices, favorable or unfavorable.

The standardizing agencies, whether appointed by the state, or made up of groups representing voluntary educational activities, which may sometimes demand that an infant should be full grown.

The general public, which feels an interest in all educational foundations in the state, and which walks across the campus and through the buildings with critical eyes.

The parents, who regard the college as a parental substitute, the second home to which they commit their sons and daughters, while the professors are their proxies, standing in loco parentis.

Here are nine groups—each one of them with its own desires, preferences, convictions. The offset to the difficulties involved in the variety of contributions was that the persons in the several groups had genuine reasons for desiring the prosperity of the college, and that from their ranks the occasional sacrificial helper would come.

The DePauw faculty was loyal, quite beyond the average. Professors like Hillary A. Gobin, James Riley Weaver, Edwin Post, Henry B. Longden, William F. Swahlen, Wilbur V. Brown, Joseph P. Naylor, William M. Blanchard, who were there when I came, and who remained for my entire administration, were kindly and faithful. They did not demand the impossible of a new president; nor were they campus gossipers. I was later to discover, at other colleges, how critical certain types of teachers could become. After my second year I investigated with scrupulous care the promise of loyalty of each possible candidate toward his chief and his institution. I searched also for signs of parental instinct, believing that no teacher succeeds who does not have a splendid fund of that instinct. When an applying person exhibited more interest in "research" than he did in "students," I avoided him as a professorial plague.

I marvel that I was able to secure such efficient teachers when the salary scale was so low. Of course, the period of inflated prices that was to bring disaster in later years was distant. Still, our salary range was pitiful. The first two years cost me several thousand dollars in surrendered salary and contributed perquisites. Yet I could scarcely think much of my own sacrifice when William M. Blanchard was receiving $1,000 per year. By 1905 the support of the faculty began to move toward more comfortable figures. The no-deficit policy, which I refused to forsake, gained the confidence of patrons and philanthropists. In the year when I had no longer to spend time in paying for current debts, the supporting endowment increased more than 33 per cent. All my experience convinces me wholly that deficits are devils.

Consequently, bequests or gifts that came without designation were used for no other purpose than endowment. My conscientious feeling has been that money not specified for current expenses belongs naturally in the permanent funds. Men who make wills usually have that long-run feature in their purpose. Doubt should always be resolved in favor of the future life of the college itself. I rejoice that I worked sedulously in behalf of my successors. The confidence that results when men are convinced that they are not putting money "into a bag with holes" soon began to appear.

What I now write of the DePauw days is taken largely from Professor William W. Sweet's history of the University. I was formally inaugurated in December, 1903, the principal addresses being delivered by United States Senator Albert J. Beveridge, of the class of 1885, and President James W. Bashford, of Ohio Wesleyan University. I myself spoke on "The Meanings of Christian Education."

Many things needed to be done—the campus beautified, the buildings repaired, the boarding facilities improved, the laboratories re-equipped, and the library enlarged. But the main problem was the balancing of the budget.

For thirty-two years the deficit had ranged between $6,000 and $30,000 each year. The debt of $22,000 was soon eliminated. At the end of the collegiate year in 1904 the current arrears were only $2,400. This the trustees raised in their own circle—on my confident prophecy that the spring of 1905 would see no arrears whatever. This preview was justified. It marked an accomplishment and set the precedent for coming years. Convinced that the deficits were the devils of collegiate administration, I held sedulously to the policy of spending no funds that we did not have. I suffered unspeakably in the loss of some able professors whose salaries I could not possibly increase. When word went out to our constituency that the University was steadily meeting its expenses and enlarging its endowments, hesitating philanthropists wrote wills in our behalf. The Hon. Marvin Campbell, of South Bend, accepted a long-refused election and became a trustee. By wise and kindly industry he succeeded in raising a sustaining fund which permitted the immediate extension of work. This program covered five years. At the end of that period the University was ready to proceed in paths of normal finance.

The current budgets and the necessary outlays for improvements prevented large building plans. Yet by the persistence of the late Dr. C. E. Line we secured an agreement from Andrew Carnegie to give $50,000 for a new library building, provided the university endowed it with another $50,000. The trustees rallied to this call, and patient work produced the great result.

Meantime the endowment fund became more substantial. In 1903 that fund equaled $231,000, of which $180,000 was subject to large annuities. Indeed, in that year the endowment had to be itself supported by an added $200. The helper needed to be helped. Five years later the fund had been lifted to $530,000, the greater part

of which earned interest for the support of the college.
The faculty received strong recruits, including Professors
Adelbert F. Caldwell, Harry B. Gough, and Rufus B. von
Kleinsmid, now president of the University of Southern
California.

The discipline of the institution gave me concern. The
overdone free spirit of the time came to the campus. I had
not known that the students had occasionally taken holidays by force, refusing to go to recitations and patrolling
the buildings to "break up classes." In 1904 there had
been a holiday on Monday; Tuesday was made a holiday
on account of the national election. In their jubilancy
over Theodore Roosevelt's triumph, the students took
Wednesday and compelled the suspension of recitations.
To me it appeared as the surrender of the last citadel of
college authority. I knew that mutiny of that sort could
not dwell with my administration. So I took a firm stand
and said that any matriculant who thereafter participated
in the breaking of classes would be without debate separated from the University. The wild liberty had one or
two brief spasms and then ceased. Many able schoolmen
sent grateful letters, saying the DePauw example had
stimulated reasonable discipline over the whole state.

Our student enrollment grew steadily through the entire period. Our comparative weakness in athletics was
more than offset by other phases of campus life. The
University service held once a month on Sunday afternoon
was splendidly supported by faculty, students, and towns-
people. In a frank estimate of my own service I may say
that I came to the close of my DePauw administration assured that the public confidence had been won, general
morale strengthened, professional salaries lifted, endowment increased, and the crisis overcome. I shall always
feel that, so far as my life's work was definitely localized,
its chief token may be found in the college for which I

came near to surrendering my life. I may add that one reason for my reluctant change of work came from distrust of further physical strain.

In giving the charge at the inauguration of several college presidents I have commented on what a wonderful piece of machinery a college organization is. In reality it is the evolution of literally thousands of years. The trembling presidential neophyte enters his office, wondering how he can care for so many wheels. But he finds the machinery firmly set! He discovers, too, that the process has gone on for decades without his skill; and he is soon certain that it still proceeds in spite of his ignorance. The preceding engineers have done their work! Progressive and sometimes complaining graduates said to me fiercely, "Get DePauw out of the ruts," by which, of course, they meant that I should transfer the vehicle to their ruts. At the end of a weary day in the office my wife once said to me, "What have you been doing all these hours?" I replied in all sincerity, "The most of the time I have spent thanking God for these ruts." I know too much now to be deceived by talk about "educational statesmen." President Eliot, of Harvard, and President Warren, of Boston, became statesmen because they knew how to be neophytes. It takes far more than a pose of individual wisdom to run a modern college. The institutional fund, endowed by experience of a long past, comes into our treasury.

The state of Indiana was hospitable to a newcomer. Governor Winfield T. Durbin appointed me a member of the state Board of Education. Governor J. Frank Hanly reappointed me. The work was interesting and far-reaching. Schoolbook contracts, as made by the Board, were the largest in the world. The great publishing houses employed remarkably adept agents, who "majored" in the study of human nature. I presume that a dishonest

94

man could have made much revenue by selling his vote.
Yet I believe that the Board was composed of strictly
honorable men, not moved by filthy lucre, and able to
guard themselves against approaches on the blind side
where the subtle bribes of friendship do their work.

Within two years, also, I was elected president of the
Indiana State Teachers' Association. I went to my first
meeting without an understanding of its significance.
Professor Elmer L. Bryan and I were placed on a committee on nominations—largely for purposes of "scenery."
Three other men, county superintendents, excellent men
who had been caught in a wave of educational politics,
presented their slates for officers and members of the
Reading Circle Board. They would allow no slight
change. My feeling was that I took my educational life
"in my hand" when I felt compelled to join Professor
Bryan in a minority report. I was asked to close the debate, which I did in the most outright and frank manner,
making a special appeal for the re-election to the Reading
Circle Board of Mrs. Emma Mont. McRae, one of the
most efficient women educators of the commonwealth.
The usual phrases are accurate here: We "swept the
decks," overwhelming the three majority members of the
committee with a vote of hundreds as against approximately forty. To my big surprise, my conscience had
guided me to a fortunate, as well as righteous, road. The
next year I was elected president of the association. My
chief aide was the late Benjamin Franklin Moore, one of
the finest schoolmen I have known. Largely on his insistence, we put on a Riley Recognition Meeting, making
"The Hoosier Poet" the center. Senator Beveridge, Editor Charles R. Williams of the *Indianapolis News,* Henry
Watterson of the *Louisville Courier-Journal,* and Henry
van Dyke were the speakers, while I was president and
introducer. Mr. Riley's response was inimitable. He was

the best public reciter I have ever known. The meeting increased the membership of that session by thousands. A frightened treasurer found himself in possession of a grand surplus. Backed by this money, we entered upon a campaign to pass a minimum wage law for Indiana teachers. Several of us, notably the late William W. Parsons, of the Indiana State Normal School, framed the law and secured its passage. It is gratifying to attend County Teachers' Associations and to be aware that every official attendant has received a more just support because we were courageous enough to promote that Riley meeting in Tomlinson Hall. Shakespeare was not wholly right. The good that men do not only lives "after them"; sometimes, thank God, it lives *with them.*

Collegiate work brought me again into occasional contact with Charles William Eliot, president of Harvard. I met him often at the meetings of the Carnegie Foundation trustees. Later I was to preach frequently in Appleton Chapel, especially in the period of my episcopacy in the Boston Area. In Indianapolis one day I sat at a dinner between him and the late H. B. Brown, president of Valparaiso University. Their institutions were so very different. Valparaiso was designed to put education on an economical basis, by the avoidance of expensive buildings, the giving of self-help opportunities, and the creating of a collegiate community that turned back profits to the struggling students. At this time Presidents Eliot and Brown were heads of the two largest colleges in the land—speaking numerically. Yet I discovered that the Harvard president had never before heard of Valparaiso.

Several times I appeared with President Eliot before committees of the Massachusetts Legislature when the question of Prohibition was at issue. It was said that he became an abstainer for the most part because of the scientific argument. Feeling that he had consecrated his

life to the following of the truth, and becoming assured
that the narcotic effect of liquor was bad, he felt driven
by consistency to war against rum. The letter recorded
in his biography as sent to Dr. Henry S. Pritchett gives
the reason for his conviction. He felt that "the use of
alcohol as a beverage threatens seriously the existence of
the white race"; declared that he had seen "many cases"
of the disasters of intemperance "among the college or
university families I have known at Harvard"; and confessed that "I have known intimately the process of de-
stroying family life and of breeding sickly or deformed
children, several cases having occurred in my own family
on both the paternal and maternal sides among the five
generations with which I have been acquainted." These
arguments led him to feel that there was justification for
"some abridgment of personal individual liberty in order
to gain a great collective good." The reason sounds nobly
Christian. The liquor cohorts had no right to count
President Eliot among their supporters.

As an author he was not prolific, nor are his writings
well known. As a fashioner of cameo descriptions of
honorary-degree-receivers he became expert. His "Five-
foot Shelf" of standard books was widely advertised. The
most of the selections were fairly heavy material. More
than one reader was glad that the shelf did not reach the
length of six or seven! Though not a maker of many
books, he doubtless still inspired more readers than did
any other man of his generation; while the educational
system that he promoted made him a creator of many literary men.

His sense of humor was meager. The Henry James
biography gives two illustrations, both related to athletics.
He criticized a baseball player because he had "resorted
to deception on the diamond." When questioned as to
what he meant, Dr. Eliot replied that the man had made

97

"a feint to throw a ball in one direction" and then had thrown "it in another." Hearing the Harvard boys at a football game singing, "Three cheers for Harvard and none for Yale," the President suggested as a more sportsmanlike slogan, "Three cheers for Harvard and one for Yale." The amendment was laid on the table.

An athletic illustration helped me in a polite debate. At a banquet table he courteously criticized the Methodist movement for its "overdone emotionalism." I was certain, of course, that the criticism was not based on knowledge! He had to admit that in many years he had not attended a *regular* Methodist service, and that he himself had not seen among Methodists anything that resembled an orgy of feeling. I told him that the "shouting Methodist" had been noticeable rather than numerous, and that our present-day Church, so far from having too much expressed emotion, was really distinctly lacking in that respect.

I ceased defense and began attack by saying that "the colleges in our country were now the centers of overdone emotion, rather than our churches." Asked what I meant, I replied that I had recently attended a Yale-Harvard football game at which even "some professors became shriekers, while the students themselves yelled until they would have made Comanche Indians appear like vocal amateurs." The President did not retreat but declared that collegiate athletics should be blamed for "this abominable hysteria." He did not bring his charge back to the Wesleyan field. In the Carnegie Foundation, I never detected in President Eliot the slightest glint of humor, though he constantly gave evidence of the educational statesmanship that had made his official reports high literature.

Beneath his austerity there must have resided a reserve of tender feeling. This appeared in the death scene, as depicted by James. Expressing the hope that he might die on Saturday because his family and friends would find Sunday trains less crowded and more comfortable than weekday trains, he later astonished the nurse by exclaiming, "I see Father," and by giving a moment after the affectionate addendum, "I see Mother." The Methodists, who were fond of him because he kept the right kind of Puritanism, would scarcely have been guilty of "overdone emotion" if they had intimated that God's hand removed the veil between two worlds and sent a great soul over the border to the music of filial love.

I preached a number of times at Harvard—never without being aware of the presence of President Eliot, who always came from his pew to read the scripture lesson. My college preaching began at Wellesley, in 1895. The list of collegiate institutions through the years included Vassar, Smith, Mt. Holyoke, MacMurray, Mills, Yale, Wesleyan, Amherst, Dartmouth, Williams; universities of Indiana, Illinois, Iowa, Wyoming, Nevada, California, Washington, Virginia, West Virginia, Kentucky, Vermont, Maine, Delaware, Minnesota, North Dakota, Montana; Columbia, Cornell, Wooster, Dennison, Duke, Vanderbilt, Northwestern, Southern California, Southern Methodist; state colleges of Pennsylvania and Iowa, Purdue, Toronto, Stanford, and more than thirty other institutions. It is difficult to evaluate college preaching, inasmuch as its main purpose is to create an atmosphere that defies statistics. Often it impressed me as being an attempt to grasp what was fluid. I was much interested in a comment made by Francis Greenwood Peabody—that the preachers who invariably failed at Harvard were those who tried to be learned and deep, and those who feared to be distinctly religious because of an effort to adjust themselves to a liberal climate. I had a sense of more definiteness in lecture foundations, in six of which I have participated.

Here there was a fixed aim, and sometimes the utterances were institutionalized into a book. It can justly be said that itinerant college preaching wholly lacks the constructive quality of a pastorate.

I must particularly emphasize my relations with James Whitcomb Riley. He was appealingly lovable. The name "The Hoosier Poet" signified that he had annexed the state. He knew her nooks and corners. His days as a journeyman signpainter had revealed her to him. He could have said, "I am the state." "Out to Old Aunt Mary's" and "The Old Swimmin' Hole" were definitely in her borders.

He had moral struggles about which he was pathetically frank. There is a semihumorous and semitragic story that once, when Senator Beveridge was leaving for Washington, he called to pay farewell "respects" to Riley. The poet was reported by the housekeeper as incapacitated. The statesman insisted, however, that his card be taken to the writer's bedchamber, and that "he will see me." In a few moments the card was returned to the visitor, with this crisp penmanship on the reverse, "Too much Beverage already." Probably the tale was an invention. Riley mourned over his failing. He told me that when he was giving a kindly benefit entertainment in the Engglish Opera House, the verses he was reciting fled from him and left him in helpless silence. He imagined a funnel that whirled from himself to the entrance and felt constrained to swim through it to the door of escape. The remark to the audience that he had "a bad case of buck fever" restored his equilibrium. He completed his recitation. But he told me that his chief terror was that "the folks would think" that he had "gone to drink again." He was humbly proud of his victory over appetite.

He used to call me his "spiritual adviser," and was the first man to tell me what would be my future work. I

100

never addressed the afternoon services of the Young Men's
Christian Association without finding Mr. Riley in the
box on my left. He had a keen hospitality for religious
truth, and his face was an Amen. Once he said that he had
joined the Methodist Church in boyhood and had never
been informed of his "expulsion." He told me that if
St. Peter asked him at the gates about his faith, he would
reply, "I am a Methodist." He had a complete trust in
immortality. He was an eminent example of the thousands of our members who were cruelly marked into our
nonresident and inactive list. Whitcomb Riley abides in
my memory as a kindly, lovely soul, with windows toward
earth and toward the sky. He would never be at home in
any world prepared for the evil and the lost.

My association with him affected my ministry. He sent
me one of his books, in which he wrote, "To Dr. Edwin
Holt Hughes, with Hale, Hoosier Greetings of His Friend,
James Whitcomb Riley." As an addendum he penned
one of his own dialect couplets:

> I believe all childerns good
> Ef they're only understood.

Riley's titles take you into the eighteenth chapter of
Matthew with its glorification of childhood. His books
were schoolrooms to which fathers and mothers could
go for gentle instruction. There Riley sat in the teacher's
chair and dispensed his loving pedagogy.

After one of his visits to my home, and his reading
some selected poems to my enraptured students, I sent
him a note of appreciation. His response was characteristic, as the following holographic copy will show:

June 6,
1906

Dr. Edwin H. Hughes—
Dear Dr. Hughes
It's a hearty, wholesome message you send a fellow.—Thanks

101

good-and-plenty for it. Mr. Nicholson will be likewise pleased
with the welcome you accord his poems—for, verily, his poems
are poems, and of such spirit and uplift at times as will even
pull a brother-poet starward.—Mark, "A Prayer of the Hill-
Country," "The Heart of the Bugle," "In the Great Pastures,"
etc., etc.

Your work flourishes: I can *hear* you growing, like a field of
corn after our late liberal rains.

Always your friend,

(signed) JAMES WHITCOMB RILEY

Another incident placed one of his own poems in a
radiant light. In the office of Bobbs-Merrill, his publish-
ers, I said to him: "I have long wanted to thank you for
a poem that has comforted me personally, and has served
me well in my pastoral service. It is the one called 'Bereaved.'" He was at once alert, and replied: "How glad
I am to have you say this! I have long regarded that poem
as one of my best. Yet it has attracted so much less attention than my dialect verses have received. Shall I tell
you how I wrote those lines?" Of course I did not lose
that golden chance. So Mr. Riley gave me the tale substantially in this form:

He was at home one night in Lockerbie Street, between
his Lyceum engagements. Without any objective cause,
and as if it fell from the blue sky of inspiration, the lines
of "Bereaved" came to him. He wrote them out with his
usual care and left them on his desk. The next morning
he received a message from Bill Nye, his Lyceum partner,
saying that Nye had lost his little child. Riley sent Nye
a copy of the poem, and another copy was sent to a magazine editor who responded, "Your poem accepts itself.
Enclosed is our check." The scene at the other end of
the consoling transaction is easy to imagine—the afflicted
parent receiving the message from his bachelor friend:

Let me come in where you sit weeping,—ay,
Let me, who have not any child to die,

102

Weep with you for the little one whose love
    I have known nothing of.

The little arms that slowly, slowly loosed
The pressure round your neck; the hands you used
To kiss.—Such arms—such hands I never knew.
    May I not weep with you?

Fain would I be of service—say some thing,
Between the tears, that would be comforting,—
But ah! so sadder than yourselves am I,
    Who have no child to die.[1]

The great humorist must have taken to his heart that healing pathos, until he knew that the boon of earthly parenthood, however brief, brings one into the shared creatorship of the Father revealed in Christ. Any friend who thus gives glimpses of the Greatest Friend must be a friend indeed.

Often now my memory reviews an educational procession headed toward the DePauw campus. I see the old-time Methodists, with quaint clothes and earnest ways, as they came to found a college. There was scarcely a college graduate in all their line. Their bishop, Robert Roberts, was innocent of academic learning; but he saw the future school in his dreams, and in glad sacrifices he built its first humble walls. Years later they brought his dust to Greencastle and made the campus his sepulcher. Tens of thousands of students have marched past his grave, with its simple stone, heedless, often, of the meaning of his life for theirs. Later Matthew Simpson came with step more stately and with lips more eloquent, and with an aristocracy never concealed by his blue-jeans garments.

But in panorama that passes through my heart I see

---

[1] From *Poems Here at Home,* by James Whitcomb Riley. Copyright, 1893, 1921. Used by special permission of the publisher, the Bobbs-Merrill Co.

affectionately the later personnel: William Newkirk, the first president of my own Board; Martin V. Bieger, who stayed so short a time that his going appalled my spirit; Hugh Dougherty, my dear, dear friend, who stood by me when the hours were gloomiest—a trustees' president who himself had had no chance, because of the War of 1861-65, to secure any higher education, but who planned great things for youth; Simeon Smith, a southern Indiana farmer who caught a vision of life beyond his acres and gave me a promise for endowment that he more than fulfilled; Harry Whitcomb, who loved his alma mater as he loved his family, and gave to her with unfailing generosity; J. Smith Talley, a modest and noble soul, who made his wealth from mines beneath the earth, and lifted generous portions to treasuries in the sky; Edward Rector, Frank H. Hall, John H. Harrison, who came after my time, but who walked squarely into my heart, never to leave! Ira Burton Blackstock, a fraternity brother, an alumnus, and a trustee whose many gifts were climaxed by his wife after his death, in a splendid stadium builded on the field that bears her husband's name.

Amid them all I see the figure of Salem B. Town, the gentle financier who carried the books of the school not only on the ledger but on the tablets of his own heart. Often, too, I think of William H. Adams, trustee for many years, and kindly friend; of Charles H. Barnaby, later a most efficient trustee, but one who, as a great citizen, never yielded to the antagonism represented by the phrase "town and gown"; of Augustus Lynch Mason, an alumnus and a trustee, as fine a specialist on city charters as we had in the land, with a brilliant mind hampered by a limited body, but with a fortune that more than a third of a century before his death he promised me to give to his alma mater; and of Newland T. DePauw, son of the benefactor, who himself had large plans for the institution

104

that became the family monument, and whose Virginia plantation gave me more than one restful vacation.

Amid the steadier marching of these elders I hear the rush of students' feet; I catch the chapel cry of

> Dr. Hughes-es,
> Please excuse us!
> Holiday!

sung to the wild tune of freedom. Then do I feel like putting into far more poetic lines my farewell words to the trustees of DePauw, adding a doxology of praise for the privilege of touching so many splendid lives.

One of the railroad lines passing through Greencastle gives a view of the cemetery that slopes gently toward the south. My last letter from Edward Rector brought a deed to a lot that adjoins his own. There, near his sleeping place, and close neighbor to the graves of President Bowman, President John, Professor Longden, President Grose, Dr. Tucker, Dean Blanchard, and in hailing distance of the tombs of President Gobin and President Martin, I, too, shall come. My body shall be comrade with theirs in the fellowship of dust, while my spirit shares the felicity of that Schoolroom where we learn lessons not lawful for us here, and where we shall see face to face the Son of God whose love and light inspired so many of his servants to found and maintain a college in his Name and for his Glory.

CHAPTER V

EPISCOPACY

THE METHODIST EPISCOPACY WAS MADE UP IN CONSIDerable part from the pattern of the ancient episcopacies, combined with features demanded by a new day. Although the period of its adoption was clamorous with slogans of a democracy that had repudiated the divine right of kings and later carried its repudiation over to the divine right of priests, the transformed office was given features of monarchy. Yet in its beginning the principle of delegated powers was asserted. Francis Asbury refused to become general superintendent until his selection by John Wesley had been confirmed by the Christmas Conference. The autocracy thus received a democratic sanction.

The office quickly gained an astounding confidence. Though Mr. Wesley in a letter which contained the conciliating diminutive "Franky," mildly objected to Asbury's permitting the use of the title "Bishop," the great founder's word of protest had slight effect. To call a man "General Superintendent" would have made a bunglesome approach. Thus the alternative title departed from popular speech and remained only as a legal term.

The earliest records of Methodism in America do not reveal any deep distrust of the office. The long fight for the sacraments had destroyed confidence in strict ecclesiasticism. The spiritual democracy of the eighteenth century could not see why the first- and second-century Christians had any more right to mold an office than did

106

the later believers. Our people accepted Lord King's view as to an identity of the eldership and the episcopacy, and avoided as an approach to superstition the theory of episcopacy as a third order. Though they were not technical historians, they welcomed the views expressed by Lightfoot in his work on Philippians, and the later historical researches of Headlam—both scholars belonging to the Church of England. Efforts to prove that John Wesley had been ordained by a bishop of the Greek Church excited little interest. Doubtless many Methodists would have been disturbed by such a fact, if proved. Charles Wesley's hymns added to their rapture; his High-Church views influenced them not at all.

The prestige of Francis Asbury was transferred to the office. It was hard to argue against an episcopacy that spelled incalculable sacrifice. The hero of mountain and valley, of outdoor sleeping places, of rocky fords, of cold rains, of deep snows, of pains that racked the body but never halted the soul, defined episcopacy into a blessed meaning. The era of republican emphasis that made the Revolution and steadily increased popular government never succeeded in effecting radical changes in the office. O'Kelly found it easier to make an exodus than it was to make a transformed bishopric. As the years advanced and democracy spread over the earth, the Methodist episcopacy secured stronger foundations. If there is today a preacher in the united Church who would consent to accept reordination because he felt any lack in his Methodist credentials, I know not the man. Changes toward a strict ministerial sacerdotalism have nearly always been made under a motive of disaffection rather than on the basis of conviction.

When I was elected to the episcopacy, my friend and fraternity brother, Charles Edward Jefferson, wrote hesitating congratulations. He said that evidently the office was "the high personal goal in Methodism," expressed the opinion that a college presidency or a pastorate would have been better for me, but declared that if I really wanted to be a bishop he was glad that I was! Naturally in the later years one reviews the earlier decisions. As I have said elsewhere, I never spoke to anyone about my possible election; nor when anyone spoke to me did I ever suggest anything that could be done to secure votes. But if I did not say that I desired the office, I certainly never said that I was indifferent. I was saved from negative falsehoods. My vote came near to the two-thirds requirement on the fourth ballot at the General Conference in Baltimore in 1908. The losses on succeeding countings convinced me that the Church had concluded that a man forty-one years of age should remain in educational work. I was wholly ready for unmurmuring continuance at DePauw University. Yet when on the fifteenth ballot I was elected, I felt a great, but sober, elation. I had read of men who passed through agony of soul and nightlong vigils of prayer ere they consented to accept the honor and the task. I felt no agony and needed no vigil. Six days of voting had given abundant chance for ethical introspection. I did have some distinct emotions. When my dear friends, Bishops McDowell and Bashford, came to lead me to the platform, I turned to look at my comrades in the Indiana Conference delegation. I was leaving them now. My eyes knew the approach of tears, and I by effort restrained them because I feared that a wrong reason might be assigned for their flowing. All these splendid Hoosiers were my friends. When I had been in their conference less than four years they had elected me delegate on the first ballot, and by two more than five sixths of all votes cast. Two of them became my beloved intimates—the late Dr. Charles E. Bacon, a princely character, and Dr. Lewis Fred Dimmitt, who still dwells in California's sunshine as a vestibule of a brighter land.

My wife, having been reared a Presbyterian, did not have the background that enamored her with the episcopacy. The prophecy of an absentee husband was not to her liking. Yet when my vote was halted, and she felt that some foolish delegates needed a baptism of wisdom she became a firm believer in the doctrine of my "election," and was convinced that the slow voters were defeating a divine decree. And my parents! They had long idealized the episcopacy and its personnel. They believed that William McKinley's mother showed good judgment when she wanted her son to be a Methodist bishop rather than President of the United States. Their telegrams were not for publicity, but for a sacred reading by their son and his wife at a quieter altar.

I

I was assigned to San Francisco, California. As the balloting had been placed on bulletins at the university, one of my students had made a pen-and-ink cartoon showing the young president in his cap and gown moving away from a shrewish matron with corkscrew curls, labeled "DePauw," and snuggling closer to a gayly dressed young lady marked "Bishopric." On my return from Baltimore I was met by the student body at the railroad station, and was pulled by them in a carriage through the streets to Meharry Hall. Touched by the enthusiasm of the collegians, my second son, then ten years old, joined heartily in the cheers for his father. This lack of propriety brought grave sorrow to the older son, who had reached the adulthood of twelve, and who felt that the family was grievously disgraced by those filial yells.

Preparations began for the westward migration. My most poignant sorrow was caused by leaving DePauw Uni-

Lexington appeared. The "embattled farmers" at the "rude bridge that arched the flood" did not lack successors. The prevailing church, with a colonial title deed, was Congregational. The environment was not favorable to a connectionalism. A bishop holding the New England Conference had once declared that the time had come "to check the Congregational tendency"—only to discover that something else was checked. *Zions Herald* contributed its trumpet in an editorial and joined the marches around the episcopal Jericho until the prerogative walls trembled.

Perhaps I took too seriously a proneness to criticism. At preachers' meeting in my own pastoral days I had heard good men ask good men, "Where is the Bishop?" Being told that he had been at Albany or Syracuse, the question was, "Why is he not here, attending to his own work?" The reminder that the preachers themselves, being in Copley Square, Boston, were outside their own charges, was not satisfying. I really did prefer to plan my own itinerary. A minute censorship of my labors, together with an accurately kept calendar of my whereabouts, did not appeal to the free will of my Arminian nature. After I had been in official residence for a time, I knew that my advance surmises were not fair, and that I had exaggerated the critical disposition. But if in advance I had used Paul's metaphor about Ephesus, and had said, "A great door and effectual is opened unto me, and there are many adversaries," one of the "adversaries" to give me tremors would have been that critical attitude. All this I stated in kindly frankness to the delegates whose desire so greatly honored me.

To Boston I came—to meet assurances of loyal support. In one respect I had a fixed policy. Methodism was not as strong relatively as it was in the West. Our wonderful partners in work had arrived ahead of us—Congregationalists, Baptists, Protestant Episcopalians. There remained the open door where waited the calmly happy wife and the clamorous children! Thus began thirty-two years of itinerant service for the dear Church, starting amid California's flowers and never wholly escaping from their fragrance and beauty.

San Francisco had not yet emerged from the twisted beams and gray ashes of her ruins. Two years had not erased the dreadful memories of earthquake and fire. Over four hundred members of Central Church had been made homeless. The tremors of the earth's crust had entered their souls as well. Eight churches had been smitten into literal pieces. The indomitable Bishop John William Hamilton had begun the rebuilding work and had proved that he was one of the heroes of restoration. The church locations had been mostly fixed. The story of rebuilding would be lengthy. The Board of Home Missions and Church Extension did a noble part. By agreement, I collected thousands of dollars by lectures and in church services. At the end of eight years only slight debts remained on our properties. We made, also, steady gains in membership, and had an improved *esprit de corps,* with unbroken harmony.

Yet San Francisco was a difficult field. Ivan Bunin, the Russian novelist, heads his story, *The Gentleman from San Francisco,* with a quotation from the Revelation of St. John: "Alas, alas, that great city Babylon, that mighty city!" The proud dwellers by the Golden Gate would not accept this scripture as applicable. Certainly it was an exaggeration. After the city yielded to flames, the religious people did not declare the disaster a divine judgment. The wicked were more apt to bring that confession. It is fair to say that Northern California had not learned to appreciate the Puritans. The life there had been formed by two historic layers. The first came with the Spanish priest who left his mark in names sprinkled over the geography. The second layer came with the forty-niner in his fever for gold. This adventurer was unconventional. He rejected restraint. His admiration for California Taylor, later elected missionary bishop of Africa, was not so much for his religion as for his ruggedness. The fearless street preacher, with his long whiskers flying in the trade winds, fitted into the wild life and became a beloved tradition. Bold men, like Thomas Starr King and M. C. Briggs, were to have their brave part in keeping California in the Union. The admiration for persons, however, was never transferred to the Puritan type of life.

The mingled influence of the Spanish priest and the gold hunter held sway. My position as a Methodist bishop was a hindrance rather than a help. After the earthquake and fire many of the quieter residents went over to Berkeley or Oakland, or down the peninsula. The reputation of the city, which advertised rather than concealed Barbary Coast, and which maintained saloons for astonishingly small sections of people, did not attract the stricter populations that came from the East. The Mayor Schmitz regime had broken up in scandal. Abram Reuf, the well-educated Jew, had been sent to prison. My file still holds pathetic letters in which he urged my help in securing a parole from Governor Hiram Johnson's administration. The honest rule of Mayor Taylor was nearing its end. The whole situation did not allure Puritans.

My first distinct recognition was an invitation to address the Commonwealth Club, a sturdy organization with some well-restrained ideals. I spoke on "The Commercial Value of a Moral Atmosphere." The theme could win its way only as accompanied by humor and by appeals to civic pride. But the crowd finally heard me as a friend. I showed the company how the stream of migrations parted at Green River or Ogden, a heavy branch turning to

112

Southern California, and another to Oregon and Washington, while only a trickle flowed to San Francisco. I gave them statistics of graduates from the Puritan colleges in the Central West, showing a paucity for our own city. I told them of the relative growth of San Francisco and Los Angeles, and prophesied that, unless we secured a fair share of the migration, in a brief period "the city of the angels would in population surpass the city of the saints." I declared that to call these splendid Puritans "hypocrites," with or without "the adjective," was a civic folly, and that as a lover of my plucky city, lifting herself out of a tomb of disaster, I desired San Francisco to be so made in idealism as to win the oncoming hosts. How I worked and prayed over that address! I am not conceited when I affirm that it won. The eager applause and the later praise from individuals were my assurances. The event gave me more chances at the life of the city.

Yet the people yielded slowly to an evangelical gospel. The Protestant membership was about 14,000 of the half million. The Methodist group was approximately 3,200. First Church, Los Angeles, or First Church, Pasadena, each had more strength than did all our combined Methodist churches in San Francisco. My constituency seemed to me like a beleaguered group hemmed in by forces that were indifferent when they were not hostile. The compensations were real. Often I query whether I have ever presided over as fine a spiritual average as I had in Northern California. Rolla V. Watt, the leading layman, was as fine a churchman as I have known. With a personality that would have given him even the mayoralty, he kept his banner flying, smiled his way through all ridicule, and loved the Church as his Master did. Had his life been prolonged, San Francisco Methodism would have been saved from later disasters. Down at San Jose, D. C. Crummey, worthy father of a worthy son, John D. Crum-

mey, never forsook the Angel of the Covenant. Freeman
D. Bovard was the most influential of our Northern California preachers. A wise master-builder, he used no
shoddy material. A righteous pleader, he secured a release
of church property from taxation and made it possible to
erect beautiful sanctuaries. A constant writer, as he said,
"with nothing like flashing genius," he still made the
church *Advocate* gleam with light. He allowed influences
to pull him from his editorship, solely because he sought
to do God's will. When a tangle of difficulties for which
he was in no least degree responsible caused other elections, and his anxious friends consoled him, he made the
noble reply, "Over forty years in the ministry have convinced me that I have no reason to be afraid of the Methodist Church." Elbert R. Dille became for the entire
region "around the Bay" our pastoral symbol. A native
of Indiana, and a soldier in the War of 1861-65, he came
after the great struggle to California and secured there a
second nativity. He and Dr. Bovard were David and
Jonathan. They reminded me of the two high hills that
faced each other grandly at the far end of Market Street.
So I called them my "Twin Peaks." They were lovers of
mighty Shasta and have long since gone into the heaven
toward which that mountain lifts it solemn whiteness.

Northern and Southern California contrasted strongly.
The forty-niner ruled the one; the nineteen-hundred-and-
niners began to possess the other. The transcontinental
railways carried to the regions around Los Angeles and San
Diego the Eastern and Mid-Western people who sought an
out-of-doors sanitarium in order to avoid early entrance
into heaven! Our churches often increased a generation in
a year. A preacher could capture certificates of membership as his chief tokens of evangelism. There was ministerial migration too. The Los Angeles Methodist Preachers'
Meeting enrolled scores of superannuates. That gathering

114

was once the premier among all such clans in America. It made not merely a group, but a congregation. Though gathered from wide areas, it had a fraternal unity. The debates were able, vigorous, high-minded. The response to addresses would kindle any ordinary speaker into glowing life. In size it surpassed many Annual Conferences; and being largely free from administrative details it could devote itself to the themes of the Kingdom. Even when progressives and conservatives debated, bitterness had small scope. If from 1909 to 1916 anyone had inquired of me what gathering I loved most to face, I should have made reply, "The Los Angeles Preachers' Meeting."

The Conference was not without its divisions, but they were not *mean*. If occasionally there was a theological motive for suggested appointments, especially to Districts, the spirit was not malicious. I declined to become a "doctrinal administrator." A study of assignments will prove this incontestably. Francis M. Larkin and Harcourt W. Peck were not twins. They were as dissimilar as Jacob and Esau—though neither would have sought the other's birthright. It was amusing to see two such different men at the one cabinet table. The gentle mediations of Frank D. Mather and Alfred Inwood did not detract from my sly joy.

My brother, Matthew Simpson Hughes, came to First Church, Pasadena, in the fall of 1908; and I was his resident bishop until he himself became a bishop in 1916. He served notice that he would be "useless as a counselor"; and through the eight years he lived up to that resolution. Evidently the Conference knew that, for in 1912 and 1916 it made him the leader of its delegation. The people greatly rejoiced in his election as bishop. On his return from Saratoga Springs he had many glad receptions. Repeatedly he was asked how he liked his appointment to Portland, Oregon. Inasmuch as at three General Conferences he had not denied his willingness to accept episcopal responsibilities, his reply was given in an apt story. A timid young man had wished to propose marriage to a lady friend. Each opportunity frightened him from his purpose. Believing that one providential use of the telephone was to send your voice where you did not dare to take your person, he adopted the method of absentee speech and called the hopeful one on the wires. "Sallie," he said tremblingly, "will you marry me?" The reply came quickly back: "Of course I will. Who are you, anyhow?" The inference was that any episcopal residence was a preferred candidate.

Arizona and Nevada as parts of the Area were pathetic fields in respect of isolation. The latter, though several times larger than New York State, had been built largely on mines—an unstable base. The population had dwindled to less than 50,000. The distances were appalling. Often a Methodist preacher went to his charge knowing that he was not likely to see another preacher for months. The spiritual response was more meager than the numerical census. When he was at the height of his repute, Bishop Matthew Simpson preached at the Conference session to an audience of sixty-two—while a mountaineer Methodist, accustomed to "two or three" groups, declared that any bishop could preach a great sermon to so large a congregation. Arizona was coming to the front more rapidly. Yet even there the minister had need of courageous patience. The desert has its charm, but the sheer loneliness prevents many people from coming under its thrall. The expanses furnish abundant air, but slender company. In Balzac's famous short story, *A Passion in the Desert,* a lonely dweller is asked to give a definition of a desert. The halting reply is: "It is God without mankind." There were spaces in Arizona and Nevada that gave point to this statement, and a few that would have offered a changed form for it—"mankind without God." Yet our noble preachers often suggested Philip, who stopped a lonely traveler moving to the desert and opened to him the Scriptures until the surprising convert said, "What doth hinder me?"

That Pacific Area showed some achievements. The hospital in Los Angeles began its gracious service. The school for Mexican boys was inaugurated and, under the guidance of Frank S. Wallace as president of the trustees, made the other half of the "match factory" for the lovely Mexican girls in the DePauw School at Gardena. I took the risk involved in the doubtful health of Vernon M. McCombs and made him superintendent of the Spanish-speaking work, transforming the position from an appointment football to a sustained contest for spiritual life among an attractive people. The influx of new populations made the bishop's work a series of dedications. Hawaii called across the waves and demanded a frequent journey, as long as that from New York to Liverpool. So often Diamond Head and Pearl Harbor came into view—quite before we were made to feel that those jeweled names would in season have to be restored to appropriateness. Thither I sent Dr. William H. Fry as superintendent, that for long years he might give his loving energy to our work among the Japanese, Koreans, and Filipinos. God's providence will ere long restore to the Hawaiian crown the gems seized by the Japanese who wrongly celebrated my seventy-fifth birthday by their attack on Pearl Harbor.

The eight years on the Pacific shore brought personal reactions. If it be true that the Saviour's first great theater was the Mediterranean Basin, and his second the Atlantic Basin, and that time's noblest drama is to be worked out in the Pacific Basin, the bishops located in California and Oregon feel the call of a mighty world and catch the vision that refuses frontiers. The American mainland lies to

117

their east; the Pacific Ocean shimmers in their west. From the hidden boundary where Occident turns to Orient, they feel the pull of the Hawaiian and Philippine clusters—while China, Japan, Korea, India beckon with Macedonian calls. They live in immensity. The map of the world is written in their heart. While they do not lose the pride of their citizenship in the great Republic, God issues to them new naturalization papers, and the patriot is transformed into the cosmopolite. Yet the Saviour constantly touches that breadth with a missionary meaning, so that the Golden Gate becomes the Lord's entryway into his widening Kingdom.

II

The General Conference of 1916 named the Boston Area as my field. I had a frank reluctance. I still treasure the invitation, signed by all the delegates, urging my consent and soliciting the Conference to make my assignment. As a student and as a pastor I had lived within sight of the Massachusetts State House for more than fifteen years. Now I was asked to exchange the Golden Gate for the Golden Dome. In New England I had sought friendships and had avoided factions. Yet I felt confident that some preachers would prefer another as resident bishop. I was sure that I could go to a different Area without fear of the slightest cleavage, and almost as sure that one who had not been related to the New England work would find unity greeting him at the border.

There was still another phase. It can scarcely be stated without being overstated. I had seen four resident bishops in Boston. They were all men of blameless life, and all possessors of distinct abilities. Note the list: Bishops Foster, Goodsell, Mallalieu, Hamilton. New England soil was in the habit of producing the plant "independence." When episcopal authority came to assertion, a new Concord and

118

Lexington appeared. The "embattled farmers" at the "rude bridge that arched the flood" did not lack successors. The prevailing church, with a colonial title deed, was Congregational. The environment was not favorable to a connectionalism. A bishop holding the New England Conference had once declared that the time had come "to check the Congregational tendency"—only to discover that something else was checked. *Zions Herald* contributed its trumpet in an editorial and joined the marchers around the episcopal Jericho until the prerogative walls trembled.

Perhaps I took too seriously a proneness to criticism. At preachers' meeting in my own pastoral days I had heard good men ask good men, "Where is the Bishop?" Being told that he had been at Albany or Syracuse, the question was, "Why is he not here, attending to his own work?" The reminder that the preachers themselves, being in Copley Square, Boston, were outside their own charges, was not satisfying. I really did prefer to plan my own itinerary. A minute censorship of my labors, together with an accurately kept calendar of my whereabouts, did not appeal to the free will of my Arminian nature. After I had been in official residence for a time, I knew that my advance surmises were not fair, and that I had exaggerated the critical disposition. But if in advance I had used Paul's metaphor about Ephesus, and had said, "A great door and effectual is opened unto me, and there are many adversaries," one of the "adversaries" to give me tremors would have been that critical attitude. All this I stated in kindly frankness to the delegates whose desire so greatly honored me.

To Boston I came—to meet assurances of loyal support. In one respect I had a fixed policy. Methodism was not as strong relatively as it was in the West. Our wonderful partners in work had arrived ahead of us—Congregationalists, Baptists, Protestant Episcopalians. There remained none of the ostracism which Francis Asbury and Jesse Lee had faced. Yet the Pilgrims and Puritans had won "vested rights." Frequently men and women exhibited the quaint cards which their parents and grandparents had received as certificates that, being Methodists, they were to be relieved from tax support for a state church. The people who moved out of that dominion against which Brooks Adams so inveighed in his book, *The Emancipation of Massachusetts*, were not weaklings. In order to be Methodists, the followers had to possess convictions. The situation did effective sifting. In some aspects New England Methodism was not surpassed anywhere in America. In Boston itself no other denomination had so blessed the city with helpful institutions. Boston University, Morgan Memorial, Deaconess Hospital, Palmer Home for Incurables, all rendered amazing service; while *Zions Herald*, under the auspices of the Wesleyan Association, had won honors in religious journalism. Yet in the rural sections of Massachusetts, in the villages of Rhode Island and Connecticut, and in the northern reaches of New Hampshire, Maine, and Vermont, many of our churches were small and struggling. My fixed policy was based on the belief that our work, while needing administration, needed inspiration; and that without constant gifts of hope much of it would change steeples to tombstones! When at the end of my first four years one splendid man desired to have a bishop who would spend more time in his office and give more heed to machinery, I replied that if he represented a fair minority I would go elsewhere without a sense of grievance; but that if I were returned there would be no change in the proportionate parts of my program.

The truth was that New England responded to a warm and throbbing gospel. A review of the records would show this unmistakably. William Nast Brodbeck, Louis Albert Banks, Charles A. Crane, Lauress J. Birney were all Western imports—men with evangelistic zeal who found response among the reserved "Yankees." Statistics may be a form of boasting, yet I give the membership results in New England Methodism for the period from 1916 to 1924 as proof that then, at least, the inspirational emphasis did real work. In the first four years every Conference made an increase, while the Area as a whole lifted its membership from 113,768 to 125,661. In the second quadrennium each Conference made a further gain in spite of difficulties created by changes of population in Maine, New Hampshire, and Vermont. The record showed a fine response to inspirational evangelism.

Our local mergers resulted magnificently. In these I had the steady co-operation of the district superintendents. After patient negotiations, Dr. C. Oscar Ford succeeded in unifying two local churches in Springfield, Massachusetts; the late Dr. Charles Edward Spaulding secured articles of union for two churches in Worcester; while the late Dr. John H. Newland brought together societies at Fall River. No one could today pass Trinity, Springfield; or Wesley, Worcester; or Union, Fall River, with their striking properties, and not feel a thrill of pride. In a few other New England cities our work would today be on a far stronger basis if small counsels had not compelled fragmentary groups without power enough to impress a city's life. Sometimes the love of an old church, with its tender memories, can defeat the demands of the new day, with its manifest challenges.

There were many agreeable features in the Boston Area. The two quadrenniums there, added to former years, gave me twenty-three years of life within a twelve-mile area; while the securing of a romantic home, scripturally built on a rock in Malden, gave me sixteen years in a city big enough to attract, and not big enough to appall. I had fine associations with the Boston University School of

121

Theology. Its students were often in my domestic circle. I had the reverent joy of ordaining scores of them. While at first there was a tendency toward hasty ordination that made it only an incident, the co-operation of Dean Albert C. Knudson made the young men understand that "the laying on of hands" was to be made an event. The altar at which men knelt to give all their lives to Christ was not to be treated as a matrimonial convenience, but as a holy of holies where the Shekinah was lighted for ceaseless radiance.

At the General Conference in May, 1924, at Springfield, Massachusetts, the Committee on Episcopacy read me out for another assignment, and the Conference itself adopted the report. So I was called upon to give an official farewell to New England Methodism, to the Berkshire Hills, the Green Mountains, the Androscoggin and the Penobscot, the Connecticut Valley, Narragansett Bay, Martha's Vineyard, and the Old Man with the Stone Face in New Hampshire. Boston's successor was Chicago. Lake Michigan succeeded the Atlantic, and seemed as big because its expanse was as surely lost in the horizon. The historic Common was supplanted by fields of fertility that stretched away in a vast acreage of oats, and wheat, and corn. Since I had spent eight years on the Pacific Coast and eight years on the Atlantic Coast, it seemed wise to restore the equilibrium of the continent by placing me in its central life. The orders were: On to Chicago!

III

Once again, the packer and the van! Once again, parting words from beloved relatives and dear friends! Once again, tickets for the Hughes caravan, still large enough to win the attention of other travelers! North Shore Hotel, Evanston, four months! Then the comely episcopal residence in Wilmette! The fine office in the Chicago Tem-

ple building—obtained through the generous courtesy of
the late George W. Dixon, and William W. Dixon, and
Dr. John Thompson; and furnished in a worthy way with
gifts secured by a great gentleman and educator, Dean
Thomas F. Holgate! The study of a map that revealed
Chicago's immensity—four times the population of the
state of Maine! A great reception at which, as my discreet
wife felt, my response to Edward Rector's speech of welcome was not "quite up to the usual standard"! The
dedication of First Church, Chicago, as a sanctuary set like
a jewel in the midst of the Temple! Crowds so great that
policemen had to conduct me through a rear door! A
querulous voice, issuing from a man who gazed at the
tallest church steeple in the world and said: "Where [in a
certain location] do these [adjectival] Methodists get all
their money?" The fall breezes are sweeping in from the
lake. The Conferences arrive with their glorious problems. I know how Paul felt when he "departed from
Athens and came to Corinth." Over this figure of speech
Boston may smile, and Chicago will not frown.

My new Area was described by another metaphor. As
its geography was fairly level, so was its religious life level.
Succeeding to the work of William Fraser McDowell and
Thomas Nicholson, I found that my inheritance of tasks
was like them—solid but not sensational. The temperaments of these earnest and cultured leaders did not create
upheavals or initiate rash enterprises. No startling crises
were turned over to me. The acute situation in our Wesley Foundation at the University of Illinois was caused
by a bank failure, and not by administrative fault. The
financial depression was still distant. Once at a Chicago
dinner, when fiscal clouds were dark and heavy, two commercial pharisees inveighed against the management of the
Church, declaring that our need was "good businessmen."
I mildly asked whether we should send for the bank presi-

123

dents or the railroad presidents. I pointed out that rail stocks had sunk toward zero, and that scores of banks had closed their doors. Had church stock gone down to two cents on the dollar? Amid the crash of commercial interests had they heard of any Methodist church that had nailed up its portals? I was not bumptious enough to anger them, and yet factual enough to puzzle them.

There were contrasts between the Chicago Area and my former Areas. The likeness between Boston and Chicago was that each had a cosmopolitan university— Northwestern University, with Garrett Biblical Institute in collaboration; Boston University, with the School of Theology in organization. In these seminaries I frequently ordained the young ministers elected deacons or elders by their Conferences. If I were challenged I could not produce figures, yet I am confident that the lists of men ordained at many Conferences, added to the lists of seminarians, would show that I had used the commissioning rituals over more men than has any other bishop in modern Methodism. This has been due to propinquity rather than to popularity.

The likeness between the San Francisco Area and the Chicago Area was that each had contrasted sections. As Northern California, with San Francisco, spoke jokingly of Southern California as Southern "Cafeteria," so Chicago had a little condescension when she spoke of "down-State." For the Area itself the nonurban territory was increased when we added the Southern Illinois Conference. This brought McKendree College to our institutional roll. McKendree, like its Conference, has been a fountain for ministerial life. It would be an inconceivable blunder if any technical insistence or any halfhearted support should close doors through which some of our ablest ministers have walked to power.

There were accomplishments for which I make modest

124

claims. One was the merging of the Illinois and the Central Illinois Conferences. The latter lay like a narrow ribbon across the wide state—not only hampered by long pastoral moves, but limited in opportunities for strong ministers. I did all I could to effect this union. When at last the delegation, headed by Dr. William E. Shaw, appeared before the magnanimous Illinois Conference, the vote for the merger was overwhelming. I have never heard any minister or layman declare that this unification was a mistake.

There was a similar problem with our foreign-speaking Conferences—the German, the Swedish, and the Norwegian and Danish. These Methodists were sturdy and loyal. Their Lutheran catechetical tradition was an asset. In addition, they had kept the Methodist tradition. They were ardent without fanaticism. Their ardor testified by its generosity. They gave to benevolences far more per capita than did our English-speaking people. My children declared that after I had held these Conferences it took a month to cure me from saying "Yah." Yet their example touched my heart far more than it did my vocabulary. I prepared the formal documents of merger. In all the outcomes we did not lose a single minister or layman. The English-speaking preachers treated these incoming brethren, in the matter of pensions, with a fairness that always became liberality.

I must boast also about one achievement for Garrett Biblical Institute. The original charter relieved the school of taxes on its real-estate holdings. This provision made it advisable to put much productive endowment into real properties. But this long-run wisdom made a short-run difficulty in the depression. The charter provided, as well, for a very small board of trustees. I was soon convinced that we should enlarge the circle of official friends, though I feared that we might lose certain great privileges if we submitted our charter for change to the Illinois Legislature. So I wrote a new by-law providing for counsel trustees, as well as for the charter trustees who would still keep a power of veto. This provision was adopted without change of a syllable. It has resulted in substantial gains for Garrett's life. The magnificent work of three lay trustees, Harry A. Wheeler, James E. MacMurray, and William H. Dunham, together with the inconceivable patience of the late Frederick C. Eiselen and the unfailing wisdom of President Horace Greeley Smith, is rapidly placing this school beyond crisis, though not beyond constant current need.

I never escaped from one hindering impression of Chicago. Always I felt concealed by its immensity. The big city could hide a man. When I moved from West Virginia in 1885, the state's population was 600,000. Chicago had five times that many people. The vocabulary of Bishop Quayle, being taxed for a metaphor, fled to jungles. He likened the city to a vast and tawny lion, stretching himself along a lake. The animal was so huge that one "could not talk to it all at once." One's addresses to it moved jaw, or foot, or tail, or brought the creature to an occasional roar. But the difficulty lay in taming all that colossal living area. The simile is unique—and suggestive.

Chicago was leonine. It swallowed many a preacher into obscurity. Episcopal administration was hindered by "cityitis." Francis Asbury's journal declares that this was a common complaint in his day. Probably Chicago Methodism was the strongest city Methodism in the world. This made it a magnet. More than one preacher wanted to stay there to educate his children. When, after graduation, they settled there, his argument did not disappear. After living in Chicago parsonages for many years, one man, when removed to a fairly distant county seat by Bishop McDowell, wept "all night long"—his wife co-

126

operating with the tears. But in six months, facing larger audiences than he had ever known, and being a "leading citizen" as he had never before been, he declared that he had "been a ministerial fool for more than a quarter of a century." Leaving Chicago mournfully, he and his wife felt that they were another Adam and Eve driven from the Garden—only to discover that their Eden was elsewhere.

Yet the Area was amazingly loyal. The anti-official obsession was not vigorous enough to make wide disturbance. There was nothing like espionage on the travels of the resident bishop. The men were generous toward his itineraries. When the Area delegates in 1924 requested my assignment, I refused to make my own choice among the Areas. Bishop McConnell came teasingly and said that the Illinois men were troubled by my reserve, and had desired to approach me through him. He desired to know if this was not like an effort to reach the tropics by way of the North Pole! But the Church's decision was good for me. When I think of the Chicago Area, I know a freight of love that is abundant, but not burdensome. Someday I shall look down from the turrets of another City and thank God for the tasks that came to me beneath the towers of the mighty metropolis by the lake.

IV

The General Conference of 1932, at Atlantic City, assigned me to Washington. The Chicago Area delegates had unanimously asked for my return, but there was a general conviction of the Church that I should succeed Bishop McDowell. The change of residence helped to bring to its crisis the question of Methodist unification. I had been placed in the borderland—in a district purposely removed from sectionalism, and officially designated as neutral ground. Consequently my visits to the South became more frequent, while my associations with Southern Methodism in one of the centers of old-time debate, and with the Methodist Protestants in a field of their beginning activities, increased the intimacy that prepares for union.

William Fraser McDowell continued to live in Washington as a retired bishop, so that our long-time intimacy helped to dovetail the two administrations into unity. He gave solicited counsel, but never interference. He was a magnificent predecessor. Between us there existed that wordless affection which often marks the relations of two men. At his funeral services I pointed out that the historic friendships had been between men—David and Jonathan, and Damon and Pythias. I have elsewhere written that as he grew older he walked the path of sanctity that lies between two worlds. Yet I never detected in him the slightest self-consciousness of superiority. The surrender of the years was made complete. Life was given over wholly to God, as his deeds of kindness and his will and testament proved. The shadows lengthened for us both, but they fell far toward the eastern horizons: they never dropped between us. He moved out of this life while asking an anxious question about my sick wife—and stepped quickly into another Land to be greeted by Clotilda Lyon McDowell, his own faithful and brilliant helpmate.

He had done great work in Washington. While never an administrator of the super-promoting type, he had the way of the statesman. Methodistically speaking, the approaches to the Capitol looked as if they had been definitely planned. One main road lay by the Methodist Building; another by the American University; another by the wonderful Old People's Home; another by Hamline Church; another by Foundry Church; another by Sibley Hospital; another by an orphanage. Not one of our institutions received a dollar from the Community Chest.

Soon after my arrival the urbane and faithful chancellor of American University, Dr. Lucius C. Clark, presented his resignation. For a year I acted as the head of the institution and, by constant care, balanced the budget and assisted that noble layman, Dr. Arthur C. Christie, and his comrade trustees, in a work of reorganization.

Strangely enough, the region around Baltimore has become for Methodism an educational cemetery. The first institutional death came early in our history. Cokesbury College, after pathetic accidents, gave its foundations to the dust. Goucher College had been nourished by the Church until it reached eminence. Then came a change that made the Methodist Area bishop unwelcome on the Board of Trustees. The background of the difficulty I knew well—far better than did the most of the Goucher trustees. In my own administration Morgan College for Negroes was taken from us. After we had builded properties to the value of more than a million dollars, the Board of Trustees, largely self-perpetuating, turned the immense equities over to Maryland, leaving to the Church a doubtful right to govern in a modified Wesley Foundation, whose building was erected by our funds. The one consolation was that the state would doubtless provide well in financial ways for Morgan. In the general region American University and Western Maryland College at Westminister will keep open doors for our Methodist young people. Methodist philanthropists would do well to look carefully into the organization of the colleges that ask their aid, lest quick alienations remove the assets gathered by pious appeals.

The Methodist Building is a monument to the energy of Dr. Clarence True Wilson and to Bishop McDowell. It stands virtually on the nation's campus—with the Capitol in front, the Senate Office Building on the right, and the majestic Supreme Court Building on the left. An airplane photograph shows the strategy of the location. Under the guidance of Dr. Ernest H. Cherrington, the building itself not only houses the activities of the Board of Temperance, but meets Dr. Wilson's dream as an income producer for the educational work of the strongest church temperance board in the world.

I wish that I could write glowingly about the religious life of those who represent us at the capital. I lived in Washington in the final days of the Prohibition era, and I have lived there under the new liquor regime. The local statistics are appalling. Our district leads the nation in the per capita consumption of hard liquors. Our nearest competitor is little Nevada. Even she trails so far behind us that she does not get our dust—or perhaps the liquid metaphor is better which declares that she does not catch the fumes. If the cocktail is not omnipresent, it is the usual mark of feasts. Already some of the elected representatives of the people, once pleasantly Puritan in their ways, carry with themselves the perfumes of excess and move toward a dreadful habitude. Men and women who ten years ago were moral exemplars are now following a multitude to do evil. Washington newspapers debit the excessive use of liquors to visitors. Yet the plenteous spigots and bottles and steins in the capital contribute to the flood; the disconcerting statistics remain for our reproof. Ere many years pass the reaction of fashion will come once more, and a wiser era will revive the Bible's declaration that wine is a mocker and strong drink a raging. Until then we will have the label of fanaticism pinned upon us whenever we hint at Paul's statement that no "drunkard" shall inherit "the kingdom of God."

Amid these shadows much sunshine abides. We have many office-holders who do not yield to the flowing bowl. They maintain a smiling Puritanism in what William

130

Allen White's biography of Coolidge calls "Babylon." The merger of Methodism has brought with it the union that is strength. It not only solidified our ranks, it diversified our work and provided worthy appeals to different temperaments. The Methodist Union was never so strong and so useful. None of the disasters prophesied by the opponents of unification have come to pass. In the wider borders— Maryland, the Eastern Shore, Delaware—noble groups move forward under the banner of Christ. If Asbury should revisit the scenes of his earthly labors, he would be entranced by the material changes from dismal swamp to broad avenues and high domes. If his first impressions might lead him to question whether the ancient fervor had vanished, his closer inspection would give him pride in the service of his spiritual children. He would share the dream that Washington might win the features of the New Jerusalem and become Augustine's City of the Redeeming God.

CHAPTER VI

PERSONALITIES

THIS CHAPTER IS AN ACCOUNT OF CERTAIN PEOPLE WHOM I have known.

I

The impressive figures of my childhood included men who were the political pioneers of West Virginia. My father became pastor of the state's first United States senator and, later, of the state's first governor. The latter was Arthur I. Boreman, a distinctive citizen of Parkersburg. He was a mnemonic of the tragic days when the little mountain commonwealth was sundering herself from Virginia. Among the leaders in that struggle there were marked resemblances. They were rugged men, silent men. After the fashion of the period they wore plenteous beards, as did the presidential candidates such as Grant, Garfield, Blaine, and Harrison. They carried a residue of tragedy, in their eyes, in their reserved bearing, in their constant seriousness.

I stood in awe of Governor Boreman. In the church services I studied him as he sat in his pew. When social life began and I was with his lovely daughters, Miss Rena and Miss Maud, my speech became hesitant as the Governor drew near. I have wished that I had been old enough to interview him concerning his experiences in guiding a state in its initiation and in adding a new star to the flag.

The senator was the late Waitman T. Willey, of Morgantown. He was a stately person. The early records of

West Virginia often carry his name. A recent history of the place of the Baltimore and Ohio Railroad in the 1861-65 war period is sprinkled with mention of his work. He was affectionately regarded. Children were named for him. Usually, too, there was no compromise made by abbreviation. W. T. W. would not suffice.

Senator Willey was a deeply religious man. My marked impression of him came when I was fifteen years of age and I heard him give an exhortation at one of my father's revival meetings. He had a combination of head and heart that made him overwhelming. The critical students from the state university were deeply moved, while college professors were driven from their dignity to an evident emotion. If the other founders of the state were like Governor Boreman and Senator Willey, they helped to put into the civic unit a religious consciousness.

II

When I became aware of the ecclesiastical realm, I was greatly influenced by the Methodist bishops. At Conferences I looked from a respectful distance upon Randolph S. Foster, Stephen M. Merrill, John P. Newman, Isaac W. Joyce, Cyrus D. Foss, Daniel A. Goodsell, and Earl Cranston. I came into the episcopacy early enough to be associated with the two last named. The area system arrived slowly, so that my boyhood and my younger ministry had the benefit of varied episcopal talents. The bishops were strikingly different. Doubtless there has been definite advantage in the continuous administration of one bishop over a group of Conferences; yet as young preachers we looked forward with eagerness to seeing varying powers at work in sermonizing and administration.

Presiding elders, later district superintendents, touched me to my good. My first one was Dennis Murphy, a native of Ireland and a convert from Roman Catholicism—

133

a man immense in body, fertile in mind, and eloquent in utterance. Then came James B. Blakeney and Charles L. Stafford, in Iowa; George S. Chadbourne, George F. Eaton, Joseph O. Knowles, Edward R. Thorndike, and Joel M. Leonard, in New England. I never had a superintendent who did not do efficient and faithful work, or one toward whom my maturer memory would lead me to feel hostile or critical.

III

When I followed my father to Iowa in 1885, my relations with the state were too slender, and my years were too few, to allow significant relations to public men. The days of hero worship had not passed, either from myself or from a sophisticated world; and I watched prominent persons for the instruction they would give. If a really great and worthy man were announced to speak, I claimed a seat at the front. No social event could keep me from a meeting where I could observe some able speaker at his work.

The Iowa statesman who most commanded me was Jonathan P. Dolliver. The reason was domestic. The Dolliver family and the Hughes family had been together in the West Virginia Conference. The Senator's father was a big itinerant, noticeable in any assembly. The sons of the two families played around the lobbies of the Conference sessions and were about equal in their repute for "prankishness." Our names were all abbreviated—to Prent, and Vic, and Bob, and Matt, and Ed.

Senator Dolliver was a majestic speaker. To a mind that compassed political questions he added the fervor of his father's evangelical habits. The picture of his father returning from his gospel circuits, and dismounting to recite to the anxious wife the victories won for the Saviour, was an unforgettable classic. Jonathan P. Dolliver became known as the most eloquent man in the Senate. As a fraternal delegate to the General Conference of the Methodist Episcopal Church, South, he delivered an address that melted antagonism from the fiercest anti-unificationist. Reluctant tears flowed over the faces of unmitigated opponents of merger. This address claimed a place among the influences that steadily worked toward the healing of the Church division. Many believed that if the Senator had lived longer he would have made a natural compromise for the conservatives and progressives as a presidential candidate when a midnight caucus gave to Warren G. Harding a doubtful nomination and election. But the Iowa giant fell on sleep prematurely, and his golden voice was silenced for the forums of earth. He was a delegate to the General Conference at Baltimore, and was intensely interested in the election of another West Virginia preacher's son to the episcopacy.

IV

I have had the privilege of meeting every President of the country, save one, since Grant's time. The General himself I met when I was still a wondering child. I can see him now—a square block of a man, fully bearded, unsmiling, severe. His appearance did not indicate greatness. Later I appreciated the story of the youngster who had heard much of the warrior, and who, failing to see in Grant's demeanor anything that would cause a brave army to quake, said to the President, "Let's hear you holler." I myself felt that General Grant needed a supplement.

President Rutherford B. Hayes was a trustee of my alma mater. Hence he appeared on the campus many times. His wife, Lucy Webb, had graduated from the woman's college that merged with Ohio Wesleyan. The country had much respect for its former President. The Southern states appreciated his generous policies of reconstruction.

135

He would have attracted attention anywhere, with his large size, his bearded face, his formal dress, his silk hat, his gentle bearing. Though not a formal member of the Methodist Church, the former President was a faithful and constant supporter. His pastors noted his deep interest in revival services and his conviction that the Christian faith, in its program, was an essential factor in the strength of our republic. When I was entertained in his home and by his children at Fremont, Ohio, and spoke at an anniversary of the family church, I walked beneath the trees of his broad lawns and thanked God that I had known, even slightly, people whose ethical convictions had not surrendered to the temptations of public life.

President Garfield I never saw. I did see his successor, Chester A. Arthur, a preacher's son—and a New York politician whom responsibilities developed into a statesman. Without question the Republican party blundered in not nominating Arthur to follow his "accidental" years in the presidency. James G. Blaine had waited long for the nomination—too long. The funded enmities had increased. He carried his magnetism over the land, speaking from train platforms and courthouse steps, and receiving wild plaudits. His popularity was like a madness.

His opponent was Grover Cleveland, a preacher's son, whose Buffalo career was not a hopeful prophecy. Yet the heavy-set man, with stern face and gruff voice, steadily gained the people's confidence. When I met him in a receiving line he grunted a greeting and pushed me swiftly forward along the procession of handshakers. How different he was from his rival! With Blaine, suavity was an art. With Cleveland, bluntness seemed to be a specialty. The recalcitrants who distrusted the Republican candidate won eloquent voices. Beecher's profession did not keep him from maledictions against the "White-Plumed Knight." Dr. Burchard's profession did not prevent his

136

blundering phrase about "Rum, Romanism, and Rebellion." Thus clerical words against Blaine and for Blaine assisted in his defeat. The silly treatment of the temperance women headed by Frances E. Willard, who found their petition with its thousands of signatures lying tobacco-spattered on the floor of a committee room, and who in indignation persuaded John P. St. John to run on a Prohibition ticket, completed the debacle. Blaine saw his apple of gold turn to ashes. Not so long afterwards he lifted his emaciated hand toward heaven and said to his wife, "The only hope now is up yonder."

Grover Cleveland's assets were a terrible honesty and an unflinching courage. His growl was superficial and his heart real. Out of vilification he moved into a popular admiration that became affection. Long after he ceased to be President he sent me a letter so kindly, gentle, and human that I filed it with such care as to conceal to this day its alphabetical hiding place.

Benjamin Harrison I met and heard, but that was all. In my Indiana days I was told so much of his amazing legal abilities, of his splendid character, of his unremitting service as an office-bearer in the Presbyterian Church, as to give me regret that my touch with him was so slight.

William McKinley, as a Methodist layman, had won a place in church circles. He was a charming gentleman in social life, as he was a persuasive speaker in public life. His assassination shocked the nation immeasurably, while his sincere words of trust ere he passed into the other land left an impression of Christlikeness. Memorial services took on something like a revival quality. Pastors testified that church attendance increased and that professions of faith became more frequent.

Thus Theodore Roosevelt stormed into the White House. A breathless citizenry queried what a tempestuous leadership might do. I once had a personal conference

137

with him in Washington. While I talked he walked nervously about the room, making for my words a difficult target. Yet I discovered that he had caught the full substance of my errand. In season the people felt that his impetuosity was more in his manner than in his mind and will. In spite of his thin voice, he was an effective platformer. A sense of humor enlivened his discussions, made emphatic by facial expressions that resembled gestures. He would end a playful sentence in a falsetto tone—as when I heard him declare that, at a station on the Zambesi River in Africa, he "met a missionary who was engaged in teaching the natives some of the more obvious of the Ten Commandments."

My conference with him having related to an international matter, I was sent on to John Hay, then Secretary of State. I had read some of his earlier poems, about Jim Bludsoe and Little Breeches, productions in which he had little pride in his maturer years. His verses on "The Stirrup Cup" were a literary joy, though a mournful sentiment. I had been touched by his lines, "In Church," depicting his sad feeling when he caught on his wife's face the rapture that he himself could not gain. The Secretary was co-operative with my purpose. In response to an anecdote concerning a well-known Methodist official whose appetite made hardship for an afflicted stomach, Mr. Hay related the following: A certain Justice of the Supreme Court had a friend who was a gormandizer and who, after meals, often had distress. On one occasion he played silo rather than man, and then ran his hand over his pained front and expressed the fear that he had appendicitis. The Justice replied, "No! No! The trouble with you is not with your Appendix. It's with your Table of Contents." Hearing this triple pun, one is not disposed to say that it represents the lowest form of wit.

I admired Willam Howard Taft. He had an engaging

138

frankness, and a wonderful smile which was not a mere facial readjustment. I do not enter into the controversy that led Theodore Roosevelt to accept a third-party nomination, making his Republican successor's re-election impossible. In a humiliating defeat Taft proved himself a gentleman and a hero, and he grew back into the people's loving confidence.

I enjoyed a story that Mr. Taft related to Bishop Cranston. The President had been obliged by international courtesy to attend a service as a memorial to a royal personage of another land. The dead man had been far from saintly. If crimes other than heresy had been as surely punished by his religious communion, his soul would have been excommunicated into outer darkness. Our Chief Executive was criticized for attending the service, knowing as he did that the deceased had no right to belong to any church. Mr. Taft declared that, sitting amid the alleged mourners, he thought of a shrewd Negro preacher who was called upon to officiate at the funeral of a disreputable character. The ebony Solomon began his discourse by saying, "My friends, we ah heah to 'spress the hope that this man am gone whah we know he ain't." The knowledge that such thoughts as this passed justly through the mind of a President on so solemn an occasion gives wings to imagination.

With Woodrow Wilson I had more association than I have had with any other of our Chief Executives. When he was president of Princeton and I was at DePauw, we joined a group of about twenty college presidents at Mr. Andrew Carnegie's request and became members of the Board of Trustees of the Carnegie Foundation for the Advancement of Teaching. He had endowed this work with ten million dollars, which had been deemed sufficient after "expert calculation." Evidently the expertness was not so expert. The little gray-haired philanthropist was

139

compelled to lift the supporting funds to fifteen million. Later it became apparent that this huge sum was not adequate for the purpose of providing pensions for retired college teachers. Still later the Foundation, on the strictly financial side, became virtually a generous insurance board, rendering a valuable service through its own program, and stimulating the gathering of pension endowments in colleges. Woodrow Wilson, as a member of the Foundation, was a wholly "silent partner." I do not recall that he ever entered into the discussions. The report was that he was an active member of the Executive Committee. At the time of my election to the episcopacy, when I felt that ethics called for my resignation, I was no more acquainted with Dr. Wilson than I was at the initial handshake. The old-fashioned hearthstone was not in his nature. The furnace was out of sight—in the cellar of his being. My experience may be construed into a compliment. His strange advance to world influence was not explained by magnetic sociability, but by a colossal mind. His fiercest foes could never deride his intellect.

Some of President Wilson's friends and enemies classified him as a partisan. They felt that if he had selected a more representative Republican for the Versailles Commission, the outcome might have been different. But when the partisan moods of Woodrow Wilson and Henry Cabot Lodge clashed, the League of Nations was the victim. The imagination has freedom in fashioning a future that never arrived. Yet it is at least possible that, had not party and personal enmity wrecked an ideal, we might have been saved from the crimson terror that now stalks over Europe, agitates Asia, and threatens the world. The two-party system doubtless has its value for our democracy; yet it may be a dangerous thing in the broader regions where it has no genuine home.

Whenever I think of Woodrow Wilson pathos claims me.

140

His appearance after a stroke weakened his body represents something equally pathetic in his career. He reached many important goals, but he failed to attain the supreme one. William Allen White's biography ends with the explanation:

They took him to an Episcopal Cathedral, where he lies outside the fold of his father's faith; there in the tabernacle of a creed in which kings and powerful persons go to rest. He is not of the royal blood. So lying in the shadow of an alien covenant, he seems shy, remote, aloof—a Woodrow to the last, even in death! [1]

I met Warren G. Harding but once. His nomination made me anxious. His legislative history could not offer for his credit any large and constructive thing. I had the heaviest difficulty in persuading my hand to cast a ballot that bore his name. I feared that the nomination had been made on the basis of jovial fellowship where the symbols were cards and chips rather than manuscripts of high counsel. It may be that someday a kindly writer may rescue Harding's name from its doubtful setting. The sufficient advocate has not yet appeared.

In her book, *Crowded Hours,* Alice Roosevelt Longworth tells how her curiosity carried her upstairs when a party was on at the White House. There she found that all kinds of liquors were being served—and this under the auspices of a President who had taken his solemn oath, with his hand on a personally selected verse of the Bible, to defend the Constitution. Is it a wonder that disaster visited other departments of the administration? There is a deep sadness in Harding's last earthly journey. His Denver speech indicated awareness that the arm of flesh had failed. It betokened, also, a desire to return to the God who demanded the humble walk, the just dealing,

[1] *Woodrow Wilson, the Man, His Times, and His Task,* p. 483.

141

and the love of mercy. The administration ended in a funeral—in more senses than one.

Then came Calvin Coolidge—fresh on his slow-speaking lips the oath of office given by his father amid the Vermont hills. He had been my Governor in Massachusetts, where he accomplished his silent climb from the Legislature to the chief place. He had honored me by appointing me one of the three trustees of the state library, located in the Capitol building and holding one of the finest book collections of the civic sort in America. This gave me a modest place in the commonwealth's official life. On one occasion I was suddenly summoned to represent the Governor. Mr. Coolidge was ill. A state dinner was to be tendered to Cardinal Mercier, the ecclesiastic of Belgium, whose heroic stand against the German invaders of his land had made him a renowned figure. The Massachusetts officials were present, and the visiting Cardinal was accompanied by Cardinal O'Connell. The contrast between the two men was striking—one slender, the other heavy; one smiling, the other grim. They both wore the tiny red cap as the symbol of their office. So far as I have heard, I was the only Protestant bishop in America who had the opportunity of bringing a public, face-to-face tribute to the great guest. Though my period of preparation was brief, my prayer to God for right words was answered. Cardinal Mercier was moved as I offered him such an affectionate benediction as a Protestant clergyman could bring. He caught my spirit, did not seem embarrassed by his own moist eyes, and, not quite able to escape what I had offered in tribute, finally said, "You must excuse what I say so feelingly. This Methodist Bishop put me in the way of it."

I appreciated the editorial comment which the *Boston Herald* gave of the event, and am putting its first paragraph into these pages.

PERSONALITIES

MAN TO MAN

When half a dozen men are making successive addresses on a common theme, it happens now and then that one of the first speakers strikes a chord so deep and strong that it reverberates through all the later speeches. This was the case in the felicitous and earnest tribute to the Belgian Cardinal at the state dinner given in his honor Sunday. Early in the evening Bishop Edwin Holt Hughes voiced so hearty a welcome to the guest and spoke such manly and eloquent praise of his heroic stand for Belgium, that all present were touched. Coming from any source the words of appreciation would have been applauded as true and moving; but as coming from a Methodist Episcopal Bishop to a Roman Catholic Cardinal they carried in addition a finer sentiment. Immediately Cardinal O'Connell's stirring address caught up the tenderness and breadth of spirit with which Bishop Hughes had characterized Cardinal Mercier; and later the guest's own response took its warmest colors as he thanked the Bishop for the words of admiration and affection he had spoken.

Calvin Coolidge made an excellent governor. His taciturn ways were not a disadvantage. He never had to withdraw statements that had been uttered in haste. I myself suggested to Mr. Frank W. Stearns, close friend and campaign director, that Mr. Coolidge's silence should be turned into an advertisement. Yet I never had the slightest difficulty in conversing with him. He was no expert in speech about the weather. Yet, when the talk turned to subjects in which he was interested, he was not sphinxlike. His sense of humor was emphasized by his drawling tone. Pleasantry that was slow and staccato appealed to him. At luncheon at the White House one day he was much amused by my tale of the stuttering man who achieved a mischievous attitude toward his own limitations, and who, being asked by a sympathetic lady whether he "stammered all the time," made reply: "N-n-n-no! Only when I t-t-t-t-talk!" The President kept repeating the last phrase and returned to it for periods of laughter.

I have read the appraisals of Woodrow Wilson and Calvin Coolidge as written by William Allen White—as a man and an author one of my chief admirations. The biography of Wilson seemed to me the fairer of the two. The frequent reference to President Coolidge's speech as a "quack" gave a wrong impression, while his caution was overemphasized. The Governor who vetoed a liquor bill passed by the Massachusetts Legislature, declaring the measure an attempt to set aside the Constitution, and the President who vetoed the Postal Employees' Bill, and the so-called Bonus Bill, must have had genuine courage.

In fact, it was a brave action that led to Calvin Coolidge's nomination to the Vice Presidency. Officials in public life have usually been considerate of the Labor and Capital vote. Congressmen and senators have not always played David before the industrial Goliath. Few public men have faced such a crisis as came in the police strike. If the primacy in meeting the desperate situation in Boston must be credited to Edwin U. Curtis, the political brunt was borne by Governor Coolidge. The city, left without adequate protection, became a Mecca for thugs and roughnecks. The railroads brought carloads of iniquity. Central stores became ravaged by thieving bands and sections of the Common became resorts for gambling. If the condition did not deserve the name of a Reign of Terror, it did deserve to be called the Season of Shivers.

To Samuel Gompers, Governor Coolidge sent his famous reply, "There is no right to strike against the public safety by anybody, anywhere, anytime." The granite of his native hills illustrated his will. Mr. Coolidge did consult with various citizens ere the state militia was summoned into the confusion. I deem it an honor that I was among those with whom he counseled. When

144

obduracy seemed final, it was met by the even more un-yielding obduracy of a quiet Governor. The telegram to Samuel Gompers was one speech that nominated Calvin Coolidge for the Vice Presidency and moved him into the providence that placed him in the presidential chair. Apparently losing his political life, he saved it for the larger realm.

First and last, I had abundant credentials of the man's patriotism. I know not what was in his mind when he gave the country his quaint and enigmatic telegram: "I do not choose to run." Perhaps a fluttering heart gave him a red signal. Or perhaps some canny prevision warned him of the commercial reaction. Or perhaps, again, his form of words left leeway enough to allow him to respond to an importunate call. But he walked without an open tremor into the quiet places. Ere long his dust was borne, not to a stately sepulcher that did not belong to his people, but to the native state where his own church stands guard near at hand, and his own mountains are the sentinels of his tomb.

My last conversation with President Coolidge gave me a thrilling satisfaction. The Hon. Roy O. West, Secretary of the Interior, invited Mrs. Hughes and me to the dinner given by custom to the President and his wife by a member of the Cabinet. Mr. Coolidge asked Secretary West, after the dinner, to seat me next to him. He expressed profound relief that he was soon to drop his vast burdens. Then he said to me, "Do you know that you were the first person who nominated me for the Presidency?" I recalled the Home Market Club banquet at which we had both spoken, and asked if that was the occasion of which he was thinking. He replied, "Yes." And he added, "Little did I dream then that a current of events would carry me where I have lived in these years." Naturally I was pleased to have him regard me as the pioneer

145

in naming him for the climax of his career, and I smilingly said, "I shall certainly narrate that to my children and grandchildren." I now so inform them—and not without pride.

Soon after I came to reside in Washington, Herbert Hoover invited me to lunch at the White House. Later he conferred with me confidentially about the campaign that issued in his defeat. I came from the interview feeling that he saw the handwriting on the wall. I have at times quoted the remark of the New Englander who said that "the man on top of the wave was frequently mistaken for the wave itself." The opposite of that statement is as true—the man in the trough of the wave is often mistaken for the trough itself. A depression is a heavy handicap for an administrator who has met the shock of a financial reaction. The people think that contemporaneousness is causation. The exhibit of a world floundering in commercial problems does not convince them that their own ruler was not at fault. So Mr. Hoover moved from the White House, not wholly into privacy, but near an occasional platform where he uttered his economic instruction and where he continued the career of earlier days which had made him the engineer of mercy for feeding the hungry millions.

Franklin Delano Roosevelt is now in the presidential chair, striving to meet the multiform emergencies of a bleeding world. While I make no claim to a friendly intimacy, I have found his door always open to me. To meet him is to feel his personal charm. His smile is a welcome. His voice over the desk is even more musical than his voice over the radio. Though I myself proudly dwell among the Puritans, and so distinctly disagree with the policy that has brought on the debacle of the present liquor excess, I still give unfeigned admiration to the man who, in spite of a physical handicap, has traversed

146

the ways of power and achieved an assured place among the world figures of our mid-century tragedy.

While my relations with President Roosevelt have not been intimate, they have been friendly. My definite opposition to his Supreme Court plan and my objection to the third-term proposal did not cancel our pleasant dealings. In December, 1941, he appointed me a member of the United States Muhlenberg Bicentennial Commission, the appointment being signalized by a document signed personally by the President and by Cordell Hull, as Secretary of State. When the time of my retirement from the active episcopacy arrived, Mr. Roosevelt sent the following letter:

THE WHITE HOUSE
WASHINGTON

June 3, 1940

MY DEAR BISHOP HUGHES:

My hearty good wishes go out to you as you retire as Senior Bishop of The Methodist Church.

Although I cannot attend in person the dinner in your honor, I have much pleasure in joining the Methodist Union of Washington in this tribute of admiration and esteem.

Yours has been not only a long but a distinguished career, embracing service in such important fields as San Francisco, Boston, and Chicago, before your coming to Washington. In all of these posts of responsibility you have not only rendered faithful service to The Methodist Church but you have been active in good work wherever your labors have taken you.

I wish you joy and happiness in the years that lie ahead and feel certain that even in retirement you will still find work to do for God, for country, and your fellow man.

Very sincerely yours,

(signed) FRANKLIN D. ROOSEVELT

Bishop Edwin Holt Hughes, D.D., LL.D.,
100 Maryland Avenue, N.E.,
Washington, D.C.

Though William Jennings Bryan did not reach the presidency, my admiration for him compels my heart to

147

give him tribute. His last days were clouded, not so much for himself as for his friends. The trial in Tennessee, relating to the teaching of evolution, was not a full representation of the man who thrice shook our nation with his campaigns. If Mr. Bryan had taken courses under Borden P. Bowne, he would not have been confused under the questioning of Clarence Darrow. Yet it is no more fair to judge the Commoner by the events in that courtroom than it would be to judge Moses by his conduct before the smitten rock. Wayne Williams' fine biography of Bryan is not overdone as a character tribute.

Arriving at Creston, Iowa, one day I found a note marked "Urgent." It contained a request from Mr. Bryan that I wait for a late lunch, as he desired to confer with me about an important matter. When he breezed into the dining room, he came to the point. He had heard that at a summer assembly I had paid tribute to a prominent man who had become a victim of intemperance. My word in this man's favor had related solely to one reform. I defended myself courteously, but Mr. Bryan felt, after my explanations, that I was at fault in promoting in public opinion one whose appetites gave an evil example. So I said: "Not in the way of reprisal, but for the purpose of satisfying my thought about yourself, may I ask how you secured the consent of your moral nature, in your first presidential campaign, to speak under the auspices of Tammany Hall, and to praise one of its leaders?" His reply was disarming: "Bishop Hughes, you are not the only one of my friends greatly puzzled by that episode. I have two things to say about it: first, that it was done in a political exigency; second, that I would not do it now for anything in the world." How could one avoid admiration for such honesty!

The second experience with him touched a domestic line. He came into the Pullman car at Ottumwa, Iowa,

148

just before midnight. He was sociable—and talkative. Directly I reminded him that he had spoken three times that day, and was to speak three times the next day. So I commended him to his berth. He went, but returned to tell me this story, which I give as nearly as I can in his own words.

"Today I had a long letter from my dear wife, who is an invalid. Our grandson, on his voyage to Europe, met an English cabin boy who was reading good books, keeping his idealism, and hoping to get to the United States and secure an education. The grandson had written to his grandmother, 'Grandfather has helped many American boys. Ask him if he will not give my English boy a chance.'"

Said Mr. Bryan to me, "I at once wired my wife, 'Cable Billy that I'll take care of his cabin boy.'" The man who had twice been a serious candidate for our White House sat on the edge of my Pullman couch, tears falling down his splendid face, as he said, "Bishop Hughes, you can hardly imagine how happy it made me to have my grandson show such sympathy."

These stories are typical. When William Jennings Bryan left us, the United States lost one of its finest moral assets and one of its noblest servants.

V

In Indiana I was often in the company of Senators Beveridge and Watson. Courteous rivals as students at DePauw, they maintained seeming truces amid their state's political struggles. Governor Winfield T. Durbin and Governor J. Frank Hanly were also members of the Methodist Episcopal Church, Governor Hanly being conspicuous in our General Conferences. He was no compromiser, and his unyielding convictions did not always produce harmony. He met a tragic death. It can be said

149

of him that he never trailed the banner of a Puritan conscience in the mire.

Vice President Charles Warren Fairbanks I knew well. We had the bond of our alma mater, Ohio Wesleyan. Few men in our public life have been more misunderstood. He was often compared to an ice wagon, or called an iceberg or a dweller in the frigid zone. There was nothing in him to justify the charge of coldness. He was kindly, hospitable, companionable, and, at times, finely emotional. His grief over William McKinley's death was touching. As a fraternal delegate to the General Conference of the Methodist Episcopal Church, South, he became a persuasive promoter of union. One humorous thing occurred as he was making his address. He intended to say "Fellow Methodists," but his long habit betrayed him into saying, "Fellow Republicans." There was an uproar of merriment, renewed when Mr. Fairbanks had a chance to say, "You will not find that phrase in the written copies of this speech." I am confident that he had a White House dream. But Theodore Roosevelt so changed the political climate as to make impossible the nomination of a conservative. When it was apparent that presidential hope must be abandoned, Mr. Fairbanks gallantly accepted the situation. The remainder of his years he gave to Christian work. As a trustee of Ohio Wesleyan, DePauw, and the Methodist Hospital of Indiana, he rendered service that indicated an understanding of the deeper meanings of institutions baptized in the name of Christ.

My chief friends in the public life of Illinois were five men of distinctly different types. A person of the dignity and character of James E. MacMurray was not adapted to abide the elections of Chicago's wards. So his service as state senator was not lengthy. Perhaps this was good! For he turned quickly to Christian philanthropy. He was

150

a chief aid in saving Garrett Biblical Institute. Then he crowned his life by his splendid gifts to Illinois Woman's College, which now, without his demand or consent, bears his name and becomes his monument.

John Higgins Harrison, editor and part owner of the Danville *Commercial News,* was my wonderful friend. I performed his marriage. I buried his dust. I loved him much. His career spelled romance, and included stations all the way from the circus tents to the national capital. His able and gentle wife became the dear friend of our home.

United States Senator Charles S. Deneen, the son of a faithful Methodist minister, won his first fame as a district attorney. Threats and reprisals could not daunt his honest conception of public life. A kindly and lovable spirit, he took his chosen friends into his heart and never allowed them to escape his gracious empire.

My association with Roy Owen West began in 1888 when we were both delegates to the National Convention of Delta Tau Delta, our college fraternity. Soon there came a re-enactment of the David and Jonathan tie.

Through him I first met Edward Rector, one of the great patent lawyers of our nation. He was a handsome man. In any group his face stood out like a strong cameo. Roy West and George Richmond Grose were responsible for Mr. Rector's development into the DePauw University philanthropist. They were more than abetted by Mrs. Lucy Rowland Rector. I have never known two people who had more joy in their benevolence. On the campus they were the centers of the affectionate Rector Scholars. They did not need to wait for a greeting in "the Eternal Tabernacles" by those whom they had helped by converting "the mammon of unrighteousness" into the funds of God's Kingdom. The Saviour fulfilled his promise in advance. The doors of hundreds of youthful

151

hearts swung open to them long before heaven's gates were set ajar for their coming.

Roy Owen West sought no office for himself. Having a genius for loyalty, he became agent of the fortunes of Charles S. Deneen. He was a candidate for nought save unfailing friendship. His activities as a party leader brought him into some strange associations. But he walked through the fires without the touch of flame on his garments. I never heard either friend or foe charge that Roy West had sullied himself by wrong machinations. He had his surprising reward: Calvin Coolidge appointed him as Secretary of the Interior. The man who sought nothing gained much. As a loyal Republican, a loyal Methodist, a loyal alumnus, a loyal fraternity man, a loyal husband, a loyal father, and a loyal friend, he had lifted his allegiances to the highest. One of his intimates now records the feeling of his heart and confesses confidence that he could ring Roy West's doorbell at any midnight hour and have his hands filled with three loaves or with any other gifts that friendship could offer.

I close this section with a disclaimer. I have never directly sought the companionship of the great and influential. Some kindly comrades felt that, in Washington, I might well have knocked at more doors and put myself wisely in the path of rulers. I could not do that. Having seen examples of an "inferiority complex" that led men to call notables by their first names and to claim an intimacy that never existed, I have allowed my closer affiliations to come naturally out of life itself. I have felt that obsequiousness was unworthy of a minister of Christ. But now I find myself grateful both for the vagrant contacts with the passing hosts of prominence, and, more, for the fellowships that came where the servants of God's Kingdom worked together in joyous Love.

CHAPTER VII

CONTROVERSIES

THE WORD "CONTROVERSIES" MAKES A FIERCE HEADING for a chapter. Yet other terms appear too mild. "Discussion" does not give an adequate idea of the verbal violence often involved. "Debate" suggests a procedure under parliamentary rules—instead of those eager tilts where feeling overran order and caused scrimmages. Bitterness often entered into the contests now to be described. The questions related to what were deemed priceless issues. The explanation of the vigor of religious warfare is not so much that people became wicked as it is that they considered that the matters involved were of eternal consequence. The word "anathema" is in the spiritual dictionary. Men who have either no convictions, or slender convictions, do not become sacrificial in their devotion. Calvin and Servetus both believed utterly in the worth of their views. Reaching heaven, they may have talked in celestial calmness over the fiery episodes of earth. It may be that each conceded that the other had lived up to his mundane conscience. The period of my own life has been marked by intense hostilities—and marked as well by reassuring progress toward solutions of friendship. A review gives not only an interesting history, but also a hopeful prophecy.

I

The slavery issue would not have been classified by Mr. Wesley as a debate about a trifle. His last great letter went to William Wilberforce—a vigorous protest against human bondage. When the issue shifted in the political region toward the issue of national unity and states rights, or in the ecclesiastical realm toward a doctrine of the episcopacy, the intensity affected both sides. My earlier years were spent in the swirling aftermath of the War of 1861-65. The thunders did not cease at Appomattox. They reverberated down long corridors. The survivors of the original struggle are not many. Federal and Confederate reunions have dwindled in attendance, until the roll call is brief. The parades are no longer marked by swinging strides of marchers. Among the veterans the "infantryman" has been mustered out of the ranks. The heroes are carried in upholstered automobiles.

The feeling has not been so readily discharged. Especially has this been true in the invaded regions. Those who saw Sherman march through Georgia bore tragic memories. The commander could not keep track of the pillagers. Bishop Candler used to remark that one trouble with Sherman was that he was "very careless with fire." The child whose terror-stricken eyes saw his home become a bonfire, or who saw the face of his mother slapped by a soldier's hand, has no quick oblivion for his memories. For years the word "Yankee" in certain Southern sections called for an adjective.

Yet the case was not one-sided. Sections of the semi-North knew invasion. Only recently have the tides of feeling lapsed in the near-geography of Gettysburg. Thaddeus Stevens nurtured his ferocity in that region. He carried it into Congress and sat there day after day a monster of bitterness. Much of the destruction in Pennsylvania was caused by the looters who, in spite of the command of Lee, brought in the rough customs of battles. In wartime enemies are superenemies. The imprecatory

Psalms come back to life. Western Virginia was subject to ravages. When either the regular troops or their unrestrained partners, the guerrillas, arrived, flames and thefts were the tokens. My grandparents' home was laid waste, while my parents, fleeing from a burning parsonage, found resort along the mountain bridle paths. Ere long western Virginia became West Virginia. The feeling was sufficient to rend a commonwealth in twain and to send into the courts of two generations feverish suits that dealt with the equities of the old-time state expenditures.

I now see clearly how the years worked for harmony. My mother had intense feeling. For her the dear little parsonage burned for more than half a century. Yet her admirations began their influence. She appreciated the lofty character of General Lee; became proud that her native county adjoined that in which Stonewall Jackson was born; was glad that in her girlhood she had lived not far from Jane Lew, where the coming General spent much of his boyhood; and even boasted that her uncle, Jonathan Bennett, had given Jackson one of the letters that admitted him to West Point. My father remained the Grand Mediator. He could deal with the war as history, not as irritation. He laughed at the growling of men who wanted to make the struggle perennial. When he found on his church roll those who had been in the opposing armies, he rejoiced in their brotherhood and made their associations prophetic.

He was one of many whom God appointed as pacificators. Two chiefs in that healing process were Lincoln and Lee. There was an odd difference of sectional attitude. The South moved toward admiration of the North's President. The North moved to admiration of the South's General. Robert E. Lee never fanned the flames of discord. He lived out Grant's word—"Let us have peace." Had he permitted himself to become a disturber, his immense influence in the South would have made for turbulence. But his speeches and his silences were always contributions to harmony. Amid all the memories of destruction and sorrow, Lee remained a steady and gentle figure.

Lincoln, unlike Lee in many ways, was like him in kindness. The tragedy of his death softened hearts. The smile made slow by many griefs rendered anger difficult. As he looked like the giant with the broken heart, a brokenhearted South found him a comrade. The partners of the wine press know each other. Southern voices began to bring him eloquent tribute. Watterson and Gordon gave eulogies that became proclamations of good will. A verbal coincidence reveals the likeness in Lee and Lincoln. One book about Lee bore the title "Marse Robert." Often Lincoln was hailed by the negroes as "Massa Lincoln." The word, glorified, moved from slavery days to nonslavery days. The two men became "masters" of that nobility which made them agents of conciliation.

Through the period of spiritual reconstruction I lived in a state that was itself a controversy. I learned the lesson of tolerance, of wise silence, of the uniting word. I could not have originated this mood within myself. My Methodist-preacher father was its kindly environment, his heart the generous school. In his presence fiery controversy could not prosper. When I think of the hatreds that were evolved; read the indictments that men hurled; consider the relations of two groups once so hostile; and then remind myself that Christian hearts, North and South, have wrought this transformation of brotherhood, I have faith that the Divine Grace can win against any bitterness and will continue to effect "peace on earth," because it produces so many men of "good will."

156

II

The second controversy was wholly different. One would suppose that the last thing to make for unholy feelings would be an emphasis upon holiness. The trouble was caused by a label rather than by a fact. The advertisement of a perfectionist is naturally a challenge to the imperfect. If a man were to proclaim himself as brave among soldiers and insist that he had received a second installment of courage, he would cause a disturbance in the camp. The proclamation is an irritation. The most of us do not have enough love to keep us from classifying the claimants of "perfect love" among the Pharisees. We are able to detect a scorn of spirit even among the elect when one declares that he himself has joined the ranks of the super-elect. A college teacher, giving testimony as an expert before a court, affirmed that as a chemist he was "second to none." The phrase became the jibe of opposition attorneys, even as it became among students the professor's nickname for the rest of his days. His degree was S.T.N.

In spite of this disadvantage, the attainment of perfect love as a "second work of grace" played a large part in the first century of Methodism and sent a wave of its influence rolling into the second century. The syllogism seemed resistless: God is all-powerful; man is by nature sinful; and the conclusion came surely. The man-made taint could not be stronger than the God-made cure. Those who sought to argue against perfect love came upon that stubborn logic. Nor could they evade the feeling that they were debating against an ideal. But a syllogism must contend with other syllogisms. One can put the promise that where two or three agree as touching any one thing, it shall be done, into the form of a major premise, a minor premise, and a conclusion—and leave any three believers condemned for the failure to convert a city overnight.

157

Or the syllogism could be changed into an embarrassing question: Why should an all-powerful God achieve complete salvation on the installment plan—though the installments be only two?

The theory, therefore, met logical difficulties. Often the effect was to make a church a debating society. When the claimers of the blessing insisted that their doctrine related to perfect love, and not to perfect judgment, the critics pursued them with the inquiry, Why did God confine himself so strictly to one realm in his insistence on perfection? It came to pass at last that a camp meeting was the rendezvous of the disputers rather than the resort of the mourners.

In the background John Wesley's booklet on *Christian Perfection* remained as a classic study, while in the foreground came the question to ministerial candidates: "Do you expect to be made perfect in love in this life?" Almost every neophyte showed a noble hesitation. The thoughtful young men stood in blanched reverence—as if the inquiry were a challenge to sincerity. A quick affirmative would have seemed out of harmony with the "Woe is unto me" of Paul. So the candidates searched for some frame of words that would keep the ideal and that would also avoid deceit or presumption. Tremulousness was taken by the Conference itself as an answer to the staggering inquiry. Since Wesley's time every applicant for the ministry has been compelled to make reply. There has never been a prescribed answer. If it be true that few votes could be secured for the removal of the question, it is just as true that fewer votes could be secured for a ritual response that claimed perfect love.

For many years the preaching of this perfectionist doctrine awakened little opposition. The earlier itinerants, while claiming the blessing, expressed the possession in sacrificial ways. Many preachers died this side of middle life, wearing themselves out in a ceaseless evangelism. When men were doing that, the living itself was certified as a token of the love. When, however, the preaching of the theory fell into the hands of specialists, the proofs did not seem so vital. A divided local church was a frequent occurrence. At times the second-blessing advocates became ferocious. They used the doctrine as a weapon rather than as a persuasion.

This forbidding result made its impression upon me. My father had completed the term in a pastorate where hundreds had been converted. His successor was a good and attractive man who was ardent for "sanctification" in its technical meaning. Ere six months passed the church had been badly rent, while stronger members fled from a totalitarian sanctity to other societies where a Biblical proportion of doctrine was maintained. Of course, this man did not long remain in the active ministry. A procession of ruined charges could not serve as a good recommendation.

I passed through the throes of that controversy. There was an agony in the process—a struggle in one's heart between the idealism of the theory, and the effort to make no insincere profession. My father has often been claimed by this group. It is true that to the end of his ministry he preached the theory as both Wesleyan and Christian. *But I never heard him profess entire sanctification.* He struggled pitifully in that direction, poring over books like *Love Enthroned* and *The Christian's Secret of a Happy Life.* Yet he was too good to proclaim that he was good. The farthest reach of his experience was expressed by Paul in his claim of the ceaseless pursuit. "Not as though I had already attained, either were already perfect; but I follow after, if that I may apprehend that for which also I am apprehended of Christ Jesus." Father lived and died in that seeking mood.

159

Personal disasters sometimes fell into those eager circles. A distinguished advocate forgot the warning about "keeping the body under," and between the sermons that advocated holiness became himself a castaway. In one Conference several of its claimants were shadowed by suspicions, while in pastorates devoted largely to the specialty two ministers in succession walked the road of disgrace. Even those who repudiated the doctrine of certain modern psychologists as to the relation of religion and sex wondered whether a lack of self-control in the one did not lead to a lack of self-control in the other. One of the records about Christ's ministry comes to mind: "The high priest then asked Jesus of his disciples, and of his doctrine." The world always does that. The disciple and the doctrine become mingled. The Kitty O'Shea imbroglio put both Parnell and Home Rule for Ireland at a disadvantage. So the professor of sanctification who sank beneath waves of scandal pulled the doctrine down with himself.

The inevitable happened. The advocates of Christian perfection became subjects of ridicule—often unjust ridicule. As in Daniel's case, the foes "sought to find occasion against" the professing prophet. A great bishop of the Church, being asked whether he had experienced the "second blessing," replied: "No. I had the first, and the third, and the hundredth; but when I saw what that second one did to some of my brethren, I concluded to skip it." The humor of the remark cannot conceal its sadness, while the fact that it was uttered by a most devoted servant of Christ compels belief that it had some warrant. Another crippling tale was about one who, professing sanctification, lost his temper shamefully in a parliamentary debate. Being chided by his fellow confessors for putting the group and their doctrine at a discount, he confessed his fault, but added the doubtful

testimony that while in his anger he "had lost his sanctification," he had still "held on tightly to his regeneration."
This gave the scornful their chance. A great ideal suffered
from a devastating jocularity.

Outer events joined in the conspiracy. Gradually the
specialists were lured or forced out of the pastorate. Of
ten men whose preaching of this ideal affected me, only
one remained in pastoral work. All the rest found roving
commissions. In addition, not a few of them did not have
sanctification enough to be patient with unsanctified com-
panionships. They drifted into the more or less fanatical
groups who gave the theory an unbalanced advocacy. The
Church was not always patient. An air of infallibility
was trying and a disputing spirit was an added plague.
Some of the debaters could have been charged with living
only in "the accusative case," as Calvin was. Occasionally one of them appointed himself as the prosecuting
attorney of all the believers. Another, whom I well recall, went further, until his abusive advocacy of love
banished him from the camp of love—and he left the
Twelve Apostles and joined the Seven Devils. Yet, allowing for these harsh exceptions, the most of the claimants
were good people who were staggering toward the gleam
of a perfect Gospel. The record which recounts how a
sacred doctrine was sent into eclipse does not make happy
reading. Frequently a gesturing hand pointed to an
outward door when a beckoning hand should have pointed
to an inner altar.

There are signs of recovery. The preachers of the
specialty are more kindly than of yore. Good and able
men like the late Dr. Henry C. Morrison became welcome in great pulpits. The extension of the demanded
perfection beyond the individual soul, until sanctification
is driven to deal with life as represented in the social
gospel, necessitates modest confession. The stress upon

161

worship that comes to the rapture of God in Christ keeps the inner mood alive. There is a feeling, also, shared by secular publicists as well as by preachers, that the moral sag in men's souls has been greater than the economic sag in men's markets. Once again we must tell people that the good Samaritan must not abandon the holy standards of heart. Someday the Church will hear its Saviour repeating the awe-inspiring demand: "Be ye holy; for I the Lord your God am holy." Then the yearning for the "whole" life of the Lord will set the standard on lofty planes—so high that it may abash us, but so alluring that we can never give up its pursuit.

One episode had a marked influence on my spiritual life. I had been tormented by false dilemmas. At camp meetings those who desired clean hearts were asked to come to the altar. To respond meant that some of us would be seeking a type of experience that did not represent our desire. Not to respond appeared to mean that we were turning away "from the light." Sincere young preachers went quietly to the outskirts of the camp, in order that they might escape invitations whose acceptance would have indicated a seeking that for themselves was not genuine. We were not fleeing from the gospel; we were refusing a particular interpretation. Splendid ministers suffered grievously from this strange dilemma.

In that perplexed condition I came to a session of the Iowa Conference. I was eager to hear Bishop James M. Thoburn, reputed to be the finest preacher in Asia. The mysticism of India had been added to his faith's energy. He told of a controversy between a Calvinist and an Arminian Methodist on the subject of full salvation. The discussion raged around an illustration of a field where plants grew. How could one get rid of the weeds so that wholesome growths would have their chance? The Methodist declared that he would lay hands to the roots of the weeds and pluck forth the infesting things. The Calvinist declared that small rootlets would remain in the soil, to grow again, or that noxious seeds would be blown from the neighbor's garden. The Methodist then declared that he would build a fire and burn the weeds and roots in the purity of the flames. Again the Calvinist seized the fault in the illustration, affirming that the fire would expend itself largely in the air, and that roots growing to the depth of several feet would still defy the cleansing heat. A non-Christian bystander interrupted the fruitless discussion by saying: "You two are not getting anywhere. Why not compromise on this fact: that if you keep the fire burning all the time, the weeds will not grow?"

That illustration fell graciously on my perplexed heart. I do not say that it answered all questions. It did give me peace. If some eager protagonist would now classify it with the delusions, I could still say that its consolation has not failed me. That diminutive Bishop from India, with a quiet intensity that pierced souls, brought me to seek for an altar where the fires glowed with ceaseless effect.

III

It is not easy to give dates to controversies—because their starting points are often as subtle as their goals. The next warm discussion had an intellectual center. The heart did not figure greatly. Emotion came in as the accompaniment rather than as the essence. The usual name given to it was Liberalism. Some declare that its effective origin came from the theory of evolution, though on the Biblical side its pioneers were enlisted long before Spencer and Darwin. Professor Bowne used to say that in religious quarters evolution was at first met with nought but fright. Gamaliel Bradford felt that the Darwinian theory made faith all but impossible. One of his scarcely high-class poems gave a sad celebration of this fact. All this meant nothing more than that Bradford became an exemplar of shivers. Bowne's pupils were saved from consternation. Their teacher convinced them that evolution as a theory of origins was worthless, and that as a theory of progress it was harmless. The evolutionist' had to have some Power that could furnish the raw materials, and he had to find some Power that offered the dynamic for the advance! The insistence was that the watch, made quickly or slowly, required a watchmaker.

The truth is that the most vigorous opponent of evolution for a considerable season in America was not a preacher, but a scientist—Louis Agassiz. There was a parallel in colonial days. Benjamin Franklin opposed vaccination; Cotton Mather was its champion. Several religious teachers were chief agents in popularizing the theory of evolution. Henry Drummond, the great lay evangelist, gave it a winsome treatise in his Lowell Lectures. Lyman Abbott adapted it in his volume on *The Evolution of Religion*. The "monkey-scare" was driven from the realm of theology. Soon the minister who raised the false dilemma of "Christ or Darwin" became an anachronism. Some of the religious teachers who declared the Darwinian theory an unproved hypothesis would scarcely have been disturbed had it become a proved surety. The ghost ceased to be the terror of the sanctuary. Believers in evolution knelt at the altar of Christ and were not afraid.

Naturally the debate about evolution came to the Bible. The first chapters in Genesis were searched anew. Professor J. D. Dana, of Yale, had once given a unique parallel between the scriptural account of creation and the scientific order. For a time this treatise had much currency. Ere long, however, the feeling prevailed that the Bible, being the story of God's dealing with men, had not been given as a textbook on astronomy, botany, or geology.

164

The spiritual meaning assigned to such phrases as "the Morning Star," "the Lily of the Valley," "the Rose of Sharon," and "the Rock of Ages" was primary. Even in the case of the Book of Jonah the instruments for measuring the whale's throat and the possible size of the inner chambers were placed aside. The emphasis fell on the penalty that visits a man who flees from duty, and on that missionary love of God which embraced the men and women and little children of Nineveh.

In one respect the theory of inspiration presented by the liberals found ready minds. All Bible readers had experienced difficulty with the imprecatory Psalms. It helped little to tell intelligent young people that though the sentiments of some of the Psalms had not been inspired, the recording had been supervised by the Spirit. John Wesley had declared that in the Psalms there were some things not fit to be read to a Christian congregation. Such a remark made at least a fair start for a higher critic! I was not the only young Christian whose soul had been tormented by the tone of some of the Psalms—as well as by other parts of the Old Testament where a "Thus saith the Lord" was attached to the writing. In college a shrewd fellow student put his finger upon Biblical statements that bewildered my mind, while I fled vainly from one redoubt to another. Even more than I then knew I was saved to a love of the Bible by an implicit theory of broad inspiration. When the Psalmist appeared to get God into trouble, I had recourse to the greater passages where the righteous Jehovah called his people to the glory of his character and the service of his purpose.

I have narrated elsewhere the effect of this controversy upon the Boston University School of Theology, and upon the fortunes of Professor Hinckley G. Mitchell. There

165

was bitterness of debate. Epithets were not lacking. Printed articles scorched the theories of opponents, and the opponents themselves. *The Andover Review* and *The Methodist Review,* the latter under the editorship of Dr. James W. Mendenhall, took over the thunder and lightning of Sinai and made them weapons. There appeared two tendencies toward pharisaism. The liberal often mounted a pedestal and ruled out the conservative on the ground that the conservative lacked scholarship. The conservative got even by mounting his pedestal and ruling out the liberal on the ground that he lacked piety. The name-calling was often distant from the saving Name.

There were other effects. Men who were released from the embarrassments of the theory of verbal inspiration appeared to some reverent souls to find delight in pointing out deficiencies in the history or sentiment of the Bible. Alleged errors were offered as disproofs of the orthodox view—and as if they were witnesses for the new view. I can recall my own shock of spirit when I heard a group of fellow students ridiculing what they called the "rib" theory of woman's creation—becoming hilarious over what they called "a mere side issue." That attitude carried into a pulpit and placed before saintly conservatives did not make congregations joyful in God. The claim of modernity occasionally became exasperating. Condescension and pride are not mentioned by Paul as among the fruits of the Spirit. In a New England church I heard such a mistaken prophet confuse and grieve the people who had come to him for the Bread of Life and had been given the husks of a pert criticism. The farmers wended their way over the hills—wearied by the toil of the week, but not refreshed by the uplift of the Lord's Day. After a few years the church building itself became a tombstone—because an actual Ebenezer, or Stone of Help, had been thrown down by supercriticism.

This scholarly confidence frequently imagined itself under attack. Disagreement with one's views was construed as interference with one's liberty. The suggestion that certain discussions were meant for a classroom rather than for the congregation was scouted as cowardice. In one instance a man preached for thirty-two minutes from the fortieth chapter of Isaiah, taking twenty-one minutes for the discussion of the date and authorship, and eleven minutes for the sublime assurance of a comforting God. The Second Isaiah was presented not as an added evidence of the Lord's work, but as an irritating intruder into conservative minds. Blamed for unbalanced teaching, the pulpiteer enrolled himself with the noble army of martyrs, and listed his people among the persecutors.

An amusing illustration occurred in a preachers' meeting. One of the ablest among the younger preachers read a paper whose views were defiantly progressive. The discussion that followed brought out courteous opposition. The young minister in his later years recalled the episode as a delightful embarrassment. In reply to the criticism he vigorously declared that he must be allowed his liberty of thought. He was determined to nail his thesis to the door of the church without interference from the modern popes. Dr. Samuel F. Upham inquired whether he could ask the essayist a question. The young prophet, with Chesterfieldian manners, replied, "Certainly." Dr. Upham then said substantially, "Will Dr. —— please give us the names of any parties in the Methodist Church who have recently sought to interfere with his thinking spells?" This humorous event was a lesson to the group of youngish clergymen with whom I was myself identified. The actual fact is that the Church was astonishingly patient. Our people were conservatives. Their teaching for several generations had made them so. Then the bibliolaters discovered iconoclasts standing behind their altars. I recall my surprise when hesitatingly I told my father of my "new views." Expecting a debate, I really found a sanction. It was accompanied by an earnest warning that I should keep my attitude toward the Bible "religiously constructive." The transition in our Church was like a miracle. We were saved from wrangling because the Articles of Religion had committed Methodism to no particular theory of inspiration. The statement that the Holy Scriptures "*contain* all doctrine necessary to salvation" was in itself a salvation. If the view commonly held among our people had been hardened into creedal form, the controversy might have made a disastrous division.

All this now sounds like reverberation from a distant battle. One matter had a distinct bearing. Prior to the first World War many prospective teachers had gone to Germany for postgraduate work. The terrible strife not only made it impossible for students to go to Germany for a period, but it caused a prejudice that changed the later fashion of graduate study. The center of influential scholarship was moved to Scotland. But there was a deeper effect. When criticism had wrought out a proper historical study of the Bible, and when it had given adequate attention to negatives, it turned again to the Scriptures to say, "Speak, Lord, for thy servant heareth." So efficiently did this change come that the echoes of a bitter discussion have almost ceased. The debaters have become codefendants of the literature of Redemption. The times seem ready for a return to the Holy Scriptures which are able to make men wise unto salvation.

The Andover controversy was an extension of the Biblical controversy, but one that gathered into itself other features of the liberal movement. I came to Boston when the agitation was at its crest. As the seminaries were neighbors, the ripples of the debate came over to our school, and sometimes the ripples were billows. And-

168

over had been one of the best known of our theological
institutions. An excellent history of the contest that
stormed there has been written by a young professor in
Chicago, Daniel Day Williams. Boston was the headquarters of Congregationalism; it was inevitable that "the
Hub," as well as the rims would be agitated.

I watched the struggle eagerly. Twice I listened to
addresses by men who were personal foci of the controversy. I believed then, as I believe now, that the difficulty
was not wholly doctrinal. These two teachers were frigid.
They chilled the atmosphere—like icebergs driven back
to frozen fastnesses instead of out into the Gulf Stream.
Someone has said that competition is the life of trade, and
the death of the trader. The Andover debate may have
been the life of the participants, but it brought something
like death to the institution. The glorious name started
toward migrations and mergers, the saving remnant of its
endowment becoming an asset of other schools. Its abandoned buildings are mournful monuments. Save when
revived by research, the literature of the discussion has
largely lost currency. Yet back of those noisy pages the
religious world reaches occasionally for a tiny volume of
Andover's days of peace. *The Still Hour* of Professor
Austin Phelps calls the people of Christ to an altar of devotion and unites them there in worship and trust.

Methodism was kept from the fiercer struggle by an
emphasis on experience. This made for a democracy of
intellect that was warmed by emotion. Let me confess,
however, that in this season of perplexity I was helped by
the so-called heretics. Newman Smyth's *Old Faiths in
New Light* brought me an intellectual relief. One illustration given by Professor Hinckley G. Mitchell had a
steadying effect—the story of a poor family that found in
the deep soil a metal casket. They dug around it carefully
so as to wreak no injury, and lifted it to the surface. They

opened the rusted lid and discovered that the contents consisted of gold coins of such ancient mintage as to pass ownership on to those who owned the hiding place. Immediately discussions began: What was the nature of the casket's metal? What the meaning of certain strange characters, like "Selah," engraved on the sides? What the most likely date of the vessel's making? Who the probable authors of these strange vaults? Were there several whose work was combined by a redactor? What would scholarly assayers declare to be the amount of alloy worked into the assured gold? The debates became disagreements. Finally a sensible member suggested that the family was poor; that the casket offered means of comfort; and that the secondary critical questions could wait for answers until the immediate needs of life had been supplied.

This parable came from a specialist in the Biblical problem. The larger liberalism can still catch its lesson. In due or undue season the progressives themselves became introspective. They examined their souls, and their work. One of the foremost of them sounded a warning that the liberal movement was not fulfilling its promised mission, and that, in spite of its achievements, there could be listed against it some sobering failures. Doubtless the derision of liberalism has gone too far, and the need is for strengthening rather than for banishment. The movement demands a recovery of the heart. The world is not to be converted by intellect alone. Any crusade that seeks redemption when it does not proclaim a Redeemer is doomed to failure. No idealized system of ethics is equal to the task of world salvation.

IV

The fourth controversy relates to the application of the gospel to social relations. It had several John the

Baptists—men like Washington Gladden and Walter Rauschenbusch. The latter wrote a volume endeavoring to put this gospel into semitheological terms, and another volume endeavoring to give fit forms of prayer. These men have had a marked influence. Methodism's fervor became allied with the movement. "The Social Creed," often hailed as a pioneer pronouncement, originated in a General Conference and moved out to wider fields. The first World War checked some of its aspects; yet, as men meditated on the frightful outcomes of slaughter and hate, the cohorts of this gospel became premiers in a crusade for world peace. Doubtless the second World War will shunt agitation in other directions, much as the War of 1861-65 diverted earnestness from the temperance reform. But inevitably the breakdown in international life, which is simply a broader area of social life, will make a greater demand for a gospel that is more than personal and meditative.

For reasons difficult to analyze, this gospel of modern reform has created intense feeling. Perhaps some statements taken from the Episcopal Address as given to the General Conference in 1936 may present the issue. No quotation marks are necessary. The words "individual" and "social" are often made rivals rather than partners. They gather partisan groups about themselves. Both camps are tempted toward pharisaism. The religious individualist prides himself upon the thoroughgoing nature of his gospel, and may accuse the religious socialist as being a fussy ethical tinker. The religious socialist feels that the religious individualist flees to a doubtful spirituality in order to avoid the cost of a righteous crusade. It is not wholesome to set these two emphases into hostility. Each is a phase of the genuine Gospel. There is a personal world; there is a social world; and they are both regions in which redemption works. The twofold commandment of the Old Testament was placed in the New Testament and abides as a charter of the Kingdom. Christ presented an individual gospel to Nicodemus, and a social gospel to the Young Ruler. Each emphasis has a divine warrant.

But we have been prone to assume that the social gospel is itself a new thing. The Christian sanctuary has always opened upon the street of life. Methodism started campaigns against usury, smuggling, slavery, intemperance, dishonesty. Some of its insistences must have seemed impudent to an age that had staged a Revolution for Independence. This special demand for outer applications of the faith began more than a century and a half ago. Long prior to that time this gospel was at work. A claim could be made for the thesis that the Christian Church has been an agent of social reform in every century since our Saviour came. Its power in this respect is particularly evident as we move toward the modern period. We usually date Magna Charta as of June, 1215. In June, 1212, Stephen Langton, nominated as archbishop, became the ally of the barons against the imperialistic king. In August, 1213, a national council was held, one session in St. Pauls Church at St. Albans, doubtless called by the archbishop. In the later negotiations that led to John's signature at Runnymede the prelates were with the barons, both as partners in reform and as mediators toward peace. Pope Innocent III published a bull declaring Magna Charta null and void, but the papal word did not avail.

In later contests the Church had its part, whether in agitating against imprisonment for debt, or for the abolition of the Corn Laws. Frederick Denison Maurice started certain attempts at co-operation among working people. The soul of his so-called Christian Socialism went marching on, and Charles Kingsley came into its company. Both

172

of these preachers had warm sympathy for the poor. They were also intensely devotional. The wife of Maurice said that "whenever he woke in the night, he was always praying," while others felt that he walked efficiently on earth because he dwelt near heaven. John Wesley gives an example of personal evangelism and social crusading. In England, Hugh Price Hughes became the champion of the social gospel in modern Methodism. He was an earnest evangelist as well. For years in his London mission he held no public service in which men did not profess allegiance to Christ. This great leader in his balance of the two phases of the Gospel set an example that we should heed.

Not only has the social gospel, in all its aspects, been an irritant to some persons, but its present major emphasis makes for added nervousness. When that gospel comes into the industrial realm it moves into a sensitive region. Nor is the goal clearly definite. In slavery and in temperance the beacon was fairly distinct. The economic problem allows no such simplification. The last half century has brought wonderful ameliorations. We have seen the arrival of employers' liability, minimum wages, eight-hour day, inheritance taxes, excess profits taxes, housing laws, better working conditions, and our statute books have received many other fine entries. The history convinces us that revolution need not replace evolution, and that dynamite of feeling should not be substituted for the leaven of judgment. My own ministry has covered largely this period of legislative change. It is comforting to say definitely that every item of these advancing provisions has had my personal support.

Yet when one deals with extremists a balanced attitude is labeled as reaction. There are men whose views with reference to an economic situation are surely known in advance. Some are always for the capitalistic side. Others

173

are invariably for the labor side. One of my friends, on hearing my views, declared hotly that I was a socialist, and probably a near-Communist. He even intimated that my very mildness of statement made me a more "dangerous person." Another declared that my main effect was to pour sand upon the wheels of progress, and that I was "an example of antique views." I have lost confidence in epithets. The efficient promoters of the social gospel have not been abusive; neither have the best advocates of the mystical element employed scorn. In other great contests the final victory was won by the right spirit. It will be so in this artificial struggle between two worthy viewpoints. Many preachers, being most earnest in declaring either the individual or the social gospel, have kept themselves free from harshness and so from needless cleavages. Some of their sincere comrades could afford to study the kindly methods of those who combine passion with wisdom and who work toward distant goals with patience. We should maintain the spirit of Christ not only in fixing our goals, but also in our efforts to reach them. If the Gospel is equal to producing a society of redemption, it is also equal to producing individuals who live under untoward conditions in the mood of redemption. We do not further our faith by cultivating schismatic souls. Like Moses we may be compelled to say to quarreling partisans, "Ye be brethren." But it will be well not to kill too many taskmasters lest we be driven to mountains too lonely for social accomplishments. We may be assured that as we learn to follow Jesus to the Temple, we shall duly learn to follow him to the carpenter shop. Our Gospel has many phases: but the phases are not foes. The personal applications and the social applications abide, and are certainly so big and meaningful as to give us programs whose difficulties are their challenge and their glory.

174

There is a parallel between this controversy and that relating to second-blessing sanctification. The social movement represents a shifting of the old Methodist doctrine of holiness into the wider life of society. The logic seems inevitable. Christ is no Lord of fragments. He desires to command all the individual life and all the social life. He is to be proclaimed as the complete Saviour. The old movement and the new movement show other likenesses. As some advocates of personal holiness went to extremes and put their teaching at a disadvantage, so do some advocates of the individual and social gospel imitate their ancient brethren. Again, even as the debaters against subjective holiness felt that the doctrine was largely a syllogism, and that its representatives were not models of their own insistence, so now do the debaters against social holiness hurl charges of inconsistency and make the difficult demand that the promoters of objective holiness shall live their creed in spite of a hostile system. However, personal indictments do not serve. Moody and Rauschenbusch are in the comradeship of heaven. The grace of God in this present life is equal to bringing the advocates of varying emphases into the unity that spells peace.

One reason for interest in evangelism is that it makes a larger force for social righteousness. Doubtless I have won some reputation for stressing the importance of evangelistic effort. Yet departments and boards of evangelism have not claimed my official connection. My intensity has come from a conviction that a weakening of the evangelistic life meant a weakening of every other phase of religious life, I could name scores of places where, unless we gather new forces into the Church, there will not remain in another decade societies with sufficient numbers and motive to influence social changes. The outreach that made the Wesleyan movement strong is the program

175

that will keep it strong. For the sake of the social gospel we may earnestly advocate the individual gospel; and we may urge the social gospel because it can become a motive for the individual gospel. My date books show that I have made far more pleas, for example, for the abolition of industrial child labor than I have made for revivals. Perhaps I have been wrong in this. There was a crisis in our land about child labor. I have never recovered from my astonishment that so many warm promoters of the social gospel took little interest in winning the proposed amendment for the protection of childhood. Indeed, their apathy toward a concrete possibility angered me—until on several occasions my speeches against child labor were so fierce as to cease to be winning.

I have felt so about the temperance situation. The growing social menace calls for growing antagonism. There is here a bearing on character. A great reformer once advised that every young man should espouse some sacred cause and continue his crusade until he brought it to triumph. This counsel had been fully illustrated by the counselor himself, who made a lifelong contest against a mighty evil; lived to see the plague banished, and united his name with this specialty in an honored way. The reformer is not now popular if his reform relates to an appetite. William McKinley may give his life to a high tariff; George William Curtis to civil service reform; Thomas Mott Osborne to prison welfare—without achieving the label of fanatics. Yet a clergyman's life inevitably carries him toward endeavors that demand "re" as a first syllable of a noun. Call it re-formation, re-clamation, re-pentance, re-newal, re-vival, or re-generation—the root idea of vital change lies in each word. Long since it was said—"Better one former than a thousand reformers." If, however, one is to follow Him who came "to seek and to save that which was lost," the task of convincing either

176

the individual or society of a "lost condition" implies a message that is not altogether pleasant. The good shepherd has often found a protesting sheep that preferred the mountain to the fold.

V

This prelude leads to a consideration of causes that have figured in my life's work. I wonder sometimes where and how I was initiated into hatred of the beverage liquor trade. My father was a foe of rum. Yet he was never obsessed by that one crusade. When I have met people who spoke feelingly of his lifework, no one of them has long dwelt upon his work as a temperance reformer. There was symmetry in his service. Of course, I must have received from him an inheritance of conscience as to this phase of the social gospel. To this were added boyish impressions that came from beyond the home, such as loitering about the market place in Wheeling, West Virginia—because I knew that saloons would entice the husbands, and that directly their drunken helplessness would give me a chance to carry the laden baskets homeward for the troubled women. I recall the agony of one wife as she passed from saloon to saloon in search for her "man." While I had in mind the dime that his recreancy would let me earn, my heart went out in sympathy for her. Later I heard my father tell of a young man whose debauch ended with a suicide's bullet. The saloonkeeper, brought by the landlady to see one of his products, had sneered at her righteousness. A stricken father came to bear back to his home the casket of tragedy. There were many scenes that educated my heart into indignation.

So I have given strength to the temperance reform. Scrawling for my mother a total abstinence pledge when I was eleven years old, I have never dishonored the promise. Ere I was through college I was making antiliquor speeches. A while ago I found one of these—so boyish that it made me smile, so earnest that it made me glad. I have been a member of the Anti-Saloon State Committee in California, Massachusetts, and Illinois. For eight years I was president of the Board of Temperance, maligned and honored by the falsehoods of cheap congressmen. My closest companion in this long moral crusade was the late Colonel Frank Baker Ebbert, my wife's brother. He gained a lofty character and was so highly gifted in the art of sincere public solicitation that he was rated as our financial genius. Through him, as well as through the college fraternity connection, I came into a delightful and rewarding intimacy with W. Branch Rickey, who in professional baseball circles has kept his Christian banner flying over all moral fields.

I shall go to my grave glad that when the temperance cause came into its unpopular days I did not retreat. One of the most discouraging experiences in Washington has been the sight of cringing office-holders fleeing from one false redoubt to another, seeking to hide their souls within shelters of crookedness. Our nation will some day see the folly of this present spree. Some alleged statesmen who now give the name of prudence to their cowardice will creep back to their former allegiance, but will receive no credit from a good God or from good men.

In one respect the temperance forces have been blamable. They have never attained unity. In the movement that secured national prohibition, they came to measurable oneness—though there were two big banners, the Anti-Saloon League and the Woman's Christian Temperance Union. When both were put at an undeserved discount by the ridicule of a metropolitan press and by lying cartoons, and when the depression halted the flow of funds into moral treasuries, unified weakness was not adequate. Organizations with a temperance attachment,

178

individuals with a glib eloquence, and independent groups that fought in guerilla fashion all swept into the field of solicitation. There was no generalissimo—only a council without authority to centralize, but with liberty of discussion. I labored to secure an efficient merger. But traditions and preferences were stubborn. When my motives were questioned and I was accused of seeking to dislodge, leadership that I might substitute representatives of my own church, I retired from the field. Our forces still continue their split tactics. Some day a vast enthusiasm or a vast debacle will compel our scattered troops to form an army.

The references to evangelism and temperance may somewhat illustrate my thought—and my aim. Perhaps my repute for promoting each of the two is about equal. The first deals with the individual gospel, the second with one phase of the social gospel. Let me repeat that the time has come to do away with the "either-or" fallacy. Our Gospel must always command the complete logic of "both-and," if it is to be complete.

I may without indelicacy use a personal illustration. Bishop Francis J. McConnell has been for years a leader of the social-emphasis group. The quarto-centenary of his episcopacy was celebrated in meetings in New York and in Chicago. In the first I had the privilege of offering the prayer; to the second, by request, I sent a letter. The anniversary was celebrated, also, by a book, *Religion and Public Affairs*, edited by Professor Harris Franklin Rall— a book that has not had deserved circulation. Its opening chapter is Dr. Rall's estimate of Bishop McConnell—a revealing study of one great man by another great man. The Bishop has himself been the calm center of long agitation. He has willingly carried the burden of the more extreme views of some of his fellow agitators. He has, as well, smilingly endured blame for the views of men

179

when his plea was not for their opinions, but for their liberty. The people in our land who believe in free speech so long as it does not lead to freedom could not appreciate either standpoint. No one has justly accused Francis J. McConnell of hysteria. Nor has he ever been the abuser of his antagonists. Unshaken by criticism, he has kept his quiet course, believing that changes in the economic system are necessary in order that the good in that system may be preserved. I offer a copy of the letter, which, since I felt obliged to attend the meeting of the bishops, I sent for reading at the McConnell dinner. I do this not only because this letter states what I conceived to be my function, but also because it shows how affectionate relations may be maintained where two men have moved along the lines determined by their temperaments. The changes in the epistle do not at all modify the original meaning:

DEAR FRIENDS:

It is my great regret that I cannot be with you all personally. I should like to tell Bishop McConnell what I think of him—in apostolic fashion, "face to face." Only once in thirty years have I failed to attend the Bishops' Meeting. Then I was prevented by a death in the family. Our meeting this May is important, and my conscience sends me to its duties.

I became acquainted with Frank McConnell in the early nineties of the last century. The mediator of that acquaintance was the late George H. Geyer, a dear friend of us both, and a lofty character long since transferred to the service of the Inner Shrine. George felt that Frank was a ministerial "find." Soon I was reviewing an oration written by young McConnell. The subject was "Statesmanship in Reform." The idea was that there were two phases in every reform—agitation and legislation. Wendell Phillips represented the first, Abraham Lincoln the second. The implication was that it was not fair to expect either man to do the work of the other. Both were needed—the shaker and the steadier. Often I have thought about that oration as a statement of the situations we have faced. In a wholesome measure Bishop Mc-Connell has been a quiet and solid Phillips. I make no claim to being the Abraham Lincoln. But I have felt that conviction made me a humble companion in Lincoln's general group. So I have not abused the Phillipses; and I have attempted to keep the Phillipses from abusing me.

Although the above contrast is overdone, I think that it gives a basis for a rule. Agitators are needed: and I have sought to defend their function and their personal rights in their advocacies. Again and again I have conferred with friends who had more capitalistic spirit than they had capital. To them I have courteously protested that it seemed unfair to inveigh against a good man with a stainless record when they seemed to have no guns ready to turn upon the dishonest members of their own group. Personally, I am a believer in the so-called capitalistic system, with distinct modifications: and I think that these modifications are coming along about as fast as we can absorb them. I believe, too, in a wider doctrine of private property than do some of my friends—though I practice it less than a few of them. But in days that have often been feverish I have never sought to estop the so-called radicals. As for Bishop McConnell's relations with them, I have been glad that we had a leader so well poised—an unexcited voice amid the tumult. I hope that, as this is being read, he will not yield to his impulses and cry out emotionally against my statement. I am following the thesis of that deliverance known as "Statesmanship in Reform."

Our personal relations have been fully in harmony with this principle of tolerance—and division of labor. Perhaps no two men have been more intimate than we have been—since 1894. Damon and Pythias and David and Jonathan could give us no instructions. The letter that Bishop McConnell wrote me last December, for my seventieth birthday, I have carried ever since; and in some type of archives I shall bear it into the Other Land. I secured for him his first charge in the New England Conference—for his support in the School of Theology. It paid one of the best student salaries. Indeed, in those days he was almost a capitalist. Several times I borrowed money from him. He demanded no usury. We have been different men—with a different emphasis. Yet there have been no shadows between us. He has never intimated that I

181

was a reactionary. I have never declared him a wild radical. And we are both right. He "ain't," and I "ain't."

I have thought that this spirit, as between two persons, might well be fostered as between two groups. Much of the irritation has seemed to me silly and needless. So on this big night for my dear, dear friend, tell him to his face that I have loved him much, and love him now, and shall love him forever. In mists and shadows, and beyond them all, nothing can shake our fealty, or mar our partnership in the work of God. Though not always comrades in precisely similar service, we are comrades in spirit: and no power can break that inner bond.

I can see him now, as you read this. He is looking at his nose. So often that organ seems to be his favorite scenery. But his heart will smile at me over the years and the distances; and he will accept what I have herein written with an open heart—accept it not as an anointing beforehand, but as an undying sentiment of his friend.

Once I heard two radicals, one conservative and one liberal, discussing their personal views. Their faces became livid with hatred or its counterfeit; the voice of each rose into accents that made the air tingle with anger. Their discussion did not abide within the realm of Christ's spirit. The two things of which they were speaking were partners and not foes. With God's good guidance we shall duly reach that spiritual geography where the sanctuary of evangelism and devotion has windows and doors open to economic paths, and where the Christ of the Altar walks with us over fields, through factories, and within shops—bringing the gospels into a union not to be sundered by man's petulant hand.

182

CHAPTER VIII

BISHOPS

THE FOLLOWING OBSERVATIONS DEAL WITH THE PROBLEMS of the episcopacy rather than with any theory as to the nature of the office. Two facts appear in the history of our legislation: the first, that there would not be the slightest possibility of securing a vote in any General Conference declaring the bishopric a third order, with a sacerdotal meaning that leaned toward superstition; the second, that attempts to modify seriously the functions of the office have always come to failure. Certainly the latter statement would indicate that the episcopacy has had a defense in its personalities. If a third of its representatives had been deficient in ability and service, it is likely that its powers would have been more limited, or that the office would have been abolished. Yet for more than a century and a half an ecclesiasticism that had autocracy delegated to it has stood the shocks of an increasing democracy. This means that the men behind the office must have given it protection by the integrity of their administration.

When a man begins to travel as a bishop he meets an assortment of episcopal stories. Being a gentleman, he never tells the reciter that he has heard them before. If one advantage in an itinerant life be that it constantly gives a new market for old tales, one disadvantage is that the man himself becomes the constant receiver of jocular goods that are far more than secondhand. One joke, aged enough to command respect, is that a boy, being

183

asked in an ecclesiastical catechism, "What is an episcopal visitation?" made reply, "An episcopal visitation is an affliction sent of the Lord." Phillips Brooks, then pastor of Trinity Church, Boston, reported in a letter that at an Episcopal General Convention two bishops had preached for him on Sunday—and that his people had been "saturated with commonplace." This being true, the visitations were afflictions. But Methodism, at times critical of its officials, has kept a peculiar pride in its episcopal line.

I

The men who have had the closer knowledge of that line have been the chief admirers. Of the bishops in the old Methodist Episcopal group I have personally known all but twenty. I have been associated in the Board with every bishop beginning with Henry White Warren, who was numbered thirty—except the eight who died prior to 1908.

The first bishop I met was the sixteenth—Bishop Matthew Simpson, a parsonage hero for whom my older brother was, in part, named. When I was eleven years of age he put his hands on my head and gave me his benediction. How little could I have dreamed that I would be one of his successors in the presidency of DePauw University, and in the episcopacy!

The first bishop that I heard preach was Randolph S. Foster. I slept for more than an hour. Then the enthusiastic West Virginia preachers interrupted my slumbers. When the sermon began I was twelve years old; when it ended I was two hours and twenty minutes older.

The first missionary bishop that I encountered was William Taylor of Africa—a fair duplicate of Michelangelo's "Moses." He wore an astounding beard. In dealing with him a cannibal would have had to be selec-

184

tive. One of the most marvelous sermons I ever heard was delivered by Bishop James M. Thoburn, of India. Of our seventeen missionary bishops I have known all but two, and I have met in close range all of our Central Conference bishops.

I have greeted all but seventeen of the fifty-eight bishops in the former Methodist Episcopal Church, South, group. Alpheus W. Wilson was a wonderful preacher. Elijah Embree Hoss was a sparkling person, especially when scornful or semi-angry. John J. Tigert was massive in appearance, in thought, in utterance. Walter R. Lambuth was a glorious, gentle soul, with a missionary passion. Eugene R. Hendrix was a courtly gentleman, who escaped from sectional feeling and willingly took some blows as an advocate of Methodist union. Warren A. Candler had a gift of drawling wit, coupled with a background of mind and a foreground of fervor that made his utterances unforgettable. Atticus G. Haygood, by his book *Our Brother in Black*, made millions of hearts tender toward the Negro and introduced the sable hosts as candidates for sainthood and service. Charles B. Galloway had unassuming majesty, a musical voice, a restrained emotion, and an alert intellect that classified him with the very great speakers.

On the Northern side the best-informed bishop was John M. Walden. Bishop Goodsell made a fine phrase when he said, "Our Brother Walden has a noble avarice for work." I depart from my rule by mentioning a grand bishop still living, and saying that tributes for wise industry belong as well to Thomas Nicholson.

The most symmetrical bishop was Edward G. Andrews. The best ecclesiastical lawyers were Stephen M. Merrill, Charles W. Smith, and Luther B. Wilson. The best financial promoters were Charles C. McCabe, Willard F. Mallalieu, and John W. Hamilton. The best-known builder of a popular institution was John H. Vincent.

The most constructive in European missionary work was William Burt. The most ornate and melodious in public address was Robert McIntyre. The one most scintillating in his use of words was William A. Quayle—converted in a little room as he prophetically knelt at an unabridged dictionary converted into an altar. The largest in size was Bishop Peck; his name should have stood for a larger measure. Over the continent he scattered a procession of broken chairs and beds. Daniel A. Goodsell, too, would receive notice for his avoirdupois. He was sensitive about his size, and unaware that his felicitous use of English, his charm in personal conversation, his ventriloqual play with parsonage children, all removed him from oddity and made love reduce him to normal stature. The wittiest bishop was Naphtali Luccock. The best platformer was Homer C. Stuntz. The most distinctive in manner and speech was William Fraser McDowell. The most strenuously energetic was Theodore S. Henderson. The most prophetical in educational and missionary outlook was James W. Bashford. The most torrential in a grand, old-fashioned oratory was Frank M. Bristol. The most patient in the carrying of great burdens was Wilson S. Lewis, who once diffidently told me that he would not be represented by a race horse that sped to the tape, but by an ox that pulled heavy loads over rocky ways. The most persistent in his advocacy of the reunion of Methodism was Earl Cranston. John L. Nuelsen had a sadly exceptional career in his office. After a brief residence in America he was assigned to the Zurich Area, which included Germany. His remaining active years were spent in Europe—years that were soon involved in the first World War and that closed in the awful tragedy of the second. Amid all the seasons of storm he played a wise and noble part.

II

A closer inspection of the episcopal group reveals a fine domesticity. Francis Asbury was a deliberate celibate. A slender reference in one of his letters indicates that he kept in memory the face of a lovely English girl. But his journeys in the American wilderness never indicated romance. He was not a woman hater, but he was a wife avoider. His notes do not show that in this attitude he was influenced by Mr. Wesley's unfortunate experience. Asbury felt that matrimony would interfere with the itinerancy. He could not ask any woman to share the homeless roads of the frontier. The first bishops of American Methodism were old bachelors. That tradition was broken by Robert Roberts. After once the precedent was established, it was unanimously followed.

The episcopal households have been wholesome models. No bishop in my day has felt any painful self-consciousness as he has asked candidates to promise to make their families worthy "examples for the people to follow." Thus glowing hearthstones and lighted windows have waited for all the bishops elected in one hundred and thirty years. Each has known where a door would open and a hand would beckon. The homeless Asbury died in the log house of a friend. Later bishops dropped their loads at diverse points. Coke died alone in his cabin on a ship, and they buried his dust in the ocean—the only fitting sepulcher for his missionary heart. Kingsley died at Beirut, Syria; Fitzgerald, in China; Erastus O. Haven, in the vestibule of an Oregon Conference church; Moore, in a Pullman sleeping car. McCabe died on the streets of New York and was soon singing in Paradise; Joyce, on the platform at a camp meeting, with an exit appropriate to an evangelist. Hartzell traveled safely over Africa and then died at the hands of American robbers. Spellmeyer died in an Atlantic City hotel; his brethren, alarmed when he came not to the Conference session, found him in peaceful sleep across the couch where he sought to ease a fluttering heart. Matthew Simpson Hughes died at a Sunday's dawn in a Cleveland inn—hoping to the last that he might preach three times on that Easter Day. Seth Ward died on a vessel returning from China. When they fell into their scattered graves these men knew that wives kept lamps burning for them in earthly homes.

The several deaths recorded in this list of necrology in connection with Oriental visits suggests the tragic problem of Oriental assignments. To send men ordinarily beyond middle life to a new land, a new climate, a new diet, a new language, a new civilization, naturally means risks. Consider these names involved in these foreign appointments—Bashford, Lewis, Bickley, Fisher, Lowe. The first three show that the long stay in the Orient meant a short stay on earth. Frederick Fisher passed from one physical weakness to another. Titus Lowe had, as a young man, spent a term in the Orient. Yet on return homeward from his episcopal area in Malaysia he lay for days in London at death's door, his stalwart frame smitten by ailments gathered on his gospel journeys. In these facts there was an argument for a missionary or Central Conference episcopacy, surpassing other pleas made for a changed economy.

In several senses Gilbert Haven was typical. He returned from Africa with some strange fever in possession of his body. Worn out by travels long and by crusades intense, he found peace in the home where he and Mary had lived. Though she had been long gone from him, he told a friend a few hours before death, "I am so tired! so tired! I am going to heaven soon. When I get there I am going to put my head in Mary's lap and sleep a million years." He did not sleep that long! His spirit was

188

too alert for that. But the experience was typical in its dear fashion. Each journey ends where a woman waits.

But there has been more than that. There have been cases where wives led their husbands to the Saviour and, in order to make them more ready for his call, assisted them in college, thus helping belated travelers on the educational way. They walked through the early privations of the itinerancy and did not even know that they were having hard times. They cheered us amid difficulties; consoled us amid disappointments; softened us amid asperities; and calmed us amid tumults. By their instinctive judgments they saved us from the trickeries of rascals and the advices of zealots. In our absences they acted in double parenthood and kept our children—for us and for God. They hid their tears when we faced long journeys. While cars rumbled us to distant places, their knees became altars at which our little people commended us to One mightier than St. Christopher, the patron saint of travelers. One of them said to her husband: "Whither thou goest, I will go. Where thou lodgest, I will lodge. Thy people shall be my people; thy God, my God; and where thou art buried, there will I be buried also." The wives built for their episcopal husbands colonies of the Kingdom of Heaven in homes over all the land. Their own social gatherings became centers of harmony and affection. A third of a century has passed since I walked into the Council of Bishops. In all that time I have known no episcopal home that made even mild scandal or thwarted the sanctity of the Christian household.

III

The bishops themselves, as a body, have been a brotherhood. If you name them the "College of Bishops," it is no misnomer to call them a college fraternity. Episcopal quarrels in the long past have wrought their damage. One helped to split the ecumenical Church into Eastern and Western sections. Another made a separation as wide as the distance between Rome and Canterbury. Others led rival popes to hurl papal bulls—each at the other. A fair thesis could be made for the statement that the episcopate, meant for union, has often caused disunion.

It has not been thus in Methodist history. Even in the agitation that led to the separation in 1844, the bishops did not become hotly engaged. James O. Andrew, an unwilling center of the debate, was a quiet, courteous, kindly man. The records do not show that episcopal sessions were torn by discussions, while the records of the Conferences give instances where the bishops essayed the role of conciliation. This attitude came, not because convictions were surrendered, but rather because the bishops themselves desired to be the agents of harmony. The controversy was not so much *among* the bishops as *about* the bishops.

One who entered the episcopacy in modern days was impressed with the fact of unity. Every such entrant had seen an Annual Conference cleaved into factions by rival preachers. In one such instance a bishop had lifted the two disturbers and hurled them into other fields! An episcopal quarrel might readily work its way down into the total life of the Church—as it did in one of the smaller denominations of the United States. Yet while the Board of Bishops has included such different types as to threaten unity, there has been an amazing fusion of the variety into a concord. For this third of a century the lines of cleavage have seldom gone the same way twice. A scriptural reference is apt: it often has seemed as if Christ came into our room, as he did into another long ago, and repeated the benediction, "Peace be unto you."

That prayer has been answered. I have seen quick outbursts of feeling in the Board. Usually they came near the end of the sessions, when nerves had been under long strain. Three meetings each day—from 9:00 to 12:30, from 2:00 to 5:30, from 7:30 to 10:30—all dealing with immense matters, and continuing from Wednesday to Saturday or Monday, do not constitute vacations. The little tempers were usually laughed out of court; those too serious to be banishel by a quick merriment were subdued in rooms of prayer. Some of us have had difficulty in yielding to corporate action. One bishop, who is now in heaven, had a real trial in adjusting himself to composite resolutions. He had been a premier in his own Annual Conference and had usually said the deciding word. When he came into counsel with others as strong as himself he preferred his own unity to that of the episcopacy. He discovered directly that opinions are not always convictions, and that when verbal phrases were changed or emphases modified it was not seemly to vote to oneself belligerent rights. So he became a lovely counselor when he ceased to be a lonely dictator. As I review seventy-five or more meetings of the bishops, I am amazed at the almost constant harmony—and gladdened by the remembrance of brotherhood. That harmony has not been even slightly marred as the branches of Methodism have flowed back into the one channel. The three groups of bishops have made a triangle of love, and each man would have difficulty in telling which side was his own.

From the standpoint of recognition, the episcopacy is likely to be a disappointment. Unless I have misread some hearts, a few associates failed to find the expected joy of prominence. One of them made me think of the man who was given the decoration of the "King's Garter" and was grieved because he found it empty. One other confided to me that he received more respect from Roman Catholic people than he received from Methodists. The

191

last twenty-five years have seen a change in the attitude toward the episcopacy as such. That change is an aspect of a larger one. Some say that the word "parson" is a pleasant transformation of the word "person"—much as the English people say "clark" instead of "clerk." In Colonial days the preacher was the chief "person" because of his education and position. The sentiment that has done away with artificial pre-eminence has banished, as well, the false adulation given to high-ranking ecclesiastics. The title now must gain its worth from the man. Nor can the old-time power be kept by direct assertion. The guarding of the prerogatives cannot preserve the standing of the office. Episcopal self-consciousness may be episcopal self-destruction, as some men have tardily learned. The monarch is not made by the dramatic waving of the scepter. The way to remain a king is not to make the throne too noticeable.

One change may be observed in inter-episcopal attitudes. In 1908 only two men in the Board called each other by their first names. Bishops Earl Cranston and David H. Moore had been classmates and fraternity brothers. So they were "Earl" and "Dave." Soon more schoolmates joined other schoolmates in the Board. Boyhood friends were elected—often at the same General Conference. Bishops Anderson and Hughes had been boys together in West Virginia, students together in two universities, members of the same college fraternity. In 1912 such relations in the episcopal coterie were increased. Before these intimacies titles fled. Ere we were aware, we had been "defrosted." To win the right to call given names by decades of friendship, and then to demand that this right be canceled by one day of election—this was a reform against nature. All icy etiquette was melted by the warmth of love.

IV

Episcopal ties are strengthened by the ties of administration. Mutual problems make mutual fellowships. Trade associations create good will. There are difficulties that are made by freakish characteristics. Some of these are memorable. One bishop reports the case of a preacher who made a boon companion of his huge dog and rolled for hours on the parsonage lawn with the playful animal—until bishop and district superintendent demanded that the canine scandal be removed. The preacher meekly consented—by trading the dog for two pups. Another bishop told of a pastor whose people resented the fact that their minister showed an affinity for a goat. This animal had festive hours wherein he would butt his way into the prayer meetings—to the dismay of the "sheep"—or hold up automobile traffic while his owner looked on with joy. The bishop concluded that the proper administration was "to get this man's goat." He succeeded.

These were laughable problems; others were more serious. One could overstate the difficulty of making appointments. The majority of Methodist preachers are "easy to place." Those who are etched in the following paragraphs make a small proportion of the entire personnel. Yet I have known all of the following types:

The man who felt himself able to work in the high places, but when put there by mistaken authority perished by the very altitude.

The man with whom theology was not a science, but an empirical form of commerce.

The man who would not leave himself unsuggested; insisted that others should hire the brass band for his progress; and talked as if he were a city, and all the rest of the Conference suburbs.

The man who was a prophet of disasters, and their arranger—always indulging in an excitement to which you could make no response; making you feel that if you wanted an artist to paint him, you would send for Paul Potter.

The man who became the new Jeremiah—with our apologies to that ancient prophet, now rescued from exclusive tears; the man who acted like a Jewish proselyte, making a specialty of the "Wailing Wall."

The man who often besought the bishop to put wind in his sails that he might go over his course with speed, but who soon proved that he had no rudder.

The man who urged his successes as a reason for promotion, when work such as he described would in five years make his present church one of the greatest on the continent.

The man who spoke strongly of his loyalty to our ecclesiastical system, but was so poutingly yielding as to rob his obedience of merit.

The man who mournfully rehearsed the story of his own sacrifices but whose scars always seemed less than the tale of his wounds.

The man who secured a repute for exaggeration, and who never mastered the art of drawing an accurate line between imagination and memory.

The man who prided himself on a personal culture whose chief evidence was a borrowed accent.

The man who carefully selected one ministerial qualification in which he excelled, and insisted on being estimated by that, instead of by an all-round ministry.

The man who mistook scolding for bravery, and who regarded a rude outspokenness as a credential of honesty.

The man who was himself rather dull, but who lived in the shadow of a totalitarian wife with vivacious ideas enough for two.

The man who made the art of popularity his science, and pleasantness his program—until overcultivated social

194

charm grew as distasteful as constant and unaccompanied sugar.

The man who visited the desert, or the temple pinnacle, or the high mountain, without interpreting their testing values, and who could not decipher the signposts that point toward Gethsemane and Calvary.

Some of these paragraphs are smart sayings. Yet any bishop of long experience has met the types here described. If he finds his problems in this minority, he finds his joy in that elect majority who press toward the mark of the prize of the high calling in Christ Jesus.

In one way the Methodist bishops' power of appointment seems a survival of autocracy in a democratic age. Its continuance is the more remarkable because it is based on a policy, and not on a doctrine. In a connectional system power must be lodged somewhere; and the question relates to its location. The prerogative of the bishop is not assumed by him; it is conferred upon him. Bishop Thomas B. Neely's speech at the General Conference of 1904 stated correctly the Church's intent as to the episcopacy. The highest lawmaking body of the denomination could confer it, and that body had full power of withdrawing it—for "feasance, malfeasance, or no feasance at all." Bishop Neely's words came back to plague him when he protested against his own enforced retirement. Yet in the long course of the years the appointing power of the bishops has worked like a miracle. In the last seven Conferences that I held, no church declined to receive the assigned preacher, and no preacher refused to accept his assigned church.

V

The power has been interpreted modestly by the bishops themselves. I have never heard claims of infallibility. The talk about appointments as "being made in heaven," or about being "left alone with the Lord," has been largely jocular. An amusing instance occurred long ago in Maine. "Father" Dunn was an able man, with marked peculiarities, and with a wit that scattered his sayings over the state. He loved the villages and the wide circuits. Yet his abilities would have warranted assignment to any of the city churches. Hearing that his name had been put down opposite one of the Bangor societies, "Father" Dunn protested. The bishop fled to the doubtful refuge of personal piety, and asked the objector to "remember that these appointments have been sanctified by prayer." The keen response was: "Well, if my appointment was sanctified, it was sanctified before it was justified; and that is contrary to Methodist theology." The doctrinal argument won: the waggish preacher did not go to Bangor. The illustration is more than humor. It shows that superior claims of episcopal wisdom would not be taken too seriously.

The truth is that the bishops whom I have known suffered immeasurably in their appointing responsibility. Franklin Hamilton had a brief episcopal term ere death conquered his stalwart strength. Evidently the outward calm in making assignments was a screen for an inner tumult. As he lay dying, his final delirium was administrative. He was trying to "provide for" men who needed to be placed where their children could have school advantages, to give a man with a large family a better support, to fit into a congested list a preacher who was returning from detached service. All worthy bishops could understand that haunting delirium. For myself, the making of appointments was anxiety, torment, anguish. Hesitating always to use any metaphor that applies the passion of Christ to our human feelings, I still declare that the task of assigning ministers, where the interests of wives, sons, daughters, churches, were all involved, never

196

ceased to be my Gethsemane. As I walked from the Jurisdictional Conference after my affectionate order for retirement, my heart kept repeating, "Thank God! No more appointments to make!" When as a child I sat with my parents in the final Conference session, saw the bishop arise with the authoritative rolls in his hand, and once at least heard him read my father's name for an unexpected place, it seemed to me like the Judgment Day. I never recovered from that feeling. For thirty-two years it pursued me; often it exhausted and humbled me. The power involved was not a coveted possession. The implied honor was swallowed up in terror.

The chief difficulty lay not in obduracy, but rather in that partiality toward oneself that seems a part of our human endowment. I halt sometimes over the demand that each of us should love his neighbor as himself. Really that is quite a contract. Often a figure of speech suggested by the physical body occurred to me. How strange that eyes never see themselves! that no man ever beholds his own face! Our vision is so near to its own organ that the nearness hides self from self. Unless we use outside reflection, like a mirror, we are blind to our own looks. This is a spiritual parable. The Psalmist recognized the fact: "Who can understand his errors? cleanse thou me from secret faults." The limitations were hidden from the man who had them. Perhaps that law of human life makes for the happiness of self-congratulation. It does not create episcopal happiness!

Once a layman, not disposed to be querulous, said that preachers regarded themselves as sacrosanct—that since they felt themselves called of God they could not brook correction by man. This was an exaggeration of a fact. Most men think of themselves as good workmen. Two contrasted experiences occur to me. Learning that a good preacher, and a personal friend, would be compelled to

197

move after one year's service in the best appointment he ever held, I was disturbed. The sincere attitude of the man was stated thus: "I went to that church self-confident. I did not spend much time in prayer even when I saw the larger tasks. Nor did I work in travail on my sermons. I rehashed old discourses. When the vacation season arrived, I said, I will go to work earnestly in September and take strong hold on my duties. Then sickness in my home hindered me. I soon discovered that I had lost my opportunity—and that my officials were right in asking for a change. I deserve to be demoted, and I shall take my lowered standing without complaint." He faced his losses frankly and continued to give good service until he was eighty-two years of age. It was an unusual personal inventory.

The other case was different—and quite as astounding. A youngish preacher came with an outright complaint: that I did not appreciate his worth. His immodesty made me conclude that if only the meek were to inherit the earth, he would receive scarcely an inch. He ended his self-appraisal with the statement that I could not make a list of the ten best preachers in Methodism and omit his name. Somewhat abashed as I was, my sense of humor came to my rescue, and I said to him, "Sit down at my desk there, and write the names of the other eight." Slowly the illuminating joke dawned on him. Psychiatrists hint that psychoanalysis is needed because self-examination is difficult. Not always can a man be trusted to give himself an assured intellectual or spiritual quotient. One of the bishops, long years ago, being accused of conceit, replied thunderingly, "It is not conceit! It is not conceit! It is simply an adequate consciousness of my own powers!" We must leave him there in his self-made refuge of comfort.

VI

A minister of high standing in another denomination once gave an appraisal of our Methodist system. Affirming that we had the best ecclesiastical government in the Protestant world, he still declared that our defect was "the lack of an efficient back door." Probably we have been too careful lest we make a cruel exit. It is true, also, that the back door would be less needed if the front door were better guarded. Our kindly critic belonged to a communion whose "egress" was abundant. Each Saturday afternoon its churchless ministers came to headquarters to see if any supply places were available for the next day. Methodist offices do not entertain that pitiful group. A study of our system shows that one of its chief excellencies is that it gives a chance to faithful ministers not brilliant enough to win as competing candidates, but steady enough to succeed if given a chance to prove their work. An ecclesiastical government made only for the brilliant could never be widely effective. The wisdom of God has not given the world an overplus of geniuses.

Many of the persons described in the semihumorous and semitragic list given in recent pages rendered good accounts. The growler at Conference is frequently the worker at home. A complaint may be a safety-valve—cautiously opened. I would be happy to feel that the record of thirty-two years in the active episcopacy would be as largely complimentary to myself as it is to the ministerial comrades who loyally submitted themselves to my judgment. I purposely omit the adjective "godly," found in the ordination ritual. Sometimes I have wished that I had kept count of the number of miles I have traveled, the thousands of beds I have occupied, the thousands of preachers whom I have assigned. With reference to this human element, I affirm that among these many ministers

199

I could not name twenty men who responded bitterly to such authority as the Church had conferred upon me. I would not know where to find as large a group with a higher average of consecration. In the appointment sessions I have been moved by the sight of their anxious and kindly faces. In the lull that came after the benediction I have waited solicitously for their grievances. But how rarely, in that throbbing hour, did one of them speak his accusing word! Having once put their hands to the plow, they did not lift them to strike an overseer. So many times they came to thank, and not to scold! So many times I heard the march of their feet toward difficult fields! Often when one would have said,

> The tumult and the shouting dies;
> The captains and the kings depart,

I waited until the sound of steps had ceased and the vehicles had made their noisy departures. Then I found myself saying, "God forgive me if I have not done my best." I have been confident that whatever might be the immediate assignment of those good men, their Final Appointment would be to a Beautiful City. I desire to be their neighbor forever.

CHAPTER IX

BROTHER

THE FACT THAT THE NOUN HEADING THIS CHAPTER IS singular in number does not confine it to one person. There were four brothers of us: Matthew Simpson, William Francis, Edwin Holt, and LeRoy Howard. William Francis was an example of wanderlust. He felt that the big world was a gift for the traveler's joy. When he was sixteen he disappeared, though there was not at home the slightest discord. He himself said that the itinerant life gave him the habit of journeying and that he felt obliged to do better than his father did! He had always been fearless. He would play tricks that were perilous—not only for the one to whom they were done, but to the doer. Once I saw him empty a large syringe of water through a broken windowpane into the face of a sleeping shoemaker. I stood in the modest background, and made it more safely modest when the sputtering victim emerged with a bootjack and a quick gait that indicated a punitive errand. Will loved a physical joke more than he dreaded a physical penalty.

Not being afraid, he stepped into the vastness and was at home everywhere. Conversation with him was like opening a gazetteer. He was more generous than I; where there was a question as to which should first have the new apparel, he was always ready to yield. Though his nature was sympathetic, his love of travel made him unaware of the hardship visited on his parents by his "unknown whereabouts." He did not understand that one question became his mother's refrain—"Have you heard from Willie?" He must have gone through severe hardships. But his will not to "embarrass the family" always conquered. I never received from him a request for the slightest help. His last illness halted him on the highways of California, but he sent no appeal to his people. He died "in the house by the side of the road"—because it was located there. My younger brother answered the doctor's summons, selected a grave plot at El Centro, procured a headstone, and provided for religious services. I trust that the long journeys of my brother ended at a Beautiful Gate. His only son, Thomas B. Hughes II, is an honored citizen, a police lieutenant, and the father of a promising family. If God allows the redeemed an earthward glance, my father and mother are happier in heaven when they catch sight of that Christian home in Wilmington, North Carolina.

My younger brother, LeRoy Howard, inherited his mother's shyness. He could not be socially bold. Graduating from the Law School of the Univeristy of Nebraska, he was halted by ill-health on the edge of professional life. He felt the need of outdoor employment. Years ago his progressive weakness compelled him to put aside his work. So, in comfortable quarters in a Southern California desert, he dwells with books, and magazines, and papers. Callers find him one of the best-informed men on the Western Coast. His mind now carries maps of the world's battlefields, as well as statements of the political theories that make the background of struggle. He is the only other survivor of our family circle. We dwell far apart in earthly geography, but I myself well know that a loyal brother's heart lives for me ever not far from the Golden Gate.

There were two sisters. Effa, who married James O. Barton, was lured by the sunshine of California. Several years ago she journeyed to a fairer clime. Her dust found a resting place where California flowers and palms grow into memorials. Sister Nellie married William B. Taylor, a noble citizen of Bloomfield, Iowa. He won the title of the town's "model young man." I was proud to call him a brother-in-law, and to know him as a brother-in-love. True to all the program of the Christian faith, he was still smitten by the depression. Ere the mid-afternoon of life had come, he laid down his burden at the open gate of Life; and beyond that portal several years later he welcomed my lovely sister, his faithful wife.

I am justified in giving much space to my elder brother, Matthew Simpson, who became my ministerial partner and my episcopal colleague. In the history of the major Methodisms we were the only brothers who were active bishops together in the service of the Church. His biography has not been written; therefore I enshrine here the tribute to him. In the delicate task of representing him I purpose not to put special restraint upon my pen in revising somewhat the article that I contributed to *The Methodist Review* at the time of his passing. The Gospels of Jesus were written by men who loved him, and their tributes are not discounted by their affection. Filial biographies are frequent, and fraternal biographies are not unknown. I suspect that a son would be as likely to idealize a father as a brother would a brother; yet in both cases the intimacy has its advantages.

I shall not force myself out of this estimate of him. We must be in company in this writing, even as we were in life. For fifty years we experienced a growing nearness to each other. Our careers were sent by the Divine Providence along mutual ways. Save for four years, our ministries were in close contact. We were ordained together as deacons in 1890, in the church at Grinnell, Iowa, of which my father had been pastor for five years, and to which my brother was to be appointed the next day. Within the year he joined me in New England. Later I went to Indiana, and he to Kansas City. As DePauw University lay on the direct line of travel eastward, separations were not long. When I went as resident bishop to San Francisco in 1908, he came as pastor to Pasadena. For eight years we were together on the Pacific Coast. Then dawned that wonderful day at the General Conference at Saratoga Springs, when I had the privilege of conducting, as a bishop, a brother, as a bishop-elect, to the platform. In his quadrennium in the episcopacy I was with him several times each year. God saw to it that our paths crossed frequently and beautifully; and that is one cause for thanksgiving.

We were not especially intimate in boyhood. We were almost four years apart in age; had we been either nearer or more distant in years, our fellowship would have been different. I can recall no estrangements; but I traveled so far behind him in studies and pastimes as to forbid intimacies and yet near enough, also, to prevent that cordial comradeship that often exists between a big brother and one quite smaller. But in that dear past some things stand out in my memory.

My first recollection of him is vivid. He came out of the door of the North Street parsonage in Wheeling, West Virginia, clad in a new suit. From that day until the end of his life I never saw him when he was not well dressed. In his personal appearance he was the personification of a pure gospel. Of the three symbols used in the New Testament to designate the fate of the lost—fire, darkness, and filth—he would have feared the last with a great dread. He showed unfailing taste in the selection of wearing apparel. We had a nurse, in early days, who was vice-mother to us both—a wee Irish woman, Catherine Maloney, converted to Protestantism under my father's ministry, and for half a century a faithful member of the Methodist Church. When my brother heard that she was dying in a Wheeling

204

hospital, he hastened to her side. Her face, at his coming, spoke the joy that her lips could not utter. She left for me an old photograph of my brother, taken when he was six years of age. It represents him as clad in the outlandish juvenile garments of the period—side-buttoned waist, capacious trousers, and in his hand an immense hat. Yet the boyish figure is graceful. Only a cold review of fashion's eye would pronounce it otherwise. Things fitted him—because he himself affected what he wore. To the very end, when I folded his garments in the Cleveland hotel, his outer "habits," as the old phrase went for clothes, were like the clean, fine habits that he attained in the inner life. Carlyle, in his *Sartor Resartus,* might have used him as an illustration of his picturesque figure of speech.

My other remembrance of him was as boyish, but more significant. We were fishing. I caught several prizes, while he caught none. Even older people cannot always understand the providence of the waters. So the disappointed elder brother seized my tackle and ran with it over the meadows townward. My impulse was to leave his equipment, but I pulled in his line and found dangling on it the largest fish I had ever caught. I waved it victoriously, and my brother returned. He did not make me surrender the prize. I carried it home as my own trophy. The boy in him prophesied the man. There was ever a generous largeness in his viewpoint. I have no remembrance of littleness in his nature or work.

He was born at West Union, West Virginia, on February 2, 1863—"ground-hog day." I have not consulted the weather record, but I feel confident that the animal of the tradition saw his shadow cast by a bright sun. Matthew Simpson Hughes was named jointly for the great Bishop and for the maternal grandfather.

Our parents' home was never rich or elegant. In West

Virginia it was scattered in ten different houses, none of them having "modern conveniences." The charges were of all grades—country circuits, county seats, cities, and a presiding elder's district with scarcely a mile of railroad in its borders. But my father and mother were enamored of the ministry, and they were never disillusioned. They had no better day than when their third son became a preacher, save only that still better day when their first son gave them double happiness by joining the third. Advancing years made us more and more grateful for a puritanical rearing. It was a temptation for both of us to give contempt to grown-up people who slander pious parents. When the day of final decision for his career came, my brother had no hindering remembrances from the parsonage life of his boyhood.

He referred to his education as a "medley"—public schools; Linsley Institute, Wheeling; and then West Virginia University. In the university he went through the freshman year regularly; then he studied medicine for a few months, and after that law. Evidently he did not yet see his goal. With his father's removal to Parkersburg, West Virginia, he became city editor of the *Parkersburg Daily Journal,* under Editor White, afterward governor of the state. In 1884, when he had but arrived at voting age, he "stumped" for the Republican party, debating with experienced speakers and winning repute as a keen platformer with a disconcerting gift of sarcasm. For a brief interval he devoted himself to insurance. All this was a "medley" in types of schools and kinds of study. Yet there was unity of preparation. Law, medicine, newspaper writing, insurance—are they not all curricula for the ministry?

He was not athletic, though deeply interested in outdoor sports as a spectator. He played neither baseball nor football. But he was in other college activities—debate, declamation, dramatics. In essay writing he won the premier honor of the university. A regents' prize was given for the best essay on a specific subject, the production to be elaborate and to be presented under a pseudonym. Matthew Simpson entered the contest, though but a freshman, and won a unanimous decision against the competing juniors and seniors. I recall my pride when he read his essay at commencement time. I was but fifteen, and the production impressed me as a miracle.

At the university and in the later years he was preferred in society. Handsome, witty, musical, polished, he was lured by the so-called higher social circles. He met the temptation of the newspaper reporter. For the time he drifted from the Puritan anchorage. His parents moved to Iowa, and thus another tie to that good past was loosened. But the evangel only waited for its chance. God was preparing a Damascus road.

The crisis came in 1887. Father was invited to preach at the Loveland Camp Meeting in Ohio—Dr. Isaac W. Joyce, afterward bishop, and the Rev. Sam Small to be his partners. He wrote to Matt S., asking him to spend a few days at Loveland. The affirmative response came. In our parsonage we entered into a covenant of prayer, both that the son might come, and that, coming, he might likewise come to Christ. Matthew Simpson always testified that his father's life was his call; but one of the immediate influences was the preaching of Sam W. Small, who, having been a newspaperman himself, quickly found the approach to the younger man's heart. For many years Matt kept in his Bible the note that Sam Small wrote to him on the morning when the great decision was made. The Southern evangelist never did a greater day's work! Duly my brother presented himself at the altar, and the "great transaction" came by God's forgiving grace. Of the emotional experience I know nothing. But I do know that the old words "radical," "powerful," "glorious" are none too strong. Jacob became Israel. A prince was added to the royal household.

The outer changes were sweeping. Converted on Tuesday, he tried to preach his first sermon on the next Sunday morning. In a month he was traveling the Ewart Circuit in the Iowa Conference. I can never forget his homecoming, with its solemn and tearful joy. He went back to Parkersburg, West Virginia, to close his affairs there. He had dreaded the meeting of his old friends, but let it be said to the credit of human nature that the most worldly greeted him with encouragement. He mentioned with especial gratitude a Parkersburg lawyer, Mr. Charles Caldwell, a hearty and popular man of more than local prominence, who, though not himself a Christian, was especially sympathetic with Matt's change of heart and plan. Afterward Mr. Caldwell was converted and became a local preacher in the Methodist Episcopal Church, South. Once the Hon. Charles W. Smith, a congressman from West Virginia, said to me, "It was a wonderful thing that happened to Matt at that Ohio camp meeting." Even so.

I have known no greater change in spirit and purpose. A new man moved into a new world. I have only good memories of him after that spiritual event. I never heard from his lips an unclean word; nor did I ever see the slightest attitude toward womankind that did not stand for spiritual gallantry. I recall no deceitful relations to life. There was in him an extreme of sincerity. He himself felt that he yielded to needless sarcasm occasionally. He confessed to me that very agreeable people were his great trial. Concerning one excessively pleasant man he said, "Nobody can be as nice as that and be genuine." In the petty sense he had no diplomacy; but he did have a keen insight. In many cases his judgment of men apparently was justified by later facts. He had no "politics" in his nature; yet he was sent to four General Conferences, each time as the head of his delegation, and each time by a vote that indicated growing strength. In all his peculiar relations to elections I never knew him to do a thing that would not stand earthly publicity or the full light of the Judgment morning.

I set down here an account of our own personal relations in regard to the episcopacy. When discussion of my name began in 1907, I did not take it seriously. Ere the meeting of the General Conference in 1908, however, letters and conversations made me aware that both my brother and I would receive votes for the office. Each was willing to withdraw, but neither was willing that the other should withdraw. So we agreed that the one with the smaller vote on the first ballot would request that he be no further considered. When that ballot was announced, my brother went to the tribune and with a smile withdrew his name. For eight years I was in the episcopal office with the scarcely comfortable consciousness that my being there meant his not being there. His own attitude was always magnanimous. When a delegate remarked at the Minneapolis General Conference that the failure to elect him was due solely to the "brother-argument," he gave a laughing reply—"I judge that I would have a better chance for election if my brother were in the penitentiary"— a reply that was in itself a defeat of the superficial reason.

For the "brother-argument" in one form was unworthy. A fairly intelligent minister revealed himself in the statement that "the great Methodist Episcopal Church was not so poor in episcopal material as to be compelled to elect two sons of the same mother as bishops." In that form the argument deserved contempt. In its other form it was not valid. My brother and I were less alike than were several other pairs of bishops. Besides, he was too independent to indulge in fraternal collusion. The nearly

209

four years that we had together as bishops never brought embarrassment or restricted freedom. But the "brother-argument" was not a wall of stone that could be battered down by heavy reasons; it was a wall of mist that could be dissipated only by sunshine. The sunshine had an eight years' task.

One cannot estimate joy by quantity; but I record that the moment when I led my brother as a bishop-elect to the Saratoga Springs platform was a far more joyful one than that wherein I was myself taken to the platform at Baltimore. At a reception in Los Angeles, when I was to go to Boston and my brother to Portland, Oregon, I said, half-jokingly: "I was converted before my brother was. I entered the ministry before he did. I was elected to the episcopacy before he was elected. If it happens that I precede him to heaven, I trust that no foolish angel will object to his coming in on the ground that I am already there." The playful remark had its reversal. He went before me. Someone at a General Conference started a Biblical illustration—that there were two sets of brothers among the Twelve chosen by Christ. At this late time I may express the conviction that in the land to which he has gone and to which I hasten, our fraternal relation will not shut either of us out of any counsels or labors for the Kingdom.

He came to speedy power as a preacher. I heard him preach his second sermon—usually more difficult than the first! I took him to my little church north of Brooklyn, Iowa. He chose as his text that Old Testament saying about the "fountain" opened for "sin and uncleanness." He was smitten with fright, and was soon headed for humiliation. Then he wisely turned for refuge to his experience of conversion and told the story with simplicity and feeling. This changed defeat into victory. My people went homeward under the thrill of evidence for a redeeming gospel. Months later I heard him preach again—this

210

time on Isaiah's words, "My thoughts are not your thoughts, neither are your ways my ways, saith the Lord." That sermon, in clearness of thought, in forcefulness of diction, in persuasiveness of method, and in completeness of appeal, stands among the great public utterances that mine ears have heard. Sitting in that tiny country meetinghouse I knew that he was destined to be one of the mighty preachers of the Church.

He was a diligent student. From the beginning of his ministry he toiled in preparation. He read, read, read. He wrote, wrote, wrote. He had no verbal memory, but he had a memory for ideas. He followed the order of a manuscript, but not its wording, with accuracy. His library was immense, and good. He haunted book stores and gathered treasures for his shelves. In many matters he was not systematic, but in the use of his books and the arrangement of his sermon material he was order itself. He spent too much time in his study. I fear that he there exhausted the physical reserves needed to carry him over crises. Nor did he have enough of the rest that some men get from playfulness. He had to be lured from his work. His desk was his delight, his pen a pastime, his books his friends.

He had the reserve that marks great natures. Lyman Abbott says that, all appearances to the contrary, Beecher had whole areas of reserve in his soul. Phillips Brooks always had difficulty in exhibiting his heart. It was so with my brother. They called him "Matt" familiarly, and he adopted the abbreviation in his signature. Yet that form of greeting did not represent the deeper fact. He lived much to himself. More than once I saw his affection peeping out rather timidly. Several times I watched him looking with fond pride upon his daughter's photograph, which I found in his satchel after his death; yet I doubt if he could have easily shown his proud affection to her.

211

Once I was with him when he received a fine school report of his little son. He mentioned it with quiet gladness, and thereafter repeatedly I saw him rereading it with
a grateful smile. He revealed himself more in his letters.
When the doctor told him that an incurable malady had
laid hold of our father, he wrote me, saying: "It is not
possible, as yet, for me to think of father as being mortally
stricken; he has always been so large a part of the existing
order of my life. Of course, I knew that his strong and
serene old age could not last forever; but I know nothing
of a world without his presence. I am sorry to send you
such news, but I am glad to have you to share this great
burden." Then he signed himself more intimately than
was his wont, as if he would come closer to his companion
in sorrow.

In his sermons he practiced the open heart. He did
with congregations what he could not do with individuals.
It required the pull of many souls to overcome his reserve;
the clamorous sorrow of a crowd acted upon him resist-
lessly. In the first years of his ministry, when he was seriously overworking, he had to check his emotion. Yet to
the last, nothing more surely brought his spirit to the
front than any tale of sorrow. He trod the wine press
alone, and he always sought others that they might not do
the same. When he presided over the Iowa Conference
at Bloomfield in 1918, he went several times to his father's
grave, that in the solitude he might bring his tribute of
reverent sorrow and pride. If ever this reserve went too
far, it is still true that it had its meaning for his ministry,
since it sent him away from social fussiness and led to the
quiet brooding that explains great preaching.

There was a largeness in his nature that worked into his
sermons and administrations. Details were hard for him.
He could not easily be an errand boy, unless the package
he carried were valuable or the message significant. His

212

work took on breadth. Big men listened to him, and big men did big things at his call. He said to every place he occupied, "Be enlarged," and the place answered by extending its borders. On Ewart Circuit he lifted every church into strength and took the biggest farmers and the brightest teachers as captives of Christ. At Malcolm he added a country point after a schoolhouse revival, and built a church that did good work in a fine rural section. At Grinnell he compelled the attention of professors and collegians and carried the great work of his father to greater greatness. At Portland, Maine, he saved Pine Street, the neighboring church, by declining to be a party to its disintegration and by preaching there on the afternoons of many successive Sundays; while the Maine Conference shows in its minutes that the J. S. Ricker bequests, secured by his influence from a Congregational layman, are still the largest asset for its retired ministers. At Pasadena he made his church the missionary society of a growing city; refused to feed its roll with the names of people who by right belonged to smaller neighboring churches; and did a constructive piece of church extension, expending more money on that work than he spent within his own church. True to his word, God gave to the candlestick on the altar an ever brighter glow. His episcopal work was pitifully brief. But I prophesy that the years will reveal the large wisdom of his plans, and that the great Northwest will long feel the impulse of his service.

He was, also, an exemplar of a spiritual gospel—not of the kind condemned by Mr. Wesley in his reference to the "pert, self-sufficient animal" who "bawled out something about the blood," but rather of the kind that believes that there is none other Name. His own sudden and wonderful conversion foreordained him to that emphasis. Few pastors were so often invited to the meetings

213

of local labor organizations, and few could speak to them so convincingly. Yet I fear that he had too little patience and too much scorn for the radical Christian socialist. He regarded him as an applier of blistering poultices—a sort of clumsy tinker on the outside of life. He himself had become good in his social relations by getting a good heart from God, and his experience led him to what many would regard as an extreme Christian individualism. All things had been made new for him in Christ; why not for society? He felt that the final solution for our social problems will come only when the Christian individualist and the Christian socialist combine their emphases for the saving of the world. My brother had no use for the man who edged toward revolution. His Americanism, as well as his Christianity, made him regard such a one as a menace to the Republic of Washington and the Republic of God. He wanted the great changes to come by a real evolution, out of the deeper suffrages of life under the touch of a redeeming Lord. He regarded a superficial sociology as the inevitable result of a superficial religion, believing that when men really looked up into the face of the Heavenly Father they would look around and see the faces of brothers and sisters. He had little confidence in pseudo brotherhoods that did not know the God and Father of Jesus Christ.

In 1888, at the end of his first ministerial year, he married Miss Harriet Frances Wheeler, a lady of culture, gifted in music, and a constant helper in his achievements. As the three children, Blakeney, Esther, and Matthew Simpson, Jr., came into the home, his preaching took on the domestic emphasis. He dwelt seldom on Paul's figure of the Roman courtroom, and frequently on Christ's figure of the family. His fatherhood made him know the Father better. If you would read a classic in paternity, turn to his sermons and find one on "The Mission of the Little

214

Child." Thus his sociology became that of the household of God.

Within that spiritual conviction he lived and wrought. He was in no sense a class preacher. He could never have been persuaded to be pastor of a socially aristocratic church. No salary would have induced him to become a chaplain to the merely rich. He never fawned on wealth. Once he said to me rather hotly, "That man expects me to call on him, not because he needs me, but because he has money; and I cannot go on that basis." His successors in pastorates told that the story of his personal work among the poor increased in volume and glory as humble folk added the chapters.

For thirty years he stood in our pulpits, an increasing wonder to those who heard him oftenest. He consecrated a fine presence, a musical voice, an alert mind, a throbbing heart to the evangel. For four years he gave himself to his episcopal labors—answering calls that he should have refused, going out into rain and cold and darkness when a fluttering heart and a smothered waking from sleep should have warned him to rest. But the work of God enticed him, and the soul of energy allowed the failing body no earthly respite.

Then came the end. Another of my boyish memories offers a coincidence. I query whether it is really my memory, or simply the memory of another's memory. Bishop Edward Thomson died in the McLure House at Wheeling, West Virginia. Matt S. was not quite eight, and I not quite four. Yet, as in a misty past, I see the grief in our parsonage home, and my father going here and there to do his part in tribute to a great and good man. I have, too, an indistinct memory of that father's taking his oldest son to the service in honor of the dead Bishop. How little they could have known that about a half century later another Bishop would die in a city

215

hotel—and he the boy with the wondering and tear-dimmed eyes! Between those episcopal funerals there are records of grace and glory written in the Book of Life. Preacher-father and preacher-son have finished their courses in peace, and their crowning days were not far apart, as we count time. Sometimes I have said, "O brother of mine, why did you not stop when that wonderful voice grew husky and your steps dragged on the way to the pulpit?" But I know well his thought—that he could meet his engagements, as he had said, and then go West and homeward. So indeed he did. At Easter daybreak he pillowed his face on his hand and slept himself out on a journey that ended in the wakeful surprise of heaven. God is good, and so is his will.

For many years it was my custom, on entering the pulpit, to put up a prayer for my preacher-father and preacher-brother. That filial and brotherly habit abides. I entertain no conscious heresy concerning the other life. They two do not need my prayers that they may be saved. But I do think that to the last I will continue that pulpit prayer as they two serve God gloriously day and night in the holy temple. That petition will always issue into a pulpit thanksgiving that they two were mine, and are mine, and that by the unbreakable pledge of the Strong Son of God we shall be partners forever in the Gospel of Everlasting Life.

CHAPTER X

COMMISSIONS

THE WORD "COMMISSIONS" IS USED TO INDICATE GLORIFIED committees with certain authorities, or official errands on which an individual may be sent. There are many of these functions in ecclesiastical life. Some of them are formal—to fulfill courtesy or to promote harmony; others involve duties of negotiation, or revision, or legislation. Frequently they are the advance work for legal frames; while, again, they complete tasks in verbiage that would cause lengthy discussion in a delegated body. Since I have had the responsibility of serving in several of these capacities I acount for them in their calendar order.

I

My first assignment was to the Board of Education, organized for the care and counsel of colleges and secondary schools. Its later responsibilities included the Negro schools, and still later the Sunday School and the Epworth League. In each era there has been, also, the administration of the Loan Fund for the aid of worthy students. These kindly endowments, gathered mostly from the wee gifts on Children's Day, now amount to many thousands of dollars, administered so as to be available always as assistance to young collegians on generous terms.

Membership in the Board of Education was a preferred thing. College presidents coveted a place where they might help their institutions; while always there were ex-educators in the Board of Bishops who felt that this group

217

represented their more expert interest. The administration touched the largest list of schools in the Protestant world. The University Senate was given charge of the work of standardization and recognition, but the human problems fell to the Board of Education.

There was elation in the thought that we were largely responsible for preparing the future leadership of the Church. This feeling was warranted by the statistics of the last half century. Our Christian colleges have, to a surprising degree, supplied the denomination with its foremost men. Had Francis Asbury's counsel prevailed when Cokesbury College was twice burned—that Methodism was providentially taught by these conflagrations that she had an evangelistic, rather than an educational, mission—the Wesleyan movement would have been sadly crippled. But the little man in the Oxford gown won against the grand frontiersman. The Church has had a singular passion for education—a passion that founded colleges as a solid after-result of the itinerant's preaching. The books in the saddlebags were the precursors of collegiate libraries.

The fellowship of this Board was delightful. The joviality of college life at times took possession of the meetings. Occasionally there was a riot of gladness. The only depressing feature laid hold on me because I was a member of the Loan Committee. The list of persons who had paid little heed to financial obligation, made sacred because hundreds of young people waited for help, furnished gloomy reading. Some remissness was caused by the never-sincere plea that the loan was being repaid by life rather than by dollars; more remissness came from the fact that the beneficiaries lacked either ethical sense, or a budgeted management that serves the cause of personal honor. These blameworthy delinquents were not many relatively. Yet meeting them in their homes or in important councils of the Church always brought a pang and made the knowing one doubtful about the careless debtors' characters. Against this forbidding fact stood a noble account of repayment—so that the main impression was the satisfying handling of funds that benefited thousands of promising youths.

Related to this work was a service with the Conference Courses of Study. Prior to the adoption of the commission form of administration, I was assigned to this committee. My episcopal colleagues would confess that we did not take this task with adequate seriousness. Our scattered life made meetings difficult; while other official duties pushed the cause to a third-class rank. In 1916 the General Conference authorized a commission to conduct this work as a primary thing. I was then elected chairman and so remained until my retirement in 1940. The bishops knew of my desire for this assignment, and honored the only request that I ever made for a specific election.

My prophecy of the important work was largely correct. We steadily lifted the standards for ministerial training. The late David G. Downey was a valuable member. Professor Harris Franklin Rall was the statesman, foreseeing and preparing proper laws. The late Allan Mac-Rossie became its dynamic executive, extending his enthusiasm over the Church's domain. Thus there was bequeathed to united Methodism a Disciplinary provision for the training of preachers which keeps a central place in the Church's work—with William K. Anderson as its efficient director. One of my premier services was represented by the twenty-eight years that I gave to this endeavor.

II

I participated in the revision of the Rituals and Responsive Readings. At Saratoga Springs, in 1916, a Committee on Ritual brought its report to the General Conference.

There was then much theological fever in the Church. Certain conservatives were anxious to turn the Rituals into Creeds. Consequently there occurred a debate whose pleas for meticulous statements became riotously amusing. The confusion came to a climax when a delegate seemed to handle the Burial Ritual with irreverence. For two full days the battle was a reminder of a Revolutionary struggle that had occurred near those same fountains. It was apparent that, if eight hundred delegates were to participate in revision, only the constant use of the "previous question" could prevent a full year's meeting! At length the despairing Conference sent the Ritual to the Board of Bishops, for study and revision. I assisted in making the changes deemed necessary. A willing General Conference adopted the report "without reading," when it was adroitly presented by Bishop Luther B. Wilson.

I vastly enjoyed the work of revising the Responsive Readings. The Church demanded extensive changes—especially the inclusion of portions of the New Testament. Though the technical ritualistic standards were thus violated, it was deemed that a wider range of selections was warranted by the need of familiarizing our people with the words of the new covenant. Not because I was abler than my partners on this commission, but because I worked out the titles carefully in advance, I pride myself on the fact that I selected at least three fourths of the headings that give the main emphasis of the readings. Evidently the revisions appealed to the Church in general, for the old criticism has melted away like frost under sunshine.

III

I would regard the revision of the Hymnal, as completed in 1935, as the happiest of the tasks assigned by the Church. Though we recognized the importance of the

220

work, the burden of the responsibility was lightened by singing. Our toil was set to music. For the first time in history three Methodist churches were preparing a common Hymnal. A study of the personnel of the triple commission shows that its members swept the gamut of musical life—including the deans of great schools of music, and other men whose qualification was heartiness rather than art.

When, at the General Conference in Columbus, Ohio, in 1936, I made the revision of the Hymnal the topic of the closing paragraphs of the Episcopal Address, one of my colleagues felt that the theme did not make a real climax. I myself had lost faith in the four-year succession of climaxes. They perished with the using. Unification would have made a natural peak of feeling, but that could not with propriety have been argued by the bishops. So the great achievement by the triple Methodisms was the renewal of the sacred hymnody of our people. The outcome called for a three-church expression of praise in the Trisagion, "Holy, Holy, Holy." John Wesley had been given the right of way in most of the previous messages. Charles Wesley in 1936 had a right to the sacred platform.

IV

In 1917 I was chosen by the bishops as their representative in the war camps of Europe. The tasks included a responsibility for the Methodist chaplains, and for the increasing of such morale as could come from proclaiming the motives of our faith. I sailed from Quebec in September. The submarine peril was at its height. We encountered several icebergs which were not considered good traveling companions. We had a convoy of seven vessels, steaming in triangle form. Three times we sounded submarines. But depth bombs had been made so efficient that almost certain death would have awaited any attack-

221

ing crews beneath the periscope. The horrors of the sunken submarine which turned all of its apartments into a shrieking madhouse made the divers conservative. At last the airplanes from the English coasts came out to guide us, and we knew that the peril was past.

I did not lack for funds. When generous laymen heard of my errand, my mail suggested postal savings. The eager request of the chaplains was for automobiles—vain request, both because of the colossal expense, and because the Government was commandeering the automobiles that were shipped to the European ports. For all the minor demands of the chaplains I had sufficient funds. In addition, I did not have to limit myself when I entertained our soldiers on leave in Paris or in other cities. Often restaurant tables were made into altars.

The speaking itinerary was so rapid that the camps became blurred in my memory. One day I spoke in seven different open-air fields. Seldom were there less than three engagements, some of them arranged for by bugle calls that gathered audiences by quick magic. The meetings were not conventional. Occasionally the preliminaries consisted of prize fights. The postludes were often frolicsome! More than several times the "yeast" in some "doughboy's" nature acted explosively. For three weeks prior to the Armistice, I seldom slept in a room as good as my home cellar. I discovered that rats were poor roommates. Droning enemy airplanes in the sky above one's cot were not lullabies. Only once did a shell break in my vicinity—far enough away to give me no peril, but near enough to make me pious. My health was improved by my outdoor experiences. When, in February, 1919, I reached New York, after a rough journey on the converted *Montana,* I thanked God devoutly that I had received this strange commission, but prayed even more devoutly that I might never again have so tragic an errand.

222

I came to a somber appreciation of the domestic price of war. My two sons were in Europe through all my time of service there, the older of them receiving the *Croix de Guerre* for bravery in bringing back the wounded in his ambulance, under fire, in the second Battle of the Aisne. I could never tell whether the youth felt that the emblem on his one bosom was sufficient compensation for the French colonel's kisses on his two cheeks. When the boy's mother and I met after his decoration, we had a festival of parental tears. On my return to the safety of the home, I became aware that the wife and mother was the real soldier. She had gone through the experience described in Thomas Buchanan Read's poem, "The Brave at Home." For each of us she had been

> Doomed nightly in her dreams to hear
> The bolts of death around him rattle.

She never recovered from her spiritual journeys to those crimson fields. To the end, she was a wounded heroine whose memory never permitted her to be "on leave."

Another impression dealt with the moral effect of the war. If mothers and sisters and wives be the civilizers described by our gallantry, we can scarcely believe that the homeless life of the camps would not tend to produce a Bohemianism in manners and in ethics. Great publicists have asserted that this was one outcome of the period. Certain religious organizations that had been bulwarks of religion were lowered in their tone. The soldiers who imported memorials from the fields of bravery brought back with them as well some European standards that were "duty free." Puritanism lost something of its honored standing. Even Christian workers began indulgences that would have shocked them ten years earlier. Indeed, in some respects the ethical atmosphere was so changed that, if specifications were now made, this volume would receive some angry receptions, while the author would have pinned upon him labels that are epithets.

The observation is a warning. Our young men are now going into camps without such moral protections as were given them in the former World War. Those who know declare that gambling and drinking are rife; while occasionally an officer's voice pleads for the outposts of a safe prostitution. No man is a false alarmist if he declares that, unless stronger ethical emphases are brought to bear upon present conditions, we shall have a destructive aftermath, calculated to add to the arguments of the pacifists and to halt preparation even for a just war.

V

The next assignment shifts the scene once more. In May, 1928, the General Conference is in session in Kansas City, Missouri. The late Ray Allen, of the Genesee Conference, brings in an abrupt and kindly resolution, favoring union with the Presbyterian Church. The General Assembly of that body is meeting in Oklahoma. The Board of Bishops appoints me as fraternal delegate, to carry greetings and to present the one-sentence overture. To my letter about my errand, I receive word from the stated clerk, declaring that I shall be allowed ten minutes. When this reply is read to my episcopal partners, they unanimously agree that I should not make the long journey for so short a presentation, and that a courteous and brotherly letter will have to serve our purpose. My fraternal address was prepared, but was not delivered. It is the only "unuttered utterance" found in my file.

The address would have required about eighteen minutes for delivery. I have never received any intimation as to the reception that might have been given to this slight but sincere approach of Methodism. The concordat proposed between the Protestant Episcopalians and the

Presbyterians has brought from the High-Church group a threat of secession; while many Presbyterians cannot see William Adams Brown, Henry Sloane Coffin, and John Timothy Stone kneeling before a bishop for the purpose of having something added to their apostolic credentials. Personally, I am assured that a merger between Presbyterians and Methodists, which would involve no question of reordination, is far more natural than a union that would produce two types of Presbyterian clergy—one more authorized than the other.

VI

The scene shifts again toward a still wider territory. In 1930 the bishops appointed me as fraternal delegate to the Methodist Conferences in Ireland and England. I was deputed, also, to hold the Finland Conference and the Norway Conference. The family council concluded that Mrs. Hughes, the two younger daughters, Caroline and Anna Louise, and the youngest son, Francis Montgomery, should accompany me. That decision was wise. The depression was rapidly approaching. The money invested in the family tour would have been swept away in the panicky years—unless some magic depository, unshared by its fiscal companions, had kept it in safety. The outlay for wide sightseeing gained more than ten other talents, and laid up treasures of memory and culture beyond the reach of moth or rust.

The Finland Conference interested me deeply. The voyage over the Baltic Sea, with its multitude of islands, was an itinerant charm. On the boat we easily read our newspapers at midnight. For us Helsingfors—how much more euphonious than Helsinki!—was a romance. The parades, with banners warning the Communists from Russia, made impressive danger signals. The language was a polysyllabic terror. When one saw that a simple

225

lunch was a *paviolonem,* it well-nigh destroyed appetite. The Finnish singing was of an accent wherein we all are born. When the patriotic melodies floated over the waters, to encircle isles and invade hills, one felt as if a listening John would once more hear music across the sea of glass mingled with fire.

My heart was captured by the people. They had thrown off the Russian yoke. Their national idol was Jean Sibelius, who sent from his forest home melodies that entrance mankind—one of them claiming a place in our hymnals. The fear of a new oppression was on the people, and their borders were outposts of apprehension. The sad prophecies were borne out when the Soviet Republic sent its troops against its tiny neighbor. Deeply as we may feel about the Finnish alliance with Hitler, we must believe that the union is not a real one, and that a deeper merger of hearts will bring noble Finland into more worthy company. While I detected in the Conference some tendencies toward fanaticism, I was assured that our work was making a contribution of warm feeling not furnished by any state church. So surely did Finland claim my heart that the writing of these lines was interrupted by prayer in her behalf.

The Norway Conference was a larger one. King Haakon sent me a pleasant greeting by telegram. We were quartered at Larvik, a seacoast town, in an immense sanitarium near springs whose healing repute attracted many travelers. Here the Hughes tourists came together for the first time in Europe. On the arrival of Mrs. Hughes and the children, the Norwegian Methodists placed an American flag above their church. Later they transported over many miles an excellent orchestra from one of our local societies—to render, in honor of the Bishop's family, Sousa's "The Stars and Stripes Forever." Both the sight of the flag and the sound of the music moistened the eyes of

226

the visitors. Several members and ministers from our Norwegian churches in Illinois were guests of the Conference, rejoicing with their fellow confessors and looking with quiet rapture upon their native hills. Kipling was right:

> Clay of the pit whence we were digged
> Yearns to its fellow clay.

I was impressed by the fact that Norwegian Methodists had an attitude of respect that did not become obsequious. One day I was conferring with one of the district superintendents in the vestibule of the dining room, and so was delayed. I observed that, though the meal had been announced as ready, no one was entering the refectory. When I inquired the reason, I was told that the Conference members or visitors would not proceed to the noonday meal until the Bishop had taken his place at the table. Thereafter I was careful not to stand between appetites and viands.

This recalls another characteristic of the people. While this action did not at all suggest that they were gourmands, they were frequent eaters! Breakfast came regularly. At about ten thirty the session recessed for refreshments. Luncheon came at the usual time. At three o'clock the Conference took a respite for refreshments. Dinner came at six, with cheeses and fishes in profusion. At eight thirty the revival meeting was interrupted for refreshments. There was no evidence that more food was consumed in these five endeavors than would be required, per capita, for the three usual meals in the United States. The installment plan was more in evidence. The report of this to the Norwegian Methodists in Chicago was hailed with a hilarious mood like that manifested long ago when another prodigal returned—"They began to be merry."

My chief impression was one of the sincere piety of this

Wesleyan group. They held the fervor of Methodism without allowing it to become fanaticism. The State Church offered them social advantages which their Methodist allegiance denied. It is too much to say that the conforming groups cried out "Unclean! Unclean!" It is not too much to say that Scandinavian Methodists pay a price for their faith. My slight contacts with the State Church were mediated through interpreters, but they were proofs that a Methodism that kept its traditional warmth was needed in Norway. The statistics indicated that the curve of membership had turned upward. Our church work was recovering from a pitiable episode that involved a conspicuous leader. When the statistician gave the Cabinet reassuring figures, the district superintendents came to audible thanksgiving. Two of them bowed their heads and indulged in quiet weeping. I confess that episcopal tears were in that conclave of rejoicing.

I see Larvik now, lying there peacefully beside the great waters. I see the beautiful capital city, Oslo. The tread of foreign soldiers there makes sad music for my heart. On the way back to England I had a brief stay in Denmark. I saw Thorwaldsen's statue of Christ. It affected me deeply. Involuntarily I knelt where I could look up to the benign countenance of our Redeemer. I prayed that those hands might be lifted over all Scandinavia, and that the spiritual comrades whom I had met in Larvik might not fail to receive the benediction.

We had a few days in Stockholm, Sweden, one of the world's most beautiful cities. There Bishop and Mrs. Raymond J. Wade gave us royal entertainment. The call of the British Isles comes to us, and soon we are being greeted by the mother tongue, whose varying accent, whether Irish, Scottish, or English, could not destroy the beloved melody.

228

CHAPTER XI

FRATERNALISM

M Y MISSION AS FRATERNAL DELEGATE TO THE IRISH CON-ference occurred in mid-June, 1930. I hastened from the steamer at Southampton and, by courtesy of the Cunard officials, was pushed through custom inspections so that I might surely make my connection for the Emerald Isle. The route led through the smiling fields of Devon. I had made that journey in 1902. Evidently, in the years be-tween, a change had taken place—not in the landscape, but in the beholder. Under the gentle tuition of my wife my aesthetic appreciation had grown. I was no longer a Peter Bell who could not recognize a primrose by the river's brim. I think of that day's journey as a procession of beauty in the Garden of the Lord, where those who were put there "to dress it and to keep it" had not failed in their duty. Having been accustomed to the American deserts, where irrigation could not be lifted so high as to make the mountains fertile, I was impressed by fields so utilized as to leave no waste spaces between the hedges. I had anticipated that the day on a train would give me a chance for sleep. Yet the scenery produced insomnia.

I

I am on the steamer at last for my first trip over the Irish Sea—having come early to my couch in order to es-cape *mal de mer!* I am awakened in Dublin Harbor, to be greeted hospitably by Mr. William R. Burgess, who, with his cordial wife and daughter, opened to me their cheerful home. Mrs. Burgess' father was the late Dr. Robert Crook, who had figured so efficiently in our work around New York and who had exercised a chief influence on Dr. David George Downey, another Irish lad who did great things for American Methodism.

I am not confident that my impressions of Irish Methodism were just. The Conference is not large—much smaller than the average Annual Conference in America. Practically all of the men were clad in clergy uniforms. The demeanor was quiet. I could discover few traces of the revival that, a few years before, had brought hope and power to our work. The discussions were not keyed to enthusiasm. Responses to pleas for prayers, consecrations, revivals, were not visibly keen. The Gaelic temper failed to show its consuming eagerness. Perhaps the American tendency to compare the immense General Conference with a group that represented restricted geography and decreasing populations led me to wrong conclusions. One of our preachers near Chicago who had come from the Irish Conference expressed disappointment that the session was in Dublin rather than Belfast. It may be that the atmosphere of a city not at all charged with evangelical fervor somewhat touched the services.

My credentials had been prepared by my dear colleague, Bishop H. Lester Smith, secretary of the Board of Bishops. I trust that a million years hence I shall be somewhat worthy of his engrossed estimate. Historically, Dublin offered more scope than either Belfast or Cork, though all three cities would have shared in the glory of Columbanus, Gallus, Virgilius, the leaders of the gospel shock troops that in England, Scotland, Belgium, and Germany turned thousands from unhearing idols to the listening God of Christ. John Wesley went to Ireland twenty-one different times. To Dublin itself Thomas Coke traveled again and again—as if the land of his descent were the land of his

230

love. There, in 1782, he held the first regularly consti-
tuted Conference, receiving into full connection William
Myles, the first man so admitted outside of England; there,
in 1794, he became partner of Robert Raikes in starting
the Sunday-school movement; there, in 1803, he established precedent by sending to the American General Conference a fraternal address; there he held a majority of
sessions from 1782 to 1813; and from there he sailed on
the missionary journey ending with a sepulcher in the
Indian Ocean.

There were other memories. Adam Clarke had worked
on his *Commentary* in Dublin. In that city Hester Ann
Rogers, beautiful bride of a young minister, framed devotional music that was wafted to many continents.
Thence had come to America Strawbridge, Embury,
Boardman, Pilmoor, Barbara Heck, and Henry Foxall,
who built our first Methodist church in Washington;
while from Ireland, if not from Dublin, had come Robert
Williams, who brought to Christ Jesse Lee, and who himself had been converted by another Irishman, Edward
Drumgoole. My own office in Chicago had been made
possible by Arthur Dixon, an Irish boy who became the
chief influence in holding a great corner for God. There,
after his death, we lifted higher than the Washington
Monument a steeple whose illuminated cross tells men of
a Saviour who died for a city's sins.

All this I told that group in the Dublin church. The
history was more convincing than any flattery could have
been. I felt that my mission should strengthen international bonds. The ebb tides of the after-war period
were sweeping good feeling toward the waste. Harmony
achieved on battlefields was being lost in diplomacy fields.
So I was glad to be an agent of fraternity—to tell them:

There is a visitation swifter than ocean liners, swifter even
than cable or wireless messages. The delegation of prayer

231

abides always. On behalf of American Methodists I should like to enter with you into a covenant of intercession. Dublin and Chicago, in the geography of the spirit, are both near to the altar of God. I come not to ask you to admire my country or my Church, but to solicit your prayers for both. Though you be the tribe of Benjamin in size, you can become the tribe of Levi in priestly petition. We may turn the denominational prayers into family prayers. American Methodism is one of your children, grown beyond the stature of her parent, but still your own by the rights of the family tree. That child is in a distant country, with prodigal possibilities— tempted by the power and wealth of a wide continent. If the parental and filial figure of speech be too much, we can at any rate liken ourselves to Samuel and Saul and remember that when the aged priest prayed for the young king, God gave Saul "a new heart."

I did not have any special elation as to the success of my fraternal errand. But I do treasure many appreciative words. Often I see the faces of the splendid preachers as they conferred about the spiritual interests of an Island strangely cleaved by politics and by faith. One Irish ancestor unites my spirit to those Hibernian relatives: while my spiritual genealogy reaches back to a Redeeming Lord through the mediation of John Wesley and binds me to them in an everlasting covenant.

II

I have no remembrance of my return trip from Ireland. I must have crossed the Irish Sea. But I recall no stateroom, no seasickness, no companionship. Perhaps I was so obsessed by the memory of the Irish Conference and the prospect of the English Conference as to have a spell of amnesia. Between the two representations there came the administration in Scandinavia and Finland. It may be that these events concealed the interlude. I do recall the passage of the North Sea, meeting American

232

MATTHEW SIMPSON HUGHES
Aged 50

friends on shipboard, including the present dean of the Boston University School of Theology, Earl Marlatt, and preaching Sunday morning on the two texts, "Thy way is in the sea," and "Thy way, O God, is in the sanctuary"—a parallel between the reverent feelings made by the ocean and the temple. The sermon was later published in the supplement of *The Christian Century*.

On landing in Norway I was hurried to one of our churches, where I preached through an interpreter to a great congregation. The pun about an "interrupter" is not jocular with me. I am troubled by anything that comes between myself and an audience, whether it be a radio, a microphone, or a human mediator. Later I was to have Nils Bolt as my interpreter—the most satisfying one I have ever had. We soon established a rhythm—a sort of harmony that allowed me to proceed with a "headlong" quality and made the pauses less torturing. On Monday I went over majestic heights, and looked on gushing fiords, and had renewed for myself the Psalmist's tribute to the hills of help. We came to Oslo, a wonderful city where as yet no foreign soldier commanded the streets, and no Quisling surrendered his nationality. May God bring peace to dear Norway!

III

Before I went to Helsingfors and Larvik I had one experience which I am proud to relate. The building that Mr. Wesley called "The New Room in the Horsefair" had long been in possession of the Calvinistic Baptists. These good partners in faith, convinced that the historic place had a sacred meaning for the Methodists, had consented to hand it back to our people—and this without any effort at extortion. Under the leadership of Dr. T. Ferrier Hulme, and of a splendid layman, Mr. Williamson Lamplough, the structure had been restored.

Calls for accredited relics brought in many articles—benches and chairs, a bed and a writing table used by Mr. Wesley, his pulpit desk, the clock that ticked away the minutes of his sermons. Outside there was sedulously preserved the stall where Wesley's horse had his resting place.

Dr. Hulme planned a service in this New Room for the evening of July 11, 1930. Invitation was by ticket only. The call declared that the visiting American would "be the first Methodist Bishop to address a congregation in this historic Sanctuary" since the day when Asbury had arisen from his seat and had been accepted as the apostle for the new, wild world. The occasion thrilled me deeply. I felt that I was not asked to sing the Lord's song in a strange land before jeering enemies, but that I had returned to my native house to chant before friends. The environment was magnetic.

Often a preacher gets credit for his surroundings. My feeling was one of inspired gratitude, and not of unworthy egotism. The paper accounts of the event praised me unduly:

Bishop Hughes, on rising to speak, soon showed himself to be master not only of his subject but of his audience. His Bostonian accent was piquant and arresting, his voice well modulated, and his vitality amazing. His own evident enjoyment of his theme was infectious. At times he paused a moment to laugh a little to himself or at himself, but never for a moment did he lose his grip on the sympathy and interest of his hearers. He became magnificently expansive and happy and free, as he spoke after this fashion: "Picture that Conference of 1771, with fifty-three ministers present. A volunteer is called for America—a land of wilds, of rushing rivers, of lonely prairies. A young man of twenty-six years arises and says, 'Here am I: send me.' They sent him, to another continent, and to a glory in history. He stayed in an excited land when every other preacher of English birth departed—he lived with Judge White in a forest home, but even in the

234

year of that political exile winning over eighteen hundred souls to Christ." . . . .

". . . . Francis Asbury's traveling coupon had no ticket of return. At last, after inconceivable hardships and incalculable successes, the hero of the Long Road staggered into the Log Home of his friend, George Arnold, and on a Lord's Day, amid the Virginia forests, laid down his burden at the open Gate of Heaven and quickly received the Crown from the hand of the King of Kings."

At Bristol, Mrs. Hughes and I were the house guests of Sir William Howell Davies, ex-mayor, and of his queenly wife. These kindly hosts are now in heaven. When I myself arrive there, I shall early find their mansion and tell them—as I would now assure their hospitable children—that we found their home a haven of rest. A few days more of sight-seeing, under that expert guide through the aisles of Methodist history, the late Dr. T. Ferrier Hulme, and we were off for Leeds where the Conference was scheduled for later July.

IV

The social features at Leeds were more than pleasant. There was a complimentary luncheon given for us by the late Sir Robert Perks, a preacher's son, the joint engineer of the "Tuppenny Tube" in London, and for years the leading Methodist layman of the world. There was matchless entertainment at the home of the late Sir A. Ernest Bain, in comely Harrogate. The gracious Lady Bain still lives in that English city, but Sir Ernest will greet me no more on earth. Sometimes I wonder if these noble translated Britons know of the furious perils that now shadow their island, and of that tragic reversal which removes hell from its usual location and places it in the skies.

I was at the Conference in Leeds long enough to get the flavor of that body. No delegate could have surpassed me in attendance. It was an able group. Men like Dinsdale T. Young and John Hornibrook impressed me as massive and strong. I wondered whether the younger men compared with the older men in power. But as I had asked the same question at our own General Conferences, I took both suspicions as evidences of adult conceit against which the writer of Ecclesiastes inveighed in the demand, "Say not . . . . that the former days were better than these." The singing was amazing. Without the help of the organ the Conference sang the "Te Deum" with such grand fervor that my wife's ex-Presbyterianism was stirred by a big emotion. From the angle of worship I felt that the Conference surpassed our own. The business program, arranged in iron fashion, could not estop the rush of praise and prayer. The business of the Kingdom did not hide the majesty of the King.

I asked myself more than once why the ardor of this central body failed to capture the local churches. With the exception of the missions, the congregational groups seldom impressed the visitor with a glad earnestness. The pastors and the people were following John Wesley in a stately ritualism rather than in an intense evangelism. Frequently I heard complaints that the people could not hear their pastors' sermons. I had the impression that some ministers felt that a burning ardor violated propriety. Inasmuch as the pulpiteers had not mastered the Wendell Phillips art of putting terrible conviction into the conversational tone, they were victims of a quietude that was a weak substitute for typical Wesleyan preaching. This fault I had observed in our American pulpits. The rituals of our English services only made the limitation more apparent.

This was not true of the great missions. In them the Gospel had a thrill. They showed one reversal of our American church life. We have a Sunday evening prob-

236

lem; English churches had a Sunday morning problem.
At Westminster Hall in London I preached to four times
as many people at night as I faced at the earlier service;
at Tooting Central Hall Mission it was much the same.
Indeed, I think that the most persuasive regular service
that I attended in England was at Tooting—though at
Llandudno, in Wales, I saw throngs both morning and
evening and was reverently touched by the Welsh fervor
in quick response and in wonderful song. Here Mrs.
Hughes and I were guests in the romantic home of Sir
William M. Letts and Lady Letts. Their house was scriptural, built upon a rock, while in the near distance the
waves flashed with invitations for ocean travel. Wales
was the home of my ancestors, and the streets were dotted
with signs bearing the names of Jones and Hughes. The
mountains and valleys suggested West Virginia scenery—
so that I felt a double nativity. Sir William carried us
over the sinuous roads to various resorts, in an automobile
whose comfort truly suggested that our splendid host was
one of the leading automobile manufacturers of Europe.

I must believe that the religious fervor of the Conference at Leeds, if carried over the British Isles, would halt
the decline in numbers that has given concern to our Methodist leaders. One of the speakers referred to a wise saying—that "Methodism had flourished only on its own
peculiarities." The Prayer Book was not its most distinct inheritance. John Wesley's prophetic preaching was
the chief characteristic. There can be no substitute for a
Gospel that keeps a constant and throbbing Invitation.

I do not know how to describe the service in which I
completed my fraternal mission to the Conference. I had
been prepared for "English reserve"—for compliments that
would give lessons in restraint. But the newspapers and
the religious journals almost surprised me into egotism.
If their accounts were correct, I had never before had

237

myself revealed to myself. I did not know that I had "a quaint and arresting Bostonian accent"; that I was a "tall ecclesiastic"; that I had a "finely modulated voice"; that I had "snow-white hair; clear, searching eyes; sun-burned face; and restless hands." The English looking-glass made me feel that I had neglected the Greek injunction, "Know thyself." I could not with modesty describe the response to my fraternal appeal. I am made hesitant in giving the accounts wholly written by others, fearing that the quotations may really be secondhand self-praise which becomes half scandal. I must remind the readers of the journalistic records that an epochal event does things to speaker and listeners alike. If Daniel Webster did well by Bunker Hill in a dedicatory address, Bunker Hill did well by Daniel Webster. It pushed its glory into his words. In a minor way something like this may have happened to me. *The Methodist Recorder* was known for conservative reporting. Its pages were seldom plenteous in compliments. So I put into this recital some of its account, with no change that modifies the meaning. Indeed, I omit many adjectives. "Loud cheers" did greet me as I came to the front, but I took them for my people, and not for myself. I had no feeling that I was "dramatic, rhetorical, declamatory, sententious, witty, satirical, passionate, tender, indescribable." While I knew that I was receiving a gracious reception, I had only one quick moment of self-consciousness. My wife was in the balcony on my left. Looking up toward her for the encouragement that I had so often had, I saw her leaning over the railing, her face radiant and tearful, and I was tempted to call to her, "Look out, Honey! Don't fall." I was so lost in my message that I became identified with the United States while my audience became identified with Great Britain. I felt as if I were holding the Stars and Stripes in one hand and the Union Jack in the other—

and clasping both emblems into the union for which I was pleading. Utterly prepared as I was, my preparation broke out into a spontaneousness that did not change my words, but did change my mood. When recently I read *The Methodist Recorder's* description, which soon casts the story into the third person, I wondered if I had not been glorified by a journalistic Boswell. Here is the account in part:

"I come as one speaking with an American accent," he said, "but also with the deeper accent of the heart, and of plenteous love. My voice is representing 20,000 Methodist preachers and millions of Methodist people. This hand brings to you the clasps of multitudes of your fellow believers. This heart has enlarged so that it carries to you a wealth of affection." They of the Methodist Episcopal Church, Bishop Hughes proceeded, could never make adequate return for the messengers the Conference had sent them,—"W. L. Watkinson, a slender spire among the temples of God. Till I heard him speak, I never could have dreamed that there could not only be interlude but eloquence in a sniffle. (Laughter.) Next there came John H. Goodman, whose saintly expression of a loving heart made us love him and love England for him. Then came Dr. Wardle Stafford, with an English accent and an American smile. (Laughter.) He left behind him a generous legacy in a splendid boy who, in comparison with his father, makes us believe in the doctrine of progressive evolution. (Loud laughter.) After him came Frederick Luke Wiseman who not only charmed us by his speech but thrilled us as he sang the very hymns Charles Wesley sang on the evening when his greater brother came to the 'strange warming' of his heart. Then came your Chadwick— (laughter) —Samuel. He must have heard God's voice in many a Shiloh temple. He lifted among us the Cross of the Lord Jesus Christ—though I heard one Fundamentalist say, 'Samuel Chadwick is a heretic about that.' (Laughter.) I nearly said, 'Why, you might just as well accuse of heresy either the Angel Gabriel or Dinsdale T. Young!' (Loud laughter.) Then Dr. Ferrier Hulme walked into our hearts and took up permanent residence in the affections of the American people—only he also made us

239

believe that the whole of the spiritual capital of Ecumenical Methodism was located in Bristol— (laughter) —and that he had a surreptitious scheme to transfer by some theological or geographical miracle Epworth Rectory and the room in Aldersgate Street to some point in the Bristol and Bath District." (Laughter.) How could he speak in response to men like these? He felt like wishing that one of them would go up in a chariot of fire that he might catch his mantle. (Laughter.) As far as he could discover none of them seemed eager to accept the suggestion. Perhaps they felt they were not ready!

He declined to say one word or do one thing which would make for international antagonism. He believed that the Christ of the Andes, standing there in lonely grandeur, waited to draw them all towards Himself in the love which was the gift of Heaven. And might he not say that it was his deep and happy conviction that there were no two peoples whom God Almighty had joined in such evident bonds of kinship as the English people and the American people. He had great indignation against anyone who would arouse prejudice in England against America or in America against England. Might he recall an old-time incident:

"Lloyd George and G. Grant Newman
    One day were drinking tea,
The Yankee and the Englishman
    Were friendly as could be.
'Now then, Lloyd George,' Grant Newman said,
    'If all your folks and mine
Could only sit as we do now
    And drink our tea and dine
With friendly feelings, cheerful chat,
    And happy repartee,
Our Anglo-Saxon troubles wouldn't
    Trouble you and me.'
Lloyd George's eyes began to shine,
    'Tut, tut,' he said, 'now, now,
We offered you some tea one day;—
    It raised an awful row.' "

(Laughter.) His ancestors had something to say about taxation without representation, but the Conference had given him all the privileges of representation without taxation. (Hear! hear!) He wondered how many of them had thought of the magnificent political and ecclesiastical range given to John Wesley when in 1784 he wrote those famous "Letters of Enfranchisement" to the Methodist Episcopal Church: "We will entangle them no more but leave them to the liberty with which God has so strangely made them free." These words were written when John Wesley was an old man, when readjustments were not easy to make. There was, he went on, a strange historical parallel between John Wesley and George Washington. They were both Englishmen. Each of them had a family tree not without distinction. So far as blood counted they had nothing to apologize for on either side. John Wesley was rather short, shorter than he (the Bishop) was, and nearly as short as Dr. Workman. (Laughter.) The only thing that saved them in America from being afraid of Dr. Workman, when they thought of his learning, was his providential lack of inches. (Laughter.) George Washington was a tall man, but if people could not see the likeness between his face and Wesley's, the fault must be in their eyes. They both married—George Washington a widow with a comfortable fortune, and John Wesley a widow with an uncomfortable temper. (Laughter.) After Wesley was married he itinerated more than ever. (Laughter.) Both were childless,—but God compensated by making one the Father of his Country and the other the Father of his Church.

He was pretty nearly done. ("Go on!") He would tell them how he had arranged the length of his speech. He had arranged to speak for exactly the same length as Dr. Hulme had spoken at Kansas City. (Laughter.) So if he spoke too long they would know it was not his fault. (Laughter.) He was in that Conference not as the bearer of information but as the bearer of affection, and no words could express their love.

> "Kinsmen across the seas,
> Brothers at once and sons."

That they were, and that they were proud to be.

"Years ago Phillips Brooks was asked to preach at St. Margaret's, Westminster, on a fourth of July, and at a time when the feeling between the two nations was not what it is now.

241

The church was crowded. Everyone was wondering what he would do on so delicate an occasion. How will he recognize the day in England? the people asked. This is how he did it: 'It is not for me to glorify tonight the country which I love with all my heart and soul. I may not ask your praise for anything admirable which the United States has been or done. But on my country's birthday, I may do something far more solemn and worthy of the hour. I may ask for your prayers in her behalf. . . . . Because you are Englishmen and I am an American, also because here under this high and hospitable roof of God we are all more than Englishmen and more than Americans, because we are all men, children of God, waiting for the full coming of our Father's Kingdom, I ask you for that prayer.' Did not English hearts respond?" He thought there was nothing better that he could ask from his English brethren than prayers for his people that they might be helped to consecrate their wealth and power to the purposes of God. He felt like doing an unconventional thing and asking that everyone would bow heart and head in carrying out this covenant of intercession, that the Union Jack and the Stars and Stripes might be kept in company with the white banner of the Lord until the day when all men should hail Christ as King, for ever and ever.

Perhaps this glowing account is too much. But *The Methodist Times,* then published as a separate organ, had a paragraph of interpretation:

It would almost amount to a mortal sin not to mention the constructive appeal up to which the Bishop worked. Years ago in France he pledged himself to a covenant of intercession on behalf of peace and the unity of the British Empire and the United States of America. The Bishop definitely asked that the Methodist people should join in this covenant. He has put the Conference in a debt of gratitude for a noble utterance and an appeal that will not go unheeded.

This last paragraph describes a chief intent of my address. Ere I sailed for Europe I had reread parts of John Graham Brooks's book, *As Others See Us.* It gives

242

hundreds of foreign estimates of America, most of them harshly unfavorable. Mrs. Trollope comes back to doubt-ful life, while Dickens' *Notes* are hurled at us again. The volume is "a book of damnation"—with literally hundreds of peevish criticisms. Of course, great wars had stimulated these diatribes. From 1914 to 1918, in the World War period, I had seen these unfortunate growlings brought forth as arguments against our becoming an ally when the British Empire was threatened by the German legions. Why, it was asked, should our critics in peace-times be accepted as our partners in war? That miserable logic was acting as a deterrent. I was perfectly clear in my own conscience on one point—that a part of my mission was to put up a bar against that type of censoriousness, as expressed on either side of the ocean.

At the Conference itself I had seen an example of this impolite scolding. In one of the open meetings Dean Inge, of St. Paul's, London, was the speaker. I had been introduced to him as the American delegate, and as he spoke I sat near at hand. As if he were bent on justifying the adjective "Gloomy," he took his fling at America. As a guest I could say nothing, feeling bound both by the New Testament and by etiquette. Prior to that time Kipling had written his insult to our soldiers in "The Vineyard"—lines unworthy of him as a poet, and as a prophet as well. We had shown a similar fault on our American side. I myself came to Leeds from the city which had elected a mayor partly on the issue that King George was "to keep his snout out of Chicago." That vulgarity had actually figured in a campaign, and the man who raised the false issue had been victorious in the election. We may well be alarmed by the imbecile states-manship that makes discord between the two great English-speaking groups. As the raging debate was on in our Houses of Congress as to our possible entry into the present war, a United States senator came to my office with a collection of these querulous statements, and with the question, Why should we go to the aid of our detractors? We should insist in both of our lands not merely on a temporary truce, but on a final edict against these silly speeches. They are coined in the verbal mint of perdition, and we should permit no fellowship with the unfruitful words of darkness.

There was a comical after-event for this exalting Conference. My wife had gone on to London to meet there our three children who had returned from their ramblings in other parts of Europe. She had taken with her the scintillating accounts of my experience at the Leeds Conference. I knew well that she would proudly spread them before that lively trio and expect their filial admiration! But alas! Alas! Jacob was crippled after the victory at the Jabbok Brook. And Elijah, having seen the drenched wood consumed by the fires of the Mount Carmel victory, touched the timber of the juniper tree. Ere I reached our London hotel, the very children whose traveling expenses I was paying had entered into a conspiracy. Instead of falling on my neck and giving me proof of filial pride, they had committed to memory the more ringing sentences from the English papers. So they stood in the room and in a deliberate rote, with resounding voices and Delsartean gestures, declaimed their father's praise until they turned it into jocularity:

"Then came Bishop Hughes."

"His fame had come before him."

"The Conference would gladly listen till midnight."

"He made us laugh until we ached."

"He made us quiet as mice."

"That sturdy figure, that singing voice, those merry eyes."

"He took the heart of the Conference by storm."

"Once again he made them all vibrate."

Thus did the juvenile jesters pull me from my pedestal. Their mother resisted the jocoseness for a time, and then yielded. God gives us children, I suppose, that we may educate them, and that they, in turn, may educate us. Here they restored to me the humble spirit. One of the three, a lovely girl with hair like burnished gold, has since passed from my kingdom to God's nearer Kingdom. Yet my memory often sees her in that London hotel room, laughing in the joyful teasing of her parent.

And I am glad, thinking of her glad face.

My heart still sends to her the smiles that are the token of love. When at length I come where she has gone, she will greet me in the rapture of reunion, and after a while may say in the arch way of the mischievous, "Daddy, would you like to have me recite some selections from that English Conference?"

I could not deny that evidences that I met the definite purpose of my visitation made me happier. The accounts in the press, as contributed by William Wakinshaw, John Watchorn, and Frederick Brown Harris, yielded me glad assurance. Letters from Dr. Hulme, Dr. J. T. Wardle Stafford, Dr. George H. McNeal, and Dr. Frederick Luke Wiseman added to my joy. Dr. S. Parkes Cadman, my friend, and a successful "denominational bigamist," being a Methodist in England and a Congregationalist in America, soon after the Conference sent me from shipboard the following cherished letter:

On Board Steamer Olympic
September 29, 1930

MY DEAR BISHOP:

I am happy and proud about your visit to the British Conference. I met many of the leaders later. They had but one verdict on your services as Fraternal Delegate,—*splendid and*

245

illuminating. Surely we cannot estimate the good done. These delegations are of supreme importance just now, and, as the Chairman of the American Branch of the Committee on Exchange of Preachers between the U.S.A. and Britain, I sincerely and gratefully thank you for your great ambassadorship.

Yours affectionately,
(Signed) S. PARKES CADMAN

It is not easy for me to realize that the vigorous life that lay behind this letter is with us no more. God made him a constant mediator between two great English-speaking peoples, and between the two largest non-conforming bodies on both sides of the sea.

In my informal closing address to the Leeds Conference I had said that, while I had visited England before, I had not previously visited the English! These words stated a real distinction. I had been only a tourist, "passing from one ruin to another, from one hotel to another, from one cathedral to another." I had now met the Englishman in his dear castle, the home, and in the deeper sanctuaries of his worship. I had said, as well, that, like William the Conqueror in his famous toast at Hastings, I had "taken possession of England with both hands" and with one heart.

God gave me my chance to take kindly vengeance on British Methodism, by an assignment given me in 1940. Released from official work in June, in December the bishops insisted that I should head a movement for war relief, asking our churches to contribute one million dollars for merciful uses. One fourth of this was to assist our British Methodists in making temporary quarters where destruction had fallen on the sanctuaries, and to maintain missionary work that might otherwise be crippled or ruined. My premier helper in this campaign of compassion was my good, good friend, Dr. Orien W. Fifer,

246

well-known *Advocate* editor, and a leading member of the Indiana Conference. We came within a few thousand of that one million goal. Almost two hundred and fifty thousand dollars were cabled to our British leaders. I suspect that this was the largest amount ever given in such inter-denominational and international assistance. But the springs of compassion are still flowing. Bishop Herbert Welch continues to lead in this work, and money still flows in for the relief of the people.

The fraternal visit comes to an end. We are at the dock again. *The Empress of Scotland,* creaking and groaning on her last voyage, puts down her plank for our feet. Dear Dr. Hulme is there, with his kindly camera snapping us "for a farewell." The Atlantic once more! Then Canada, the Lady of the Snows! After that the New England hills! Finally Boston's Golden Dome! Then the more golden Methodist hearts! The journey has been busy and happy. Though nothing has occurred to make us sing with less fervor the lines of affectionate patriotism, yet we share the feeling of Robert Underwood Johnson when he saw "Two Flags on Westminster Towers":

> "This day is holy,"—so sweet Spenser wrote,
> Giving to Love the world's one bridal-song.
> Oh! could he see those flags together float
> Where the gray pinnacles of England throng.
> . . . .
> For great and generous England raise your voice:
> Be yours the apocalypse of Liberty—
> A vision that shall call us to rejoice.
> Divine the omens of the glorious years
> From these free flags—if you can see for tears.[1]

[1] Used by permission of the author's estate.

CHAPTER XII

WIFE

THE CONFIDENTIAL CHARACTER OF A HOME IS NOT ALWAYS held sacred in literature. Personal files have been ransacked and letters that belonged to only two persons have been put upon the world's bulletins. When a man writes of his first home, or of his second home, his pen at once strikes a dilemma. The family is the initial and most important section of the social gospel. Yet the relations involved are so sacredly intimate as to resist ordinary publicity. There is here an extension of the "search and seizure" provision of the American Constitution. A man's home is his castle and the lock and the bar are on the inside of the door.

Doubtless the attitude of a reader toward the felicities of the Brownings or the infelicities of the Carlyles would be more or less set by the personal equation. The literary problem is increased when the wife shrinks from conspicuousness. Preferring in life to remain in the domestic background, she would doubtless desire an after-death continuation of that modesty. I met my future wife when I was but seventeen. While her appearance commanded a gaze that I had to control, her demeanor was unobtrusive. Her beauty compelled the admiration whose expression her manner checked. I cannot discuss "love at first sight" in terms of psychology. But I do say that my choice was fixed on that very day. President Payne used to affirm that "all true marriages were made in heaven," but that there was "an excellent branch establishment at Ohio

ISABEL EBBERT HUGHES
Aged 70

Wesleyan University." Nearly four years at Delaware, where daily processions of coeducational loveliness moved over the campus, never once diverted me from my heart's purpose.

She was Isabel, the daughter of Dr. and Mrs. Jonathan Baker Ebbert. Her grandfather Ebbert had been a prominent lay Methodist, a local preacher who had his part in the beginnings of Allegheny College. But her immediate branch of the family was faithfully Presbyterian. I often saw in her the effects of that sturdy training. Many times she fell back upon the will of God with gentle trust. Her mother opposed our engagement, not because she objected to me, but because she felt that her quiet daughter was not fitted to be a preacher's wife. When she declared, amid her tears, that she wished she could take her daughters to an island far from masculine intruders, I made her smile with the boast that I was an excellent swimmer. Our engagement lasted nearly four years. We were both glad that the seminary days were kept strictly for their own purpose. Our marriage did not occur until church and parsonage and the full ministerial life were ready.

I must flee to other literary refuges for protection against any indelicate exhibit of home life. But I first make mention of one quality in her nature. While she was no chilly appraiser of persons, she had a wonderful intuition. Her judgments were never harsh, but their gentleness did not destroy their accuracy. When I went contrary to her estimates I blundered. A review of the forty-six years of our mutual life does not reveal any occasion when her remarks made embarrassment. In crises of church or college newspapermen could not tempt her into imprudent speech. Let the rest be said by two witnesses. Her pastor, the Rev. Dr. Frederick Brown Harris, of Foundry Church, Washington, spoke at her funeral services and gave the Memorial Address at the Baltimore Conference.

249

Selections from these two estimates give insights into her mind and spirit.

An ancient picture frame, studded with jewels, for an ideal wife and mother has come down the long centuries. As I lift it up we see smiling at us the face of the dear one who has gone from our sight to the Painless Other Side. "Her price is far above rubies. The heart of her husband trusteth in her, and he shall have no lack of gain. She doeth him good and not evil all the days of her life. She spreadeth out her hand to the poor; yea, she reacheth forth her hands to the needy. Strength and dignity are her clothing, and she laugheth at the time to come. She openeth her mouth with wisdom; and the law of kindness is on her tongue. She looketh well to the ways of her household, and eateth not the bread of idleness. Her children rise up, and call her blessed; her husband also, and he praiseth her, saying, 'Many daughters have done virtuously, but thou excellest them all.' Favor is deceitful, and beauty is vain; but the woman that feareth the Lord, she shall be praised. Her works praise her in the gates."

Nothing that we can add would make the memorial portrait more vivid or complete as we place it reverently in this old frame of dignity and strength and kindness and find it fits the picture perfectly. We fain would voice in this sacred, sacramental hour the sense of satisfaction and privilege that this choice spirit, this queenly woman, belonged to us in this Capital City. Here her failing physical strength was made perfect through suffering. But even before the door was closed to church attendance and public functions, she endeared herself to a host of those, especially in the ranks of the ministry, who had felt her understanding sympathy and the depth of her consecrated concern for the parsonage homes.

Hers was a charm and a grace and a friendliness which endeared her to all who came within the sphere of her motherly heart. She was a broadcasting station for cheer. As her own invalidism continued, poignant loss and sorrow and bereavement were frequent figures at her bedside. Yet she looked them full in the face and was not afraid. Always she came smiling through every trial and test. Hers was a faith that did not shrink though pressed by every foe, a faith which burned but the brighter in the dark hours and which no winds of adversity could blow out; for her radiant spirit was as the candle of the Lord.

Here, as her pastor, I have witnessed a love that never failed, a faith that never waned, a patience that was never exhausted. In seasons of distress and grief I have entered a home where the abiding and abounding resources of divine grace have never failed. This has been a laboratory where the premises and promises of the Gospel have been found valid and true. A life like hers is the best apologetic for the Christian faith.

As her distinguished and constantly sought after companion, as senior Bishop of the Church, faced his heavy tasks in spite of an anxious heart, she followed him every day with a beautiful partnership of spirit. The daily letter from the Bishop which never failed in all the years of their life together brought her accounts of the inner life of the Church, headlines of the Kingdom. How she rejoiced in achievements and movements often molded by the leadership and counsel of that one who to her was always a lover! With what a thrill she received the news of the vote for Methodist unification!

How lines of loving thought went out constantly to the children of her heart! In this home where she was queen, the sham and show of mere things to live with never obscured the shining goal of things worth living for. Here marriage has been a sacrament; children have opened life's eastern windows; trees and flowers have declared the glory of God; gardens have shown his handiwork; and, even in the dark, nightingales have sung on.

At the beginning of this Conference session we sit with our bereaved Bishop as we reverently and gratefully remember the face and form of the dear lady who walked in white with him across so many pilgrim years. We bear witness to her qualities of heart and mind so full of grace and truth; to her fine discriminations and her keen sense of values; to the radiant Christian virtues which ripened and mellowed and adorned the doctrine of her Lord and Master.

Isabel Ebbert Hughes was a saint without being sanctimonious. She was in love with life, with its lilt and its laughter, its human relationships, its grown folks and its little folks, its Junes and its Christmases, its birds and its flowers.

Hers was a day of religious readjustment, yet she viewed

without alarm the dislocation of very much systematic theology. Questions of criticism and theology could no more shake her simple faith than a sword can sever a sunbeam. The dynamic of her life was not what she believed, but Whom. To her, death was never black-bordered, but glory gilded. It meant for her an ampler room in the Father's many-mansioned house. It meant that, even when she lay in weakness extreme and some of her dearest passed through the shining portals. It meant that to her when, on that day as the leaves were beginning to fall, absent from the body she was present with the Lord.

On one of the last days of her conscious life, in the quietness of a hotel room, on a Sunday afternoon, as he thought of the gentle invalid at home, the mind of Bishop Hughes wandered over the pathway of the yesterdays. For her eyes alone he penned lines which, when he gave them to her, made her radiantly happy. They sang in her heart as she entered the shadows which led out into the Land of Cloudless Day. Many have been so moved by these verses, written by a loving pen dipped in blessed memories, that I can think of nothing more appropriate in remembrance of her than to share with this Conference this lovely valedictory by our Bishop to his beloved:

"I saw her first beside a maple tree
    That grew beneath a bridge's lofty span,
    A bridge that leaped a river wide which ran
To yield its waters to the mighty sea.
        And my heart knew the tingling joy and pain
        That comes when love begins its dear refrain.

"I saw her, too, within a fireside's glow,
    Her sweet face touched with mingling light and shade,
    As to her there the trembling question made
The answer that the souls of lovers know.
        And when my hand sought hers in gentle quest,
        I knew my heart had found its place of rest.

"I saw her next where blossoms filled the air,
    The veil of bridehood haloed o'er her face,
    And friendly voices filling all the place
252

And wishing us all happy hours and fair,
    As forth we went upon that gladsome day
    From manse to manse to take our trusting way.

"I saw her when the first-born's fluttering breath
    Left the wee bosom to its peace serene,
    The parents fleeing to the Friend Unseen
Whose love alone lights up the room of death.
    And in the hour when nameless grief assailed
    She found the Refuge that has never failed.

"I saw her seven times more walk down the path
    That God ordains as price of Motherhood,
    The path of pain transmuted into good
For one who shares the life the Father hath.
    And she has borne each burden of her love
    As if it were a gift from Heaven above.

"And I have seen her in the weary years
    When days were long and nights their anguish knew;
    When patient love could not her strength renew,
She trusted still and banished all her fears;
    For always in the gloom of sorrow's place
    She kept the vision of the Saviour's face."

On one notable occasion she broke her usual rule of not taking part in great public occasions by speaking at the ordination of her own son, which happened to take place at a more informal gathering of relatives and friends and parishioners of the young minister. Here she uttered winged words that went far beyond that ordination occasion. In that charge to her son, through the window of a mother's heart we see what the Christian ministry meant to her. She lets us gaze at the holy of holies of a mother's inner shrine. Here flash and flame her ideals for the Christian ministry. Here gallantly waving we see her own white plume.

This pastoral tribute was followed by another from Bishop Francis J. McConnell, the dear and intimate friend of the family for forty-five years. Placing emphasis upon her quiet wisdom and insight; upon the constancy and faithfulness of her motherhood; upon her helpfulness in the ministerial life as it centered in the parsonage, he stressed particularly her joyful hospitality. The entertainment of her husband's church members and of personal friends was for her not drudgery, but delight. Closing his address with an unforgettable picture of this characteristic, transferred to heaven, he said that if the listeners should come at length to the City of Beauty and, walking down its golden ways, should see a mansion with an open door that framed a picture of welcoming hospitality—they could know that this was the place where Mrs. Hughes dwelt.

I would add two comments to this tribute. I have never thought of myself as a poet. For occasions of jollity I have written jingles marked by speedy rhyming rather than by laureate quality. My pride in the verses quoted by Dr. Harris is not literary. My second comment is that the estimates of her two friends had no need to claim rhetorical license. They were in no sense exaggerations. Every line of praise was won by her character and devotion.

The second witness is herself. At the ordination of our son, Holt Hughes, as a deacon, I had given a personal address. When the time came for his ordination as elder I asked her to speak as a representative mother. She undertook this task so tremblingly that I almost regretted my request. The advance strain in prayer and work gave her much anxiety. Such direct aid as she sought from me, she invariably reduced to a motherly simplicity. When I went over her last revision I knew that her charge had sent my previous one into the shadows. In the little Methodist church at Mansfield, Massachusetts, in the presence of my son's members, and of the family and the intimate friends, she stood within the altar and spoke with a firm voice words that made the audience quiver with emotion too deep for tears, too powerful to be forgotten while memory should abide.

My Son:

Perhaps no one present will be more surprised than yourself by the announcement just made, that I am to speak some words to you. I have never felt that my work was to be done in public. It has always been peculiarly difficult for me to take even a small part in a large gathering. I have felt that the home was the sanctuary wherein my main service was to be given: and that God's will for me had made the cradle of my children the altar of my work. If your ordination were being conducted at a great Conference session, I should take no spoken part. But this is an intimate place, and an intimate hour. The congregation is made up largely of your family circle, of your close personal friends, and of your own dear people. I try, therefore, to persuade myself that we are a domestic group: and that, even as your father gave you a charge when you were ordained deacon, so your mother's voice may make no discord now that you are being ordained by him as an elder in the Church of God.

I have been glad to find that there is a Mother's Bible within our larger Bible. Women with little children in their arms, and women standing beside their stalwart sons, are not strangers in the Holy Book. As I have looked forward to this hour, I have frequently thought of the tender story of Hannah and Samuel. Hannah was the wife of Elkanah. Their sorrow was that they had no children; at any rate, that was Hannah's sorrow. So she went into God's temple at Shiloh and, bowing at the altar, prayed, "O Lord of hosts, if thou wilt indeed look on the affliction of thine handmaid," and "wilt give unto thine handmaid a man child, then I will give him unto the Lord all the days of his life." Eli, the priest, mistook her moving lips of prayer for the mutterings of drunkenness. But Hannah said gently, "No, my lord, I am a woman of a sorrowful spirit" and "have poured out my soul before the Lord." The priest, believing in her sincerity, said, "Go in peace; and the God of Israel grant thee thy petition." So little Samuel came to the long-waiting mother. When he was old enough to be away from her, she took him up to the Shiloh temple and said to Eli, "For this child I prayed."

"Therefore I have lent him to the Lord; as long as he liveth he shall be lent to the Lord."

In essence, this story is our own. The two children that preceded you were wee girls, one of whom stayed with us only a little while. You were the third child. How well I recall that November day when you came to us and your eager father went over the Malden Centre parish, telling of the arrival of the parsonage son! Our lovely people immediately gave you a preacher title. You were to them "The little minister." They insisted, against your father's first intent, that you should take his precise name. That was our day of dedication: their dream and ours is being fulfilled tonight. We gave you to God. We have never taken our gift away from him. You did not go as a child to any distant temple: and I did not have the loneliness that came between yearly visits when "a little coat" was carried to Shiloh—as Samuel's mother did. But I can share the sentiment of the poet who represents Hannah as saying to God concerning her son:

> "Lord, though he rise a prophet unto thee,
> May he remain a little child to me."

We have not felt that in giving you to God we have taken you from ourselves. Rather have we felt that since the day when you concluded to preach the gospel of his grace and love, you have been ours more than ever—because our parenthood is itself from God, with whom we reverently and gladly share his own gift.

Perhaps, also, I shall not be deemed immodest if tonight I claim a small place in the company of New Testament women. When the Virgin Mary received the revelation of her wonderful motherhood, she sang her song of thanksgiving: "My soul doth magnify the Lord, and my spirit hath rejoiced in God my Saviour. For he hath regarded the low estate of his handmaiden." "He that is mighty hath done to me great things; and holy is his name." I know that this song of Mary is not all. There was Simeon's revelation to her, "Yea, a sword shall pierce through thy own soul also." It is true that mothers know their own kind of pierced souls: they do become acquainted with spiritual swords. Mary stood by the Cross

256

of Calvary: and the sword thrust into the Saviour's side touched his mother's heart as well. But, my son, we shall not find fault with any little Calvaries that may come to you or to us, if only they have their part in the redemption of the world. It may be, also, that through the years there have been times when another mother has said, "Son, why hast thou thus dealt with us? behold, thy father and I have sought thee sorrowing." It may even be that sometimes we were mistaken, as Joseph and Mary were. Yet all this sank down into a glad forgetfulness, or else rushed up into a glad remembrance when at last we heard you say, "Wist ye not that I must be about my Father's business?" Tonight our deep and sincere prayer is that you may never be about anything else.

Nor can I fail to think of another Biblical story. There are not many details in the picture which is given in Paul's second letter to Timothy. Evidently Paul had no son of his own. So his heart adopted the young disciple, and the Epistle begins, "To Timothy, my dearly beloved son." In a few moments another person steps modestly into the scene. We hear Paul saying, "I call to remembrance the unfeigned faith that is in thee, which dwelt first in thy grandmother Lois, and thy mother Eunice." So far as I know, Eunice had nothing to say, save as she spoke through her son. Yet what a message she has given us after all! Let us rejoice that she was mentioned in connection with Timothy's ordination. For the next verse contains the words, "Stir up the gift which is in thee by the putting on of my hands." So Eunice in some deep and spiritual way was present when the presbytery consecrated her son to his holy work. May we not believe that there is a maternal succession as well as an apostolic succession! God surely brings mothers and grandmothers into an hour like this. He allows us to come quietly to the altar of ordination. Probably I shall not be blamed if for this first time in my life I become a spokeswoman for the company of mothers who rejoicingly give their sons to God to be his priests and prophets, and especially to be the interpreters of that parental grace out of whose abundance our own love comes. Tonight I hear a voice not unlike that of an angel, and it says, "Hail, thou that art highly favored, the Lord is with thee: blessed art thou." My heart responds with nothing but gratitude.

257

Years ago I sat in the rear of a California church on a Sunday afternoon when your father was ordaining a splendid group of young men to the ministry. I was impressed then, as never before, with the place that the ministers' wives and children had in the Ritual of our Church. The words came into clearness. "Will you apply all your diligence to frame and fashion your own lives and the lives of your families according to the doctrine of Christ, and to make both yourselves and them, as much as in you lieth, wholesome examples of the flock of Christ?" On that day I caught sight of many parsonage homes; I saw fathers and mothers, brothers and sisters, and sons and daughters, gathered there about that altar. I knew that no geography could keep their hearts away from that solemn event, and that "though sundered far" they would still meet around that "common mercy seat." To-night we of your own near households are here—father, mother, brothers, sisters, wife, sons, daughter, cousin, your beloved aunt. Your friends and your ministerial comrades join with us, and with you, in this sacred giving of yourself to the good God.

It does not seem long since that morning when God placed you in my arms. I had no feeling then that you left his arms when you came to mine. Again tonight, as I have so often done, I place you in the arms of God. I have no feeling now that you leave my arms when I place you in his. You are my son the more because you are his son the more. I gladly give you to Christ—utterly and forever. You are to be the Saviour's minister. He will keep you, guide you, comfort you, strengthen you. If by his providence I go to the Heavenly Home before you do, I shall wait for your coming in the proud confidence that, even as once you came back to me with the decoration of honor on the worn coat of a young soldier, so then you will come to me with the badge of the Lord Jesus upon your heart, and may its inscription be, "Well done, good and faithful servant."

This address traveled around the world. It was published in no less than seven languages. It was printed in full in a leading Seventh-Day Adventist journal. Well-known religious papers gave it editorial sanction and praise. Words intended for a limited group were winged for larger and longer flight. The maternal treatise, not meant for self-revelation, became the showing forth of her heart.

My children who still speak to me on this side of the veil have adjured me that they were not to be made figures in this volume. But they know surely that one who became for them the poem of this world's motherhood would want their names herein inscribed: Margaret Rebecca, Isabel, Holt, Ebbert Magee, Caroline Robinson, Morris Sharp, Anna Louise, and Francis Montgomery. The five that remain here have been good children to their parents. They fulfill the word from Proverbs about the Madonna of our kingdom: they "rise up and call her blessed." If ever their feet feel an invitation to walk the road leading to the prodigal's dreadful resort, they will listen to a gentle voice that allures them back to the Father's House.

Margaret and Morris were taken from our garden while they were what Prudentius would have called "blossoms." The dust of their tiny bodies has long slept in graves separated by wide miles of earth, but their spirits never ceased to dwell in their parents' hearts. On each little tombstone we wrote the Saviour's words, "Their angels do always behold the face of my Father which is in heaven." By the blessed contradiction which God allows to sorrowing fathers and mothers, we were granted two compensations: our arms always claimed two little children, as the other sons and daughters grew tall and mature; and, too, our faith in God led us to conceive for our departed children an ideal future. They grew by our side, giving us no disappointment, and causing us no grief save that of their absence. Above their graves the star of resurrection has not been dimmed. We have had a vision of Another City on whose streets of beauty the Saviour whispered to us, "Suffer them to come unto me."

All of my children still living in this world have been married—Isabel, to William H. Remy, Esq., lawyer, of Indianapolis; Holt, to Miss Gladys Bebout, of Rushville, Indiana; Ebbert Magee, to Miss Edna Laurin, of Lowell, Massachusetts; Caroline, to the late Dr. Walter Simpson Harban, of Washington, D. C., a charming, kindly man, much loved and deeply mourned by us all; Francis Montgomery, to Miss Bettina Beach, of St. Petersburg, Florida. I gratefully record the fact that they are all related, with more or less activity, to the dear Church that has placed my family for four generations under such incalculable obligation. Ten grandchildren, seven boys and three girls, have rekindled the sense of parenthood and refreshed the springs of life.

Although the above words may lead to filial scolding, I know that my sons and daughters would wish me to give especial tribute to Anna Louise, who was born at Greencastle, Indiana, February 11, 1907, and passed to the life eternal from San Francisco on February 7, 1937. As was meet, she left this earth almost in sight of the Golden Gate. We fought gallantly for her life through her three decades. When she married a splendid young physician, Dr. Mayo H. Soley, graduate of the Harvard Medical School, he joined us in the loving effort to prolong her days. Always frail, her last four years were a constant struggle—with gains made and then canceled. She did not know the ritual of complaint. Her invariable reply to solicitous questions was, "Fine." When I told her on the day before her death that God would take good care of her, in whatever world, her response was, "He always has, Daddy dear."

She felt that she lacked the graces of a lovely appearance; but she surely did have what the Psalmist called "the beauty of holiness.' Her hair was of the auburn tinge that poets have loved. I used to lure her into the sunshine that streamed through the window, in order that I might see the beams of light weaving golden beauty about her young head. Once, when she discovered my proud purpose, she had her moments of rapture because one dear to her felt that she had glory in her looks. After her passing I read Mark Twain's "Jean." My faith would have added much to his comfort about his afflicted child; yet what he wrote about the beautiful "majesty of death" was true of Anna Louise.

She hinted to me on our journey back to California that her visit to her sick mother, and to us all, might claim her life, but that the affectionate experiences were worth the final cost. Through those anxious days in Washington her brothers contested for the privilege of carrying her up the stairway of the earthly home. The Heavenly Father soon completed the journey by taking her up another ascent into the joy and peace of his own House.

Though she graduated with honors from DePauw University and had a wonderful European tour, the journey from the Greencastle of her birth to the Greencastle of her burial seemed so short. I shall be forgiven readily if in these pages I give her a bit of earthly memorial. I have never known a braver young soul. All our cares and anxieties for her found a rich reward in her love. We received her in gladness; carried her in proud affection; and at the end of the triple decades were grateful to Heaven that we were hers, and that she was ours. The courageous faith that sustained her on the path of weakness never failed. When at length her wee craft swept into the Eternal Harbor, the Saviour saw her tiny flags of bravery flying still, waiting to catch the breeze from the Shores of Peace. Her only natural dwelling place is with the good. The

Everlasting Arms are her refuge, even as they are our consolation.

The mother lay in piteous helplessness in Washington when her daughter took voyage for the final Haven from San Francisco's harbor. Knowing that we could not have months of pretense, and feeling that my wife had the reserve of heroism, I counseled by telephone that my preacher-son should tell her the story of woe. The maternal instinct had prepared her heart. Ere three sentences had made the approach, she said: "You need go no farther. I know what has happened. My little white pigeon has flown away from me." Ere crimson leaves came the second time mother and daughter met once more. My faith has often seen them holding the hands of the wee sister and brother who took their flight in the long ago.

The writing of this record was suddenly interrupted by another telephone message saying that little Stephen, son of Francis, had made a stay of less than a fourth of a year in this land. He was the first to break the circle of the grandchildren. So three generations sleep together in the Greencastle Cemetery. For me the final shadows will disappear, not because they are merged into darkness, but rather because they are banished by the radiance that shines for the Redeemed Family.

CHAPTER XIII

UNIFICATION

THE PURPOSE OF THIS ACCOUNT IS NOT TO GIVE A HISTORY of unification, but to make a contribution to unification. The value of the pages will come not from their formal accuracy of record, but from their affectionate interpretation of a gracious merger. Another mind will make the researches necessary for an exact story. Indeed, the same fingers that set the type for this volume and the same machines that impress these pages, may be working contemporaneously on Bishop John Monroe Moore's historical presentment of the tragedy of separation and the glory of reunion.

I. ALIENATION

Inasmuch, also, as the 1828 and 1844 divisions long preceded my birth, and the earlier endeavors for unification preceded my maturity, the autobiographical years of the movement were not many. The gate through which I have repeatedly gone in order that I might witness the scenes of separation has never been an inviting one for me. The Methodist Protestant division in 1828 had its harsh episodes. Expulsion of a group meant the exodus of the many. The main debate did not center around episcopacy, but around lay representation. This meant that the progress of democracy would make the issue less and less. Nor did the contention give room for such lastingly bitter feeling as the later separation entailed. If with an occasional individual of the Methodist Protestant constituency there came later an antibishop mood, this represented a personal development rather than the initial difference of opinion. The more than a century of the separation had removed the issue. The larger bodies had gradually provided by law for lay participation. A wall that has been removed is no longer an effective partition. The ties within the fellowship of the Methodist Protestant people had their own appeal and were more of a kindly hindrance to union than was the original cause of separation.

The division of the Church in 1844 sent into the future a heavier freight of feeling. On the Northern side Dr. Charles Elliott was the first recorder of the "Secession." However well written his pages may be, both the provocative title and the more than eleven hundred controversial pages make a literary battle. The intense war of principles may have upon one something of the effect of a battle which, seen from a safe hilltop, still adds to life's sadness. J. Nelson Norwood's treatise, *The Schism in the Methodist Episcopal Church, 1844,* is admirably done. Its abundant references and footnotes indicate research, while its impartial tone adds to its value. Dr. Norwood is not a Methodist. The motives that led him to write the monograph, accepted by the faculty of Cornell University as a thesis for the degree of Doctor of Philosophy, would make an interesting study. Perhaps a worthy outsider could do this work better than an insider on one side of the controversy who was necessarily an outsider on the other side! There is a civic parallel. One of the best interpretations of our own country is Lord Bryce's *The American Commonwealth,* while one of the best interpretations of Lincoln is Lord Charnwood's admirable biography. President Norwood's pages make us grateful by their historical care, but they make us sorrowful by their story of passion.

Once more, I received an inheritance of tragedy. The mention of the year 1844 always sobered my father. The date for him meant just one thing—the calendar of separation. He was only eight years old when the General Conference met in New York City as one body, and marched out at the close to make two bodies. He would have admitted all the twinhood that became the South's claim. None the less, 1844 gave him the same sense of ecclesiastical tragedy that 1861 gave to him as a form of civic tragedy. He would have clad both of the years in mourning.

I declare, too, that the event of 1844 never made me desire to debate. It was all grief. I was far away from the division that in 1828 had led to the formation of the Methodist Protestant Church. Nor was there in the family life any counterpart of that division. In 1844 and in 1861 my two sets of grandparents were in opposite camps. I have sometimes said half-jokingly that God did not dare to allow my two grandmothers to meet each other. They were both Methodist class-meeting characters; but if their sessions had related to the causes of separation, the result would not have been a Love Feast. This double domestic background was helpful to the reunion of the churches. One other episcopal member of the Joint Commission had a like qualification. By a family relationship, as well as by a residence, Bishop Frederick Deland Leete had an equipment of experience that made his wisdom wiser and his sympathy more sympathetic. The danger in negotiations would naturally come from a Southerner who could not understand the North or from a Northerner who could not understand the South. The unmitigated sectionalist could scarcely be a success in harmonizing the sections. A blind Isaac is not a good judge when the birthright of two sons is before the court.

There are not found many items of humor in the long

agitation. Occasionally there is a dim gleam. Bishop Waugh was presiding over the New England Conference, and was seeking to prevent the introduction of an anti-slavery resolution. Many of the members felt, not only that the right of petition was being cancelled, but that they were denied a privilege exercised by other Annual Conferences. Orange Scott was on hand with a burning conscience, making efforts to put through a paper embodying the conviction that had already caused him heavy strain, and loss of friendships. He failed again, being much aggrieved. As a kindly overture, the Bishop called on Scott to close the session with singing and prayer. Not feeling deeply pious, the redoubtable Abolitionist declined to lift either tune or petition. The Bishop then tried another vigorous antislavery man, Jotham Horton, who started the hymn,

> Come on, my partners in distress,
> My comrades through this wilderness.

The truth in the grim humor is that "distress" and "wilderness" were really descriptive words. The agitation offers few events of laughter. One who tries to find in the accounts pleasantries that will relieve the gloom has slight rewards. The Church moved from sadness to sadness.

At last 1844 came. The General Conference met in Green Street Church, New York City. Thirty-six Conferences were represented by one hundred and eighty delegates. There were few young men. Even those who were at middle age looked venerable. The New York papers were much impressed by a kind of saintly adulthood in the body. One would have prophesied that these chosen representatives would find a path out of the dreadful dilemma, if such a path existed. The list of delegates shows impressive names—Stephen Olin, Nathan Bangs,

John P. Durbin, Charles Elliott, Jesse T. Peck, James Porter, Matthew Simpson, Phineas Crandall, L. L. Hamline, Henry B. Bascom, A. B. Longstreet, William Winans, William Capers, George F. Pierce, J. B. McFerrin, Lovick Pierce, William A. Smith—and the picturesque Peter Cartwright. Thirteen of the delegates subsequently became bishops. Any study of the personnel would have indicated a stanchness for which the "stonewall" figure of speech would have been apt.

II. Separation

The issues quickly moved to personal centers. Francis A. Harding had been suspended by the Baltimore Conference for refusing to manumit slaves that came into his possession by marriage. He carried an appeal to the General Conference. After eager debate, the body affirmed the action of the Baltimore Conference. The delegates felt that this case was a skirmish. They must have recognized, also, that the vote of 117 to 56 was a prophecy of the outcome of the episcopal case. The two issues were remarkably alike—the pleas with reference to marriage, the state laws concerning the freeing of slaves, and the aspects of personal duty being most similiar.

The bishop who was the center of the second controversy was a mild and kindly man. He had often preached to the Negroes and was their friend. The previous history of James O. Andrew would prove that his symbol was the peaceful dove rather than the stormy petrel. The quiet grave plot that holds his dust at Oxford, Georgia, is far more like his nature than was the turbulent scene in the New York church. If Bishop Andrew did not foresee that his matrimonial ownership of slaves would become a warm issue, we have proof of his naïve character. Yet accounts agree that the agitation which raged around him brought him great surprise. Evidently his episcopal duties had been irksome. He had sincerely thought of resigning months before the slavery issue focused on himself. Southern friends felt that a resignation would be a betrayal of their section and their cause. His sorrowful letter to his daughter reveals his fear that his withdrawal from office would gravely injure the Church in the South. It was the dilemma of Scylla and Charybdis. The rocks waited in either direction—bitter disappointment among his own people, or bitter feeling among the Northern contenders. So this pacific man made a decision not unlike the choice that Robert E. Lee made seventeen years later.

Considering the discussion as a whole, the phrase "more in sorrow than in anger" seems appropriate. After the Harding decision, Editor Lee of the Richmond *Christian Advocate,* knowing that the outcome meant division, still wrote, "There is no unkindness, no anger, in the body." This same Editor, after a Sunday spent in a New England town, gained a charitable interpretation. "The truth is Northern Methodism stands on the crater of a heaving volcano. . . . . If they move forward they destroy the unity of the Church; if they sit still they destroy themselves." The line of cleavage indicated that both parties had been imprisoned in their convictions. Geography does make chains. Occasionally a spirit of strong independence can break them. But the vigorous tendency both North and South had been toward cohesiveness. The separating lines in the Green Street Church were miniatures of the strict borders that were to be drawn two decades later in the nation.

The sorrow of Bishop Andrew as the unwilling focus of the trouble was characteristic of the group. The ablest speech on the Southern side was made by Dr. Augustus B. Longstreet of Georgia. Sad eloquence on the Northern side is found in the address of Stephen Olin. He was president of a New England college, Wesleyan; but he had earlier been president of Randolph-Macon College in Virginia. His heart knew the experiences of the two parties. He was not glaring at opponents on the other side of a chasm. He had lived among both contenders. To the South he said, "The men who stand here as Abolitionists are as ardently attached to Methodist Episcopacy as you all." They "seem to you to be arrayed in a hostile attitude," but they "have suffered a great deal before they have taken their position, and they come up here distressed beyond measure, and disposed, if they believed they could, without destruction and ruin to the Church, to make concession."

To the North he said:

With regard to our Southern brethren, ... if they concede what the Northern brethren wish . . . . they may as well go to the Rocky Mountains as to their own sunny plains. The people would not bear it. They feel shut up to their principles on this point. . . . . But if our difficulties are unmanageable, let our spirit be right. If we must part, let us meet and pour out our tears together; and let us not give up until we have tried. . . . . If we push our principles so far as to break up the connection, this may be the last time we meet. . . . . I see no way of escape.

There is preserved a marble-topped table used by the presiding officers of that General Conference. It is broken across the center and remains a pitiful memento—because the gavel employed to still the stormy debate made the cleavage. The broken table was the token of broken hearts. When Dr. Olin completed his speech, waves of grief dashed upon the delegates. Men that had faced the frontiers without a tremor yielded to the blasts of sorrow. Eyes that had looked unafraid at rough mountains and boiling rivers gave themselves to tears. Dr. Olin was right. There was "no way of escape." But there were two

269

ways of concentration and service. So the delegates departed. They "went forth weeping, bearing precious seed." Almost a century was to pass ere they should return for the Harvest Home, "bringing their sheaves with them."

III. CONCILIATION

There was, however, a surcease of sadness. The address of Dr. Olin left a remainder of hope, as it certainly left a remainder of kindness. When it became plain that a cleavage was inevitable, a representative committee was appointed to prepare a Plan of Separation. The full reading of the document does give prophecy of an amicable division. But the scheme needed the continued accompaniment of Olin's speech and spirit. The cold print was not as persuasive as was his warm heart. In addition, the terms were loosely defined. Border lines, even of a geographical nature, were not surely fixed; while border lines of a more subtle kind were blurred. The word "Separation" overwhelmed the word "Plan." The spirit of division went out and found seven other spirits, and they took up residence in both of the houses. The discussion was pulled into the constitutional realm. Voting to change the sixth restrictive rule began; but, as it moved from Conference to Conference, majorities favorable changed to majorities unfavorable—so that the three-fourths figure was not attained. The debates augmented the strife—and the grief. Ramparts of ice were builded between the two groups.

I was brought into the final swirls of this agitation. In 1883 my father was appointed as pastor of the First Church, Parkersburg, West Virginia. That town had been one of the fiercest focal points of contention. Eighteen years after the War of 1861-65, Parkersburg Methodism had not achieved calm. The "Northern" and "Southern" churches

270

were geographical neighbors, but they had not yet become neighbors in the deeper sense. All my remembrance of the inherited irritations gives me an increased admiration for my preacher-father. He had left the camp of his parents and had conscientiously denounced slavery and disunion. Now with equal conscience he moved into the camp of conciliation. He became a partner of the Church, South, pastor. If they did not live as David and Jonathan, they did attain a lasting friendship. That friendship made its gentle contribution to peace. With the exception of a few stubborn dwellers in the old days, the members yielded to love. Such ferocity as my heart gathered out of boyish debates was stilled by my parent's spirit. He bequeathed to his intense children no measure of scorn.

The Parkersburg situation was typical—a local example of a wide turmoil. For a long period the best plan of separation was a discussion of the Plan of Separation! The effort at union caused disunion. Threats against so-called interlopers included an irreligious immersion in a pond on the Eastern Shore, and a garb of tar and feathers in West Virginia—though both of these humiliations were avoided by a nimble resort to the itinerancy. Questions of the right of assembly; and of the ownership of churches and parsonages, and of the allotment of Book Concern equities, and of annual proceeds—all became involved in the melee. They passed on at last to the consideration of civil courts.

Nothing could be more vain than to rediscuss the issues. The heavier legal decisions were against the Northern contestants. Later arbitrations agreed upon settlement in the Book Concern case, thus giving the main claim of the Plan of Separation a valid standing. The North was not unanimous. The editor of the Pittsburgh *Christian Advocate* rejoiced at the outcome, declaring that the document embodied "real Christian sentiments" and was

271

"worthy to be printed in letters of gold." That the decision came to be deemed final is indicated by the fact that, in all the Joint Commission's conferences with reference to a Plan of Union, the Plan of Separation never became a subject of debate. The members knew that the central thing in the Plan was ecclesiastically settled by the Cape May Declaration, adopted on August 17, 1876. This document laid the only possible basis for reunion. It did away with all talk about the homeward "return of the wandering daughter," and used the word "branch" in the domestic sense rather than in the horticultural sense. Henceforth neither Church was represented by a limb torn by anger from the one recognized tree, but was "a legitimate branch" of the "one Methodist family." The unified hearthstone was distant, but it had become assured. The solid wall was making ready to become an open door.

IV. NEGOTIATION

The chapters of grief began to give way to chapters of joy. Progress toward union was slow, but it was steady. Often what seemed to be backward steps were later to be seen as real advances. If milestones may serve as a figure of speech, they may be described in paragraphs as follows:

1. The appointment of a Federal Council of Methodism by the two General Conferences of 1906 and 1908. Though this Council never succeeded largely in making local withdrawals and mergers, it did increase the spirit of federation as a prelude to union.

2. The amazing address of Dr. Thomas H. Lewis, president of the Methodist Protestant General Conference. Delivered at Baltimore in May, 1908, it brought a wholesome shame to the Methodist Episcopal General Conference, and added to that necessary repentance a splendid faith. Two paragraphs had a piercing effect. Speaking of his

272

people, President Lewis said: "When we think of going back home the question will recur insistently and painfully, 'Which home?' . . . . We are like children whose parents have separated. Do not force us to separate from each other in order that we may rejoin the family. We want to unite with a united home." The delegates trembled under that pathos. Later there came an offer that quickened our consciences. "We dare not ask it as an honor, but if it be required of us we bring all our treasure and lay all our identity upon the altar as a sacrifice; if we may but beat a drum or carry a flag, while Judah and Ephraim once more march on to the same music of peace, joyfully we will say, Amen, God wills it."

Who could resist such appeals? Lay representation had been settled. Indeed, the Methodist Protestants' relation to the merger can scarcely receive deserved recognition, because it had become so assured as to make meager debate. Yet they have a pivotal glory in the achievement.

3. The appointment of a Joint Commission which, in 1898, agreed to measures preventing competition and recommended the preparation of a common Hymnal, Catechism, and Order of Worship. By 1904 all this had received the confirmation of the General Conferences. A teaching, worshiping, and singing union was a preparation for a legal union.

4. In 1910, at the meeting of the Joint Commission in Asheville, North Carolina, there was submitted a statement of terms of union, written largely by the late Bishop Elijah Embree Hoss. If this statement be laid along the Plan of Union as finally adopted, the points of parallel will strikingly appear.

5. The article in the Nashville *Advocate* of March 3, 1911, in which John M. Moore gave a prophetic platform—followed at the next Southern General Conference

in 1914 by his report, adopted with only one major change.

6. A series of fraternal addresses which made great contributions to the steadily growing cause of unification. Read the lists: Albert S. Hunt, Charles H. Fowler, General Clinton B. Fisk, James A. Duncan, Chancellor L. C. Garland, Vice President Charles W. Fairbanks, Senator Jonathan P. Dolliver, John J. Tigert, Collins Denny, Frank M. Thomas, E. B. Chappell, W. A. Shelton, David G. Downey, Wallace MacMullen, William F. Oldham, Matthew Simpson Hughes, Merton S. Rice, William N. Ainsworth. I was the last, but by no means the climactic, visitor among these bearers of fraternity. One cannot complete the story without an effort to imagine the scene if Dr. Lovick Pierce had appeared at the General Conference of 1876. Refused an official reception in 1848, he was appointed to return twenty-eight years later. His selection by the Southern Church was not a matter of historical vengeance. His reception by the Northern Church would, however, have been taken as a glad opportunity to give a fairer form to the history of approaches. It was not to be. The grand old man, enfeebled by his long years, sent an affectionate letter as his substitute and added a loving paragraph to the story that had known one sorrow, and many joys.

V. APPROXIMATION

The first definite plan for union came from the Joint Commission appointed by the Methodist Episcopal and the Methodist Episcopal, South, General Conferences. This Commission began its work in 1916. Prior to that time some rather awkward efforts had been made. There were, also, covenants that united missionary work in Brazil, Cuba, Puerto Rico, and the Philippines—sectional unions that helped toward wider union. Yet the com-

274

missions that carried forward their work accomplished far more than the members could realize. In 1918 the representatives contributed a month of actual working time; and in that year the Church, South, by overwhelming vote continued its commission, with some change in personnel.

The Plan was given form in July, 1919. It provided for seven Regional Conferences in America, and for a Judicial Council; but left organization for foreign work to the General Conference. Agitation against the regional feature became distinct, and in some cases violent. It was evident at Des Moines in 1920 that opposition in the North made it inadvisable to submit the Plan to a constitutional vote, while definite questioning in the South added to the hesitation. Yet those who knew the sentiment at Des Moines were aware that the General Conference was all but unanimously favorable to union. Its suggestion to the Church, South, of a convention did not appeal to the Southern General Conference in 1922. That body, however, appointed a strong commission, while the Methodist Episcopal Church authorized the bishops to appoint a similar group. Thus, in 1922, I became officially identified with the movement and was to be so continued, save for a brief interlude, until the consummation.

I recall vividly the first meeting of the Joint Commission in Cincinnati, in January, 1923. Dr. Thomas D. Ellis proposed a Plan based on two Jurisdictions. I was a member of the committee to which this Plan was referred. After slight editing of the document, it was recommended to the Joint Commission for favorable action. The vote was 31 for; 3 against—one of the negatives being cast by my good and dear friend, Bishop Collins Denny.

This Plan was transmitted to the churches for constitutional decision. I presided over the General Conference at Springfield, Massachusetts, in 1924 when it approved the measure by a vote of 802 to 13. At a special session of the General Conference of the Church, South, at Chattanooga in July, 1924, the Plan was sent on to the Annual Conferences by a vote of 298 for, 74 against. The Annual Conferences of the Methodist Episcopal Church gave a majority for the Plan—of almost 96 per cent. The Church, South, Conferences gave a vote of 4,528 for, and 4,108 against the measure. This was a majority, but not a constitutional majority. I recall my elation over this result. Since a Plan that was far from perfect had received such endorsement, the dissidents in both churches had been informed that they were a minority. I had, too, seen so many instances among my Southern friends where the fathers had been against, and the sons had been for, the union, as to give assurance that the real battle had been won. The defeat was only apparent. The official figures convinced me that no man's hand could stay the inflowing tides of the Spirit. I had a subdued shout in my heart and a prayer of thanksgiving on my lips. I saw God's day, not distressingly afar, but gloriously near; and I rejoiced.

VI. REALIZATION

The day was even nearer than I thought. One of my great hopes had been to see union ere I joined the united hosts in heaven. While I was confident of the ultimate outcome, I had no assurance of dates. The General Conference of the Church, South, in 1926 wisely recommended that there be no agitation for the present. It appointed a committee, or commission, to consider all matters possibly involved, and to arrange for feasible exchanges of territory. The Methodist Episcopal General Conferences continued a commission with similar powers. This latter

commission negotiated with a Methodist Protestant commission. In 1928 the prospects for a merger of the *two*
Communions approached certainty.

The conditions indeed became so promising that they
created a new conscience. I had many interviews with
princely Bishop McDowell. We appreciated the causes
of Southern reluctance. One could overdraw the parallel
between the ecclesiastical conditions that resulted in the
division of the Church, and the political conditions that
almost resulted in the division of the Republic. The
parallel, however, is more interesting than it is useful and
pacific. Still, great statesmen saw in the Methodist cleavage a foretoken of a possible national cleavage. Daniel
Webster referred to it in his Seventh of March speech and
expressed "great concern." Henry Clay wrote to a friend
that the division was to be deplored on account of its
"political tendency," and as an "example" that "would
be fraught with imminent danger." On March 4, 1850,
John C. Calhoun made his farewell speech to the United
States Senate, declaring that "the strongest" of the cords
that bound the states together were those "of the great
religious denominations"; and that "the first of these
cords which snapped under the explosive force was that
of the powerful Methodist Episcopal Church." The civic
meaning of the division was apparent. The political
feelings constantly had their effect on the ecclesiastical
life. We who in periods long after 1861-65 went into the
South to deliver addresses and sermons discovered that
we had no reason for caution in our spiritual references.
Methodism remained a theological unit. Nor did the
nature of the episcopacy often call for treatment before
popular tribunals. Our care centered on political illustrations. We needed to be circumspect in the mention
of our heroes. But the decrease of sectional feeling was
making a steady contribution to the cause of church union.

Bishop McDowell and I both felt keenly that another ecclesiastical wedge should not be pushed into the South. There were already several wedges which might be roughly described as the Holston wedge, the St. John's River wedge, and the Oklahoma wedge. The Methodist Protestant Church had a fine constituency in North Carolina—approximately 30,000 members, with an excellent college at High Point. A Methodist merger that did not include the Church, South, would have completed a quartet of disconcerting wedges. This fractional union was not at all ideal. Our Methodist Protestant comrades shared this conviction. They were willing to be God's agents in fulfilling the prophecy of Dr. Thomas H. Lewis' Baltimore speech.

Then came the historic breakfast at Bishop McDowell's episcopal residence in Washington on June 18, 1934, preceded by a much earlier meeting where three representatives of each of the three churches had conferred prayerfully and had recommended to the General Conferences of 1932 and 1934 that they take "definite steps" for the union of the triple Methodisms. The preliminary service of Bishop Herbert Welch and Dr. John C. Broomfield in the Methodist Episcopal–Methodist Protestant negotiations had been most valuable. I was not at the time a member of the commission of my own Church. I felt that I ought not to be—for several reasons: (1) Bishop McDowell should, by all means, be a member. Two bishops from Washington seemed scarcely fair. (2) I believed strongly that Bishop Robert E. Jones should be a member, to represent his race. (3) I knew that Bishop Frederick D. Leete was needed in the conferences. (4) I had a conviction, also, that Wallace E. Brown of Chattanooga should represent our white constituency in the Southern states. I solicited several of my colleagues *not* to vote for me.

But Bishop Brown vigorously insisted that I must serve

278

in his place, affirming that he was not at all "adept in framing constitutions and by-laws." He declared that he would not be present at the commission meetings, and that I would neglect an actual duty if I did not attend. Later, he insisted that the Board of Bishops should elect me to the regular membership. So this affectionate colleague was responsible for what service I was able to render for unification. He was the first of the bishops of the united Church to enter heaven. I shall meet him there some celestial day and shall tell him again how greatly I appreciated his loving insistence.

On August 28, 1934, the three commissions met in Chicago. "Actual union" was set as the "goal" of all "deliberation and planning." A Committee of Fifteen, of which I was chosen chairman, was appointed for the study of basic materials. Our work moved forward so efficiently that at Louisville, Kentucky, on March 15, 1935, we were ready to make comprehensive reports to the full commission. No one of us expected that our plans could be developed so quickly. Who could then have foretold that in less than four years the Uniting Conference would be doing a service unparalleled in Christian history?

VII. Appreciation

It is not possible to assign credits to the members of the commissions. The chairmanship of each section was changed in the midst of the final negotiations. Bishop Edwin DuBose Mouzon, as majestic in mind as he was in appearance, passed to heavenly counsel in the chariot whose quick transit gave no chance for pain. Impressive as he was in his bearing, he was really a shy man in his social life. In my close relations with him I never knew him to boast of anything he had said or done. He had given incalculable service. God had provided for a worthy succession. Bishop John M. Moore had mastered the history of the separations and had culled from the records the points of emphasis for reunion. He served God day and night in the holy temple that made the vestibule for the sanctuary of unification. With an ever-busy pen he had prepared the paragraphs used as bases by several committees. His pockets were the filing places of possible legislation for the united Church. The careful historian became the accurate prophet. So well informed was he that he restrained himself at the door of committee rooms, lest he seem too forward. Yet the final action usually fell into the terms that he had worked out in day thoughts and night watches. As one who passed intimately through all phases of the movement, I declare that the angel of the record will be compelled to write the name of John M. Moore in golden letters.

I recall my poignant sorrow when I was informed that Bishop William Fraser McDowell had taken the one step necessary to cross the border into the Everlasting Country. Without any torture in a heart that had long been frail, he fell in a moment into the kindly arms of God. There was united to my personal grief a sense of burdensome responsibility. As I had been chairman of the Committee of Fifteen, and as I came next in episcopal seniority, I could scarcely escape a more distinct leadership in the crusade. Ere the sun went down on that day of my dear friend's death I had resorted to prayer and had promised God that if he would lead us to our goal, he himself could distribute all credits in justice and in love. Afterward I felt that my petition was like asking him to distribute the shares of the ocean.

I cannot adequately exalt Bishop McDowell's work in all endeavors for the merger. He did not enjoy details, yet he cared for them faithfully. In the broader ranges of our work he was a master. One of the members of an early Southern commission said that when Bishop Mc-

Dowell arose in his grand and simple way, pausing often as if he were searching for the phrases of diplomacy, he wondered what ruses were working in that episcopal mind. He found that there was no need for suspicion. I have no remembrance of anything said in the separate meetings of the Methodist Episcopal Commission that could not have been uttered in the presence of the members of the other two commissions. Out of the entire movement I carry no legacy of indirection or concealment.

One experience in the negotiations was memorable. The actual discussion of the race problem was neither lengthy nor prominent. It may have been more in the background than it was in the foreground. The two Negro commissioners, Bishop Robert E. Jones and President Willis J. King, admirably represented their group. I felt from the beginning that it would not be sportsman-like for the Methodist Episcopal following to demand racial legislation wholly beyond what we ourselves had given to our Negro constituency. In other respects we had to guard ourselves against efforts at reform through the process of reunion. Our commission was not set to remake the Church, but to reunite the Church. We were compelled to resist the good radicals who tried to slip into the government of the union Church provision for their favorite theories. The Methodist Episcopal Church actually had separate Negro churches, separate Negro Conferences, separate Negro Areas, a separate Negro *Advocate,* and two bishops elected by separate ballots from which votes for white ministers were excluded. These conditions had prevailed among us and had excited little controversy. Could we now demand that the union should go beyond what we ourselves had peacefully accepted?

My conscience, however, could not sanction a constitutional provision that hardened the racial question into a form utterly difficult to modify. I felt that the absence

281

of legal provisions as to racial standards for membership in all three of the negotiating bodies indicated the proper line for the unified Church. Yet the framing of an enactment that allowed this flexibility was not an easy task. We went to our couches one evening at Louisville with that problem unsolved. Bishop McDowell spent the night in Gethsemane. This statement is no irreverent exaggeration. He told me afterward that he lay in agonized wakefulness until five o'clock in the morning. His vigil was a long petition to God for guidance. The whisper came to him at last, "Boundaries." He arose from his bed and drew up the outline of legislation, not so difficult to change as a constitution, or so easy to change as an ordinary enactment—an outline protecting all Jurisdictions. Bishop Mouzon and his colleagues accepted the agreement. So we crossed that Rubicon. The hand that led us over the pass was that of Bishop McDowell. He felt devoutly that God had given him light. Often still I see his drawn and quivering face as he went to his room on that night—and the glowing countenance with which he came to me on the morning of his illumination.

Another significant change was made in the personnel of the commissions. Dr. John Calvin Broomfield's term as president of the Methodist Protestant General Conference had expired, and Dr. James Henry Straughn was elected as the successor. Meantime, to the great grief of us all, Dr. Albert Norman Ward had passed suddenly into the heavenlies. This college president had been one of the ablest of the commissioners. For one insistence he became marked. Whenever any proposal was advanced for a change in the episcopacy, he was at once on his feet, declaring that since the united Church would surely retain the episcopal office, we must not put a weakened form of it into our government. The debate usually stopped at that point. Under the Plan's provision, both Dr. Straughn and Dr. Broomfield were elected as bishops at the Uniting Conference in Kansas City—by the suffrage of the Methodist Protestant delegates. In the negotiations each was singularly qualified for his part—Bishop Broomfield for the aggressive work in the earlier months, Bishop Straughn for the kindly utterances that made him the final mediator of Methodist Protestant emphases. In the lengthy efforts for a united Methodism, God seemed to have specially qualified servants ready to meet the emergencies.

These paragraphs have departed a bit from the chronology. So much fine service was done by the commissioners that adequate acknowledgment would demand a volume. Dr. James R. Joy was ever ready with abundant knowledge and flawless diction. Dr. Harry E. Woolever and Dr. J. Lloyd Decell were admirable joint secretaries. As the presenter of the Plan, and of the resolution for its adoption at the Columbus General Conference, Dr. Woolever moved with faultless discretion. After election to the bishopric, Secretary Decell changed several tumults into calmness and by kindly poise and religious counsel brought skirmishes that might have become insurrections into the ranks of union. Coming late into the commissions, Bishops Arthur J. Moore and Paul B. Kern became invaluable counselors as to missionary organization. President Henry N. Snyder, of Wofford College, was an expert adviser in all educational provisions. Dr. Ernest H. Cherrington had made a study of the judicial system and became a leader in that phase of the planning. The extensive knowledge of both Northern and Southern interests helped Bishop Frederick D. Leete to give us charts against rocks and shoals, while his power of succinct statement, upon which Bishop McDowell often commented, added value to his service. As his administration of the Puerto Rico Mission necessitated his absence, Bishop Ernest G. Richardson resigned from the commission, with the hope that Bishop Edgar Blake might take his place. The bishops unanimously concurred and thus brought into the final counsels the mind that had been so influential in the former commissions, and that had been credited with the authorship of the jurisdictional scheme for the Conferences. Dr. Thomas D. Ellis was helpful beyond all possible statement, both as an active member of the body and as the matchless floor leader of the debate that preceded the final vote in the General Conference at Birmingham. As a courteous and effective example of parliamentary management, his work was never surpassed in all my observations. Dr. Frederic W. Mueller became our expert in charts, maps, and statistics, and gave visual arguments that were revealing. Although, at the last, ill health halted his work, the late Bishop William N. Ainsworth was incomparably helpful. His splendid plea for placing Kansas and Nebraska in the South Central Jurisdiction helped to offset the objection that Maryland, West Virginia, and Virginia were being dismembered and pulled away from their cherished nativities. Though not a member of the commission, the late Bishop Charles L. Mead, by the persuasion of his great and noble heart, scattered a splendid mood over Kansas and over other parts of the Kansas City Area. The all but unanimous votes for the Plan in his Conferences brought them into the union without dismay.

VIII. RATIFICATION

The time of voting was awaited with that strange feeling of certainty that is never quite certain. The Methodist Protestant section that Dr. Lewis had called little Benjamin surely did carry its flag and beat its drum. Twenty of the twenty-five Annual Conferences approved; and the General Conference gave a majority of 142 for, and a minority of 39 against, the Plan. These results were the more noble because they meant that after union there would not be an Annual Conference that had been predominantly of the old connection. Their approximate constituency of six hundred thousand suggested the heroism of the Six Hundred at Balaklava. The God of all spiritual battles will see to it that the life that thus lost itself will be gloriously saved.

In the Methodist Episcopal Church the voting process passed from the General Conference to the Annual Conferences. My episcopal colleagues generously changed the order of presidency and placed me in the chair when the question came to decision at Columbus, Ohio. The debate centered on the issue made by the Central Jurisdictional Conference for our Negro Annual Conferences and Missions in the United States. Overnight a shift of sentiment had been wrought among the Negro delegates themselves. There was, however, nothing like unanimity. While their major vote was against the separate Jurisdiction for Negroes, some of their wisest delegates heartily espoused that provision. When men like Matthew S. Davage, W. A. C. Hughes, Edgar A. Love, and Willis J. King favored a scheme that created the Central Jurisdiction, the disaster that some feared must have been measurably doubtful. In reality, the vote of the General Conference was never uncertain. The question mark related solely to the size of the majority; the only peril was that some foolish things might be said, or that some foolish resolution might be offered that would create confusion in the South. I tried to recognize the two sides equitably, giving opportunity to the strongest anti speakers, scattering recognitions with regard to geography, and avoiding giving the floor to two men from any one Conference. The opponents had one more speaker than did the proponents, and were given more time in the total discussion. I could later think of but one section that had not been given its

285

chance. As at times fully a hundred delegates were clamoring for the floor, only a careful plan of recognition with reference to sentiment and section could have provided for impartiality. I was gratified that after the vote was passed only two men felt that their divine rights had been thwarted. The vote was 470 for, 83 against. So far as the General Conference was concerned the issue was settled. The Plan was at once sent on to the Annual Conferences by the bishops. The results were:

	Lay	Clerical
For the Plan	6,747	10,195
Against the Plan	585	1,284

The outcome was graciously accepted by the conscientious minority.

In the Methodist Episcopal Church, South, the reverse constitutional procedure was followed. The Annual Conferences voted first—as follows:

For the Plan	7,650
Against the Plan	1,247

So the great question came to the General Conference at Birmingham, Alabama, for final judgment. Again my colleagues honored me by making me the fraternal delegate. I was present through the entire debate, my heart anxious and yet assured. I have already written of the grace and skill with which Dr. Thomas D. Ellis conducted the procedure of the unificationists; I add here that his speech closing the discussions was a masterpiece—forceful, and yet persuasive; confident, and yet pleading. The men who opposed the Plan's adoption were given the fullest liberty. They were not many, and some of them did not care to take the floor. Three things impressed me.

The first was the fact that no argument based on the War of 1861-65 appeared to have influence. It was invariably met with ripples of kindly laughter. The delegates did not intend to allow 1865 to dominate 1938. They loved their grandfathers, but they were voting for their grandsons. Posthumous polemics had lost their power. The cannons that thundered in the ruinous years from 1861 to 1865 could not defeat the persuasion of the still, small voice.

My second impression came from Bishop James Cannon's reply to the paper presented by my greatly admired friends, Bishops Candler and Denny. As Bishop Cannon claimed the floor I was sure that any reply to his colleagues would be a mistake. In this I was using faulty judgment. Evidently Bishop Cannon's paper had been meticulously prepared with an uncanny preview of what his episcopal partners would present. Without going into unfavorable comparison, I still declare that Bishop Cannon's response finely offset the presentment of his distinguished colleagues.

My third impression was gained from two speeches— one by a layman, Harry Denman, a deeply religious plea for the union of Christ's people. The second came from Dr. Clare Purcell. For reasonable listeners he did away with the Negro bogy—as he asked those who had hinted at the racial question to quote any legislation by the Methodist Episcopal Church, South, that had forbidden or regulated Negro membership in local churches or Annual Conferences, and as he declared that this problem remained, precisely as it had been in the past, subject to nonlegal influences that had kept a kindly sway since 1844. That brave speech crowned Dr. Purcell with deserved honors.

Soon the sonorous tones of Secretary Lud M. Estes were calling the votes. There was small need for bated breath. Every *Aye* vote made for me a Hallelujah. The *No* votes were so relatively few as not to make many interludes

between the Hosannas! The counting showed: for the
Plan, 434; against the Plan, 26. At once several of the *No*
voters expressed loyal acquiescence. The Conference dis-
persed in a solemn mood. As I started to the hotel to
make my body, rather than my mind and heart, ready
for the fraternal session of the evening, my spirit held
high the flag of truce that long before I had caught from
my father's hand. I felt that he marched with me on a
path that my feet had been seeking for more than thirty
years. I knew as I knelt in my room that a tall Methodist
preacher who had known little circuits and big circuits,
little towns and big towns, little stations and big stations,
a presiding elder's mountain district in West Virginia,
and another district on Iowa's prairies, was with me at that
altar of Thanksgiving, and that an earthly father's benediction joined the one that came to me from the Heavenly
Father.

CHAPTER XIV

CONSUMMATION

THE EVENTFUL DAY'S VOTING AT THE SOUTHERN GENERAL
Conference was followed by an able decision from the
Judicial Council as to the validity of the constitutional
procedure, and by a significant action that wiped out mis-
leading records of the past. As I met the delegates, between the legal session of the afternoon and the fraternal
session in the evening, I could discover no gathering
shadows of sentiment. There was a quiet and noble
jubilation, with no unfraternal attitudes toward the minority of twenty-six. I was impressed with the absence of
loudness. The more or less mythical "shouting Methodist" was not in evidence. The lobby of the big hotel
did not resound with the usual buzz. There came no hint
of boasting. Some men avoided speech because they
wished to avoid tears.

The spirit of devotion increased as the evening of
May 4, 1938, recorded the spiritual tides. Dr. James H.
Straughn and I were to bring greetings—fraternal delegates who were to have no successors. As the representative of the former Methodist Protestant Church, Dr.
Straughn acquitted himself with the utmost distinction.
His address was keen, appealing, scholarly. Ere he had
concluded, the assembly knew that our plucky tribe of
Benjamin had come into the wider Israel with worthy
leadership. The chaste language and the interpreting
of the acute meaning of union for his people would have
made the speech adequate for any great forum.

My own address had the merit of careful preparation. Indeed, I was trebly prepared. Some of my friends, I fear, doubted my word when I stated that I had written three speeches for the one occasion. One was to be given if the decision was against the Plan; one, if the decision was postponed; one, if the voting was in favor of union. I still have the copies of the speeches to be offered as proof. The delegates had often heard of a bishop's one speech prepared for three occasions; but three speeches made ready for one occasion offered an exception in episcopal behavior! The three manuscripts contained common material; yet each was ready for its own event.

The audience was wholly prepared. Its receptiveness was the product of at least two generations. In the best sense the listeners were atavistic! They could not hear the loud guns of a long-past war; they could hear the whispered prayers of long-past councils. The meeting had been called by countless summonses issued by the pious hearts of forebears. Bishops Hendrix and Cranston, Bishops McDowell and Mouzon, and Dr. Thomas H. Lewis seemed to be present. There was no uproar, though the evening had its own rushing wind; no flashing, though this Pentecost had its own tongues of fire. The accent was that into which we had all been born in Christ's Kingdom of Love. The audience seemed to me like a splendid composite, merged into quiet joy and steady hope. I knew that, even if I possessed any tricks of oratory, I did not need them. The combined vocabulary of the hour said to me: "We are together now—ready to yield ourselves in grateful response to your unifying mind and heart. We are yours, and you are ours, and we are all Christ's. He has brought us hither. We hear you in his Name."

So did I speak to them—at first with words of pleasantry, to ease us down from Dr. Straughn's high planes, and later

290

with sentences of longing for which my lips had waited through more than a third of a century. As I have reread the address I have had no special thrill of pride. It may be found in full in the Conference records. I quote only a few paragraphs.

We can affirm with gentle dogmatism that our Methodist people in America are the best-prepared people in Christendom for a unified life. Canadian Methodism united. English Methodism united. Japanese Methodism united. Mexican Methodism united. Korean Methodism united. Our sister Canada, known as the Lady of the Snows, showed us the path. Our mother, in the home over the seas, asked us to choose the merging road. Our children in the mission lands followed the example of the grandmother and the aunt; and they are now trying to bring us up in the way in which we should go! Over the world Methodism has shown a genius for union. Basing the religious life not primarily upon an intellect that argued, or a logic that formulated, or a psychology that researched, but upon an experience that felt and rejoiced, her sons have melted toward each other in unifying testimony. In no other land has a serious movement for Methodist unity failed. Heaven forbid!

God has given to us the deeper unity of a shared history. John Wesley's sermons and Charles Wesley's hymns remained as our mutual heritages. We did not have a divided glory in the ecumenical hearts of our earliest bishops. You might triple our organizations; you could not make our memories fractional. We might move away from each other in Atlanta or Philadelphia; but we came together in Aldersgate Street, our perpetual rendezvous. Two surveyors named Mason and Dixon were not as powerful as two horsemen named Coke and Asbury. As the tumult of a tragic record died we found our allegiances renewed in other Camp Grounds where the Lord of Hosts had built the altar.

Methodism has never known a theological separation. We have disagreed about bishops, but not about God. We have quarreled over earthly rulers, but not over the King of Kings. We have not been unanimous in admiration of military leaders, but we have been at one in our love for the Captain of our

291

salvation. No branch of Methodism has had a tribal God. Whenever any Northern or Southern Jacob has slept on a foreign hillside, the Spirit has given him a holy dream. The ladder with the ascending and descending angels has taught the impartiality of Heaven. We have reached the uttermost assurance that Bethel, "the house of God," is not geographical. Though the bases of the separating Churches seemed to be far apart on earth, we always found the uniting arch in the sky of the Redeemer.

We have had the unity of a shared character. It is simply inconceivable that Methodist theology, experience, and regime have worked to produce Northern saints and Southern rascals, or Southern saints and Northern rascals. The grace of God is not sectional, the love of Christ not determined by the compass. The Holy Spirit defies maps.

Are we to say that the past will not allow us to come together to fight a contemporaneous foe, but will demand that we remain apart because of an ancestral enemy? If any man may declare that my Southern Methodist grandmother failed of the genuine grace of God, I fear that I will fall from grace. He will fall somewhere else! Or shall any Southerner reverse the statement and apply it to my Northern grandmother? That, also, would be like blasphemy. I see those saintly women now. They both clasped me in arms of faith and committed me to Christ. They both sang me to sleep with the lullabies of God. They both testified to the grace of our Redeemer. They both stood in the Sanctuaries as with quavering accents they sang:

"Fade, fade each earthly joy;
    Jesus is mine.
Break every tender tie;
    Jesus is mine."

They would both adjure me that their graves should not be made an Armageddon. I shall someday find them waiting for me, their two hands clasped in reconciliation, and their other two hands stretched out in welcome. They will call me by some celestial diminutive and love me more for all endeavors to bring their Churches to the unified life which they themselves have reached. They will help me to complete the story with glad exclamations: "Glory be to the Father, and to the Son, and to the Holy Ghost. As it was in the beginning, is now, and ever shall be, world without end. Amen."

Let me add, as well, that when next I meet my father I shall tell him that the torn robe of Methodism has become like that taken from our Lord on Calvary—of one piece, woven throughout from top to bottom, a worthy symbol of a unified Methodist priesthood in the order of Christ. We now proclaim to the world that we have achieved the largest reunion of Christ's people that has ever been accomplished in the long history of Christendom. We send word to Wesley and Asbury and Coke, Simpson and Wilson, Cranston and Hendrix, Jesse Lee and Nicholas Snethen, Lewis and Ward, and Mouzon and McDowell, that a united land is now served by a united Methodism. Our three colonies have become a spiritual nation.

Do you say that we shall have our difficulties? Certainly. But God is mightier than all obstacles. Red Seas cannot defeat him. He will commission an Isaiah to say for him:

"When thou passest through the waters, I will be with thee; and through the rivers, they shall not overflow thee; when thou walkest through the fire, thou shalt not be burned; neither shall the flame kindle upon thee. For I am the Lord thy God, the Holy One of Israel, thy Saviour: .... Since thou wast precious in my sight, thou hast been honorable, and I have loved thee: therefore will I give men for thee, and people for thy life. Fear not: for I am with thee: I will bring thy seed from the east, and gather thee from the west; I will say to the north, Give up; and to the south, Keep not back: bring my sons from far, and my daughters from the ends of the earth."

This historic evening suggested again what I felt at the Methodist Conference in England. There are two parties for every address—the speaker and the audience. Sometimes the question is whether the speaker can lift the listeners to his level. Frequently, however, the question is the reverse: Can the audience lift the speaker to its grade of exaltation? The latter question belonged to the Birmingham General Conference. My gratitude is due to the hearers who on that never-to-be-forgotten evening glorified ordinary words and gave them a place in the lexicon of Love. After the addresses and the closing word of Bishop John M. Moore, the three chairmen of the Joint Commission clasped hands; and a photograph that became a flashlight symbol of Unification was hung in a gallery of remembrance.

It may be anticlimax to write of another fact. My right hand had not completed its work. The benediction being pronounced, the crowds swarmed toward the platform. With Northern energy and with Southern fervency, former Methodist Episcopal, Methodist Episcopal, South, and Methodist Protestant adherents did some general hand-clasping. My crushed and blistered fingers ceased to function for three full days. My left hand was compelled to find out what my right hand was in the habit of doing.

The jubilancy soon claimed two worlds. When at last I was alone in my room at the Tutwiler Hotel, two colleagues seemed to hail me from another Land. Bishop Earl Cranston had often been as a relative of my heart, and I had called him "Uncle Earl." When my own father went away I fled to my senior for comfort. I had had, also, an elder brother in unification, Bishop William Fraser McDowell. In the patience of long years he had worked toward this "mark of the prize." From the lobby of the hotel the glad conversation came up to my windows. But I heard other voices speaking from afar, not asking that "three tabernacles" should be builded, but rejoicing that the "three" had become one. As I mourned that they were not with me on that holy mount, I rejoiced greatly that my faith beheld them on Pisgah's height as they gazed over into the Promised Land whither they had so gloriously urged the hosts out of the wilderness into Canaan.

The movement for union was still to have a legislative climax. The Plan had provided for a Uniting Confer-

ence, whose work was to unite the three *Disciplines* into
an official manual of law. This Conference was to be
like Melchizedek, without ancestors or descendants—a lonely unit in the Church's life. The Joint Commission appointed commitees to prepare detailed plans for combined
law. These committees worked under the leadership of
chairmen, or joint chairmen. The task of the Committee
on Missions and related interests was arduous. The kindly
and efficient attitudes of Mrs. Thomas Nicholson, president of the Woman's Foreign Missionary Society, and
of Mrs. W. H. C. Goode, president of the Woman's Home
Missionary Society, were helpful beyond description.
Probably their two societies were unsurpassed in accomplishment among all like organizations in the world.
Wholly without their statement, anyone with imagination could understand their approach to anguish as they
yielded to such grave modifications. Mrs. J. W. Perry,
of the Church, South, and Mrs. J. W. Shell, of the Methodist Protestant group, toiled sincerely for some compromise for the woman's work and aided in a constructive
outcome.

The Committee on Publishing Interests faced questions dealing with historic locations and with denominational organs that had become endeared to thousands of
people. Here the skilled co-operation of the late Dr.
George C. Douglass, Dr. B. A. Whitmore, Dr. Fred D.
Stone, and Mr. William C. Perkins, and the patient industry of Bishop H. Lester Smith, resulted in amicable
plans. In the Committee on Conferences the service of
Bishop A. Frank Smith was, like that rendered on the
Joint Committee, always broad and fine-spirited; while
Bishop W. W. Peele evinced the wise kindliness that had
made him efficient in the counsels of the former Church,
South. The intricate details of Superannuate Support
were cared for by a committee moving under the guidance

of Bishops Ernest L. Waldorf and Urban V. W. Darlington, the latter the senior effective bishop of the Church,
South, whose magnanimous attitude toward unification
as it affected West Virginia was most sportsmanlike.

The delegates from the three former bodies had been
chosen by as many different methods. I had, at Bishop
McDowell's request, framed the plan of selection of the
Methodist Episcopal representatives. It had been approved and adopted by the Columbus General Conference.
It provided for a sufficient group of delegates-at-large to
give to the foreign fields a proportioned number chosen
from persons temporarily in the United States, and to give
a balancing effect to the elections from the Annual Conferences.

I looked forward to the Uniting Conference with acute
anxiety. It met in Kansas City, Missouri, on April 26,
1939. Its opening had a proper pageantry, the march
from the cathedral to the auditorium, and the advance of
the bishops to the platform under the kindly announcement of Judge Leslie J. Lyon, being striking features. I
knew that preparations had been thorough, but I knew,
as well, that serious obstacles might come as surprises. As
senior effective bishop of the Joint Commission, it fell
to my lot to preside at the opening session. The planned
program was carried through, including the admirable
Episcopal Address as read by Bishop John M. Moore. The
Conference was fortunate in its selection of chairmen for
the general standing committees, as the list indicates:
John R. Mott, George W. Henson, W. F. Bryan, Oscar T.
Olson, Alfred M. Landon, Thomas S. Brock, Orien W.
Fifer, Paul W. Quillian.

The careful industry of the preliminary committees
conquered all complications. Perhaps it was a conceited
expectation that led me to fear that I would be "pulled
and hauled" by pressure for counsel—as I had been "on the

296

inside" of the several years' planning. Yet I really lived
a fairly normal life and found myself day after day thanking God that my forebodings were not being realized. A
sentence from the account of the first great Christian
Council often occurred to my grateful heart: "It seemed
good unto the Holy Ghost, and to us." No delegates in
church history ever exhibited a more zealous consecration or moved to their goals with wiser tread than did the
members of that Uniting Conference.

The record is in a big journal. Yet formal paragraphs
can give no full impression of the thrilling toil that builded the road for the new Church. The adjournment came
earlier than was expected, due to the steady purpose of
the gathering. I was chosen on Monday to deliver the
closing address on Wednesday evening. The time for
preparation was brief. I worked through the days and
the two nights in an effort to prepare a worthy valedictory.
Bishop Blake preceded me, giving cameo sketches of "the
heroes of unification"—Dr. Thomas H. Lewis and Bishops
Hendrix, Cranston, Mouzon, and McDowell—as their pictures were cast upon a great screen.

The last likeness shown was that of Bishop McDowell,
so characteristic as to be lifelike. I was surprised into
an overwhelming emotion. The kindly applause of the
vast audience gave me time to recover from what might
have been a breakdown. I moved through my address
without elation or depression. When I came to the refrain that was really its theme, "The Methodists are one
people," I had a sense of reverent upswing, but no feeling
of the seventh heaven of speech. I was wholly unprepared
for the appreciation that came at the close, and which
was renewed in personal greetings when the benediction
was given. The total program made, without the address,
the greatest religious service I have ever attended. I
shall not experience its equal in the earthly future and

must wait for its superior until I see the white-robed throng and hear the Song of Moses and the Lamb.

It is never easy to recapture the emotion of an epochal hour. I was again debtor to a great occasion. A mighty past and a wonderful present became my helpers. The disciple on the Mount of Transfiguration must not deprive Moses and Elias of holy credit. Nor must he claim that he was responsible for the radiant face and the glistening garments. A thousand human agents from days far gone joined those in the Kansas City Auditorium, while One Sacred Presence became central among the crowds that terraced the room. The praises evoked by the address have often made me glad; they have never made me proud. I believe that what I said was what the Conference did. Many have urged that the utterance should be printed in this autobiography. Limited space forbids the full meeting of that request. The reader's imagination must supply the throbbing accompaniments that lifted the words to the peak of the Great Event. The following paragraphs are given:

This gathering is no extemporized event. If all who have wrought and prayed to make it possible should come here, we should have an audience many times larger than this. The building itself would plead for more room, while all the approaching streets would be made dense with visitors from the shadowy lands of God's other countries. We reached the altar by reverent kneeling at thousands of altars. The worship of millions of Christ's people has been concentrated here in this city, now made more truly historic. Not only have the great leaders whose faces have just been flashed upon our grateful memories brought service to this shrine, but their minor comrades in the long crusade have by countless supplications made this place the depository of their hopes and the goal of their endeavors. On this night our century plant comes to the glory of its bloom. We have waited patiently for the Lord; and he hath brought this thing to pass. Praise be to his holy name!

Some strange and lovely thing happened in our glorious

Communion service. It was as if the Lord himself were insti-
tuting for us anew the holy supper—of his remembrance, and
his companionship. We placed our *problems* at the foot of
the Cross. We were conscious of a Saviour great enough to
carry our burdens, and also to make us more nearly equal to
our sacred responsibilities. We came from that hour in
triumph. The procession that moved toward these doors
stepped to the music of victory. Our fears had been left in
the cathedral, in the care of God; our hopes came with us to
the auditorium, in the same care.

One illustration has occurred to me many, many times—a
parable gained from earth's roadways. Often as we look
ahead we see the rising hill that our automobile must conquer. We wonder whether it has the power to climb those
steeps. Yet as we move onward some miracle worker seems to
bring the ascent to the level of our powers, and we capture
the heights.

We have here discovered the secret of our future. Hundreds have said, "If we can carry to our people the atmosphere
of this gathering, unification will succeed beyond all compare."
We must be the ambassadors of this spirit. The future may
be spoiled by the mood of fear, or it may be glorified by the
mood of love. To the cultivation of that love we challenge
our companions in the faith. In all our problems the Lover
has been the Solver.

St. Paul seized the heart of his Lord's teaching and, showing us "the higher talents," showed us, too, the path that is
still higher, even the "more excellent way." He said that it
was better than eloquence, higher than knowledge, more important than the power to fathom mysteries. He made it
loftier than faith that could move hills from their bases,
more worthy than a stubborn and devoted sacrifice that surrendered the living body to the flames. He said that it is "very
patient, very kind"; "knows no jealousy"; "makes no parade";
"gives itself no airs"; "is never rude, never selfish, never ir-
ritated, never resentful"; "is gladdened by goodness"; "always
eager to believe the best"; ever "hopeful." Above the wreck
of worlds he saw its banner flying. He epitomized its con-
quests in the unwavering claim, "Love never faileth." If that
spirit has made our Conference successful, it can empower all
our coming programs whether of inner spirits or of outer

299

service. So we may repeat each to the other, and each to himself, the apostolic command, "Make love your aim."

We have not lost our old churches. They are the portable treasures that we bear into the larger associations. We have more people to love, and more kinds of people to love, and larger areas for our harvests of love. We find our lips uttering in affection the new name, "The Methodist Church," glad that the scorn that once made it an epithet yields to the tribute that recognizes two centuries of service.

Certainly the larger present, held in the days of this Conference, has seen the flow of our hearts toward union. This feeling has made its own slogans. Many have sought to make a fitting frame of words for the spirit of this Conference. Some have found themselves repeating the title of Professor Garber's book, *The Methodists Are One People*. Any unconscious attempts to discount, or check, or cancel that feeling have met resistless torrents of conviction. Looking upon the mingling of many nations, upon the meeting of the cross currents of a wide internationalism, we have uttered the words, "The Methodists are one people." Gazing with curious interest upon the racial composite, black, brown, yellow, and upon other colors not known among the primary rays, we have felt that God wrote in the rainbow across the skies, "The Methodists are one people." Knowing that here were gathered men holding all political opinions and advocating the several theories of government, we have all come to believe so strongly in this merging program as to win from our lips the cry, "The Methodists are one people." Beholding the changes in law according to which our women's societies came into a new alignment and remembering that loyal women have given us the best missionary organizations known on earth today, and yet now yield to other plans, we have politely said across the gentle barriers of sex, "The Methodists are one people." Made aware of a line once drawn by two surveyors named Mason and Dixon, and kindly regarding the differing emphases that have been fashioned by the years lived in the memories of Lincoln and of Lee, we have waved the banner, "The Methodists are one people." Amid all the clashing of temperaments, the cool statements of deliberation, and the fervencies of more eager debate, wherein Peter and James and John funded their varying dispositions, we have still declared, "The Methodists

300

are one people." Listening to three episcopal groups and
bringing into the circle of the Northern and Southern bishops
the Methodist Protestant twins, we have in differing accents
known how to pronounce the motto, "The Methodists are one
people." Carrying hither the loyal remembrances of our
spiritual forefathers, touchingly recalling the sacrificial lives
and loves of our nearer religious ancestry, we have done away
with the Jericho walls between our camps by trumpeting the
challenge, "The Methodists are one people." Gazing upward toward another world whose portals have opened to
Snethen and Lewis, Capers and Andrew and Haygood and
Hendrix, Ward and Mouzon, and Cranston and McDowell,
we have sent over wireless waves the message to the unified
hosts of heaven, "The Methodists are one people." Moving
reverently into the sacred precincts of the seventeenth chapter of John's Gospel and listening to the praying voice of the
Redeemer himself as he speaks to the Father concerning the
disciples of his earthly ministry and his disciples in this room:
"Neither pray I for these alone, but for them also which shall
believe on me through their word; that they all may be one,"
we have answered the petition of the beseeching Christ by saying, "The Methodists are one people."

Is it any wonder then that we have been lifted toward a
seventh heaven, and that we have known something more of
the mystical glory wherein one declares: "I looked, and, behold, there was a great host whom no one could count, from
every nation and people and tribe, standing before the throne
and before the Lamb, clad in white robes, with palm branches
in their hands; and they cried with a loud voice, 'Saved by
our God who is seated on the throne and by the Lamb.' And
all of the angels surrounded the throne and the Presbyters
and the four living Creatures, and fell on their faces before
the throne, worshipping God and crying, 'Even so. Blessing
and glory and wisdom and thanksgiving and honor and
power and might be to our God forever and ever. Amen.' "

This matter is too sacred for any literary climax. We must
now transfer it to the rhetoric of action. We have been on
the mountain of transfiguration where we have met the law-
giver and the prophet, and the Master himself. We must go
forward into the mightiest and most constructive movements
that Methodism has ever promoted in the name of Christ.

We must say to sinners that we know a saving Name. We must pray, and pray, and pray! We must evangelize, and evangelize, and evangelize! We must carry a throbbing gospel beyond all rivers, and plains, and deserts, and mountains, and oceans. In the program of redemption, inspired by our Lord, we must go on with the proclamation of grace until the last sinner against the infinite mercy of the Most High lays down his arms of mutiny and cries out, "Nay, but I yield, I yield; I can hold out no more." All this we do—"for the dear Redeemer's sake. Amen."

The Service of Declaration moves onward through a ritual of majesty. The myriad voices proclaim:

To The Methodist Church thus established we do now solemnly declare our allegiance, and upon all its life and service we do reverently invoke the blessing of Almighty God.

The honor of making the motion to adopt the Plan falls to Judge Horace H. White, of Louisiana, a beloved veteran of the cause of union. The seconds are given by Dr. James R. Joy, whose untiring labors for many years won him affectionate credit, and Judge Harry Shaw, of West Virginia, a commissioner who represented the Methodist Protestants with quiet wisdom. Ten thousand people hold high their right hands, pledging devotion to the Church of today and tomorrow. At 8:59 by the clock, Bishop John M. Moore puts the motion for the final adoption. The affirming delegates are on their feet— many of them casting a ballot that grateful tears baptized. The negatives are called for; and Bishop Moore utters three words that make the grand drama complete—

"NO ONE STANDS."

The greatest reunion of Christ's people in all the long history of our faith has been consummated. "The Methodists are one people." Far more than "ten thousand times ten thousand" make a jubilee on earth and in heaven. The Saviour sees the travail of his soul and is satisfied.

CHAPTER XV

REFLECTIONS

THERE USED TO HANG IN ONE OF MY ROOMS A PICTURE known for genuine artistry, and entitled "Lost Illusions." The principal figure was that of an aged man, with bent form and white hair. He sits sadly upon a seashore, while a boat is about to bear away from him the lovely dreams that he once carried in his heart. Music, and joy, and courage, and peace, and hope are all forsaking him now, leaving only a loneliness that is to become more lonely. His sun is going down in frowning clouds, and not in golden glory.

The painting gave me a negative comfort because it was so utterly untrue to my experience. The illusions of youth have not departed. On the contrary they have been enhanced. The promise about the light in the evening time is precisely true. Having passed through all the stages of the ministry, and being now in the last stage, I rejoicingly witness that my spirit knows no disillusionment. Edmund Waller put it wisely and truly when he gave a poetic version of the Apostle's statement, "Though our outward man perish, yet the inward man is renewed day by day":

> The soul's dark cottage, battered and decayed,
> Lets in new light through chinks that time has made;
> Stronger by weakness, wiser men become,
> As they draw near to their eternal home.
> Leaving the old, both worlds at once they view,
> That stand upon the threshold of the new.

I

I recall my surprise when, long since, Lyman Abbott said that the ministry was the freest among all the professions. He did not indulge in detailed comparisons. But in our period we can think, for example, of the way in which journalism may be in bondage to its advertisers. It is not easy to condemn the liquor traffic editorially while accepting immense sums for pages that promote the sale of alcoholic beverages. Often educators are subject to the whims of politicians, as recent events testify. Paul Laurence Dunbar's humorous poem describing the way in which two lawyers spoke of the same "prisoner at the bar" indicates that a barrister may wear chains imposed by his client.

My own opinion may have been influenced by my residence in Washington. I have seen among our representatives in Congress many weather-vane tokens. The colossal silence as to liquor conditions is disconcerting. Bills relating to matters likely to cause adverse votes in elections have small chance of escaping from committee pigeonholes. Pitiable efforts are now being made to avoid any record vote with reference to alcohol in our military camps. The next election may make a man a slave. I remember the endeavor of a United States senator to explain his attitude toward the Eighteenth Amendment. In moral embarrassment he fled from one false refuge to another, until at last I said, "You are having a hard time in your own soul, Senator, are you not?" His only reply was a crimson face. He sold his spiritual birthright for a mess of pottage; and then his constituents by overwhelming votes refused to give him the savory senatorial dish.

Yet in over fifty years in the ministry I can recall few cases of coercion. There have been disagreements, with vigorous persuasions following. An endeavor to persecute, by an enchained partisan who threatened to withdraw gifts to church institutions if I did not support Warren G. Harding, utterly failed—as I declined to don the price mark. The intense feeling that came out of the War of 1861-65 led to an attempt to destroy my father's liberty, but the itinerancy opened the door of the prison. Granting freely that the ministry gives a chance for discretion in teaching and consequently for the utterance of folly, I still assert that fifty and five years have shown me few instances of self-respect surrendered because of lay dictation. I have known cases where an autocratic pastor denied any liberty save his own; cases where the speaker of wildness fled to the refuge of so-called freedom; cases where ferocity of spirit made such freedom hard to endure; and cases that lifted claims for near infallibility. Yet a census of the high-minded, conscientious preachers of my long companionship makes a convincing testimony for a free pulpit.

II

I have been impressed with the Christian life as a fellowship. I have elsewhere hinted that old-time church antagonisms have often been overdrawn. There has, of course, been a growth of good feeling. Some of the most lasting friendships are now found among pastors of different denominations. Frequently the preachers of a town make the most fraternal group. John was not writing as a sectarian when he put into his Epistle the words, "We have fellowship."

The connectional government of Methodism has promoted close comradeship. If I were asked what the years have revealed of ministerial jealousy, I would be a poor witness. One who received the best appointment on graduation; came to the pastorate of a wonderful church when he was twenty-nine; was chosen as a college president at thirty-six; and elected as a bishop at forty-one,

305

has had slight chance for jealousy. Even had my nature been an envious one, my circumstances would have conquered my disposition. I have had unspeakable delight in my ministerial associations, and countless joys as I have heard the moving words and seen the splendid services of my fellow pastors and my bishop colleagues. I succeeded Bishop McDowell in two areas, once immediately. I succeeded Bishop John W. Hamilton twice, both times immediately. Bishop Adna Wright Leonard has succeeded me directly both in San Francisco and in Washington. An appraisal of the episcopal quartet involved in these successions will show most distinct individualities. Yet the relations have been amicable and affectionate, never shadowed by a semblance of misunderstanding.

I do believe, however, that Josiah Royce, of Harvard, was right in his contention, in his great book, that "Loyalty" is a proof of character and an asset in life's work. I have ardently loved my country, my state, my Church, my college, my fraternity, my family, and my friends. I plead guilty to being an affectionate partisan. Always I have been puzzled by the people who shed their loyalties as if they were outer wraps. I am assured that in this realm of adherences the world gives back reaction for our action, and regulates its "measure" by what we "mete." I reverently believe that this law applies even in our relation to Christ.

I have been grieved by any breaches of this fellowship. The men who plead for church union, but who practice exclusion, have not been my favorites. Absorption veneered by the polite phrases of union remains absorption. At the conference tables I have felt the presence of a disturbing ghost. Perhaps Oxford and Edinburgh might have enlightened me by a sense of radiant fellowship. But a Communion service in which only men ordained in a certain episcopal way could be the administrators flung before the group the very hindrance that makes union impossible.

I have not enjoyed the contrast between the courteous phrases of address and the conversational scorn of the lobbies, and have wondered whether union would not be promoted by less alleged politeness and by more outright statements. I was glad that the late Dr. William E. Barton, an eminent Congregational minister, refused homage to a presuming ecclesiasticism. His remarks to an English bishop who became dictatorial in a committee are in point. "Perhaps our chairman does not realize that in my country the branch of the Church to which he belongs includes a bare thirtieth of the membership of the entire Church. Possibly his form of address may be acceptable in this country and in the Church to which he belongs, but we are not accustomed to being talked to in that way and we do not propose to stand for it." The incident is recorded by Dr. William Adams Brown, who declares that "thenceforward the meeting proceeded to an amicable conclusion." [1]

Dr. Barton's report to the Congregational Council in 1923 frankly declares that "the High-Church element will not consent to any measure which could be accepted by any other self-respecting and democratic organization"; that the attempt to heal the breach between Congregationalism and Episcopalianism had proved "completely fatuous"; that he and his colleagues could not accept a "denial" of their orders even if the implied denial were made "as delicate and unobtrusive as possible"; and that he could hardly entertain the suggestion that "my children would appear to another more nearly legitimate if I would consent to a supplemental marriage at the hands of a Justice of the Peace." All this was sincere speech—a

[1] *A Teacher and His Times*, p. 360.

307

refusal to allow diplomacy to hide conviction. When the "Jews have no dealings with the Samaritans," the division is not cured by assigning the sacramental power either to Jerusalem or to the mountain. One who fervently rejoices in the broader fellowship of our Christian faith, and who would be disturbed if his own Church should claim a monopolistic rite or sacrament, may still doubt whether a theory of the Church which constantly prevents close association may become the basis of a union for a church without sacerdotal narrowness.

III

Yet I have had an ever-increasing conception of the importance of the Church itself, feeling that the Protestant movement has needed a sturdier ecclesiastical doctrine. There has been a tendency to set the Church of Christ over against the Kingdom of Christ—as if the two were enemies. Sometimes men appear to believe that the way to glorify Christ is to degrade his Church. Other men judge the Church solely by its devotion to their fond specialty, and seek to subject a universal institution to judgment within one limited field. Still other men have made the Church a thoroughly secondary thing, bowing to the whims of governments and rulers. This conception has developed the totalitarian state and has made for persecution. The history of Russia, Bulgaria, Italy, Mexico, Prussia may well raise doubt as to the efficacy of one Church. Without question England has been made spiritually stronger by a splendid non-conformity. In spite of all that is said, in exaggerated form, about the many denominations in the United States, it may be questioned whether any other great land offers on the whole a more efficient Christian life. The closer federation and unity of effort will be an important factor in achieving feasible mergers. I have little hope for the future of the United

308

States apart from the cleansing influence of the Church of Christ. I hail with reverent delight any growth in the numbers and influence and service of those branches of the church upon whose work God has so evidently placed the certificate of his favor. Ministers of the Gospel should carefully avoid utterances that degrade the Church. Good sportsmanship would suggest that its commissioned servants should avoid making it a constant target of attack while making it a constant base of supplies. The singing of Timothy Dwight's hymn, "I love thy Church, O God," should be made one of the emphatic orders of this day.

IV

This vigorous emphasis extends to a broader institutionalism. I have had an increasing solicitude for the corporate bodies that seem to be ordained of God. The state is one of these. A rather sacred logic prevents the religious conception of it from going to an extreme. If it is of God's ordination, it should be finally under his control. I share the anxiety that many feel when pulpits cancel respect for government. There is a spiritual nihilism that involves peril. The statement that our democratic regime has "utterly broken down" is untrue. Even under our faulty system amazing accomplishments have been wrought, and millions of romances have been written. Men who have come from other lands and have gained here wonderful developments have occasionally joined a chorus of despair and have informed our young people that they are a generation without hope. The constructive prophet has his place in every Israel; but he loses his function when he becomes the shrieking accuser of his land. Theodore Roosevelt once said that a Methodist audience was the easiest to address—because it was composed of patriotic people. It would be an inconceivable injustice if we lost that repute because of the utterances of men who keep their books with our country on only one side of the ledger.

Peevish letters received in this war period from laymen have brought a different indictment. Naturally the conscientious objector exhibits his conscience. The figures for the alternate camps change constantly. Yet their variations never fail to show that in The Methodist Church, with its hundreds of thousands of men available for enlistment, the per cent of refusals for combatant service is almost infinitesimal. The statistics can be given only approximately. Even if we were unwilling to give to a Wesleyan's conviction the recognition long given to a Quaker's conviction, it would still be apparent that patriotism among us is in no danger of extinction. I have recently found myself repeating a phrase from the Ten Commandments, "the land which the Lord thy God giveth thee." The duty of all real patriots is to prevent the land from escaping from the august Giver. Long ago the *Saturday Review* of London wrote of the American sense of incongruity—and spoke of Bishop Simpson's sentence, "God could not do without America." Many of us now believe devoutly that the Almighty greatly needs both the United States and the British Empire. We can contest the better for our countries when we relate them in their final life to God.

The like thought applies to the home. Chesterton was right when he declared that the institution of marriage was so sacred as to demand great sacrifices for its preservation. Easy divorce, in his judgment, often represented unwillingness to bear domestic burdens in order that the world might be saved from the disaster of a civil-contract conception of married life. One who does not accept Chesterton's Roman Catholic idea of matrimony may still hold tenaciously to the belief that marriage, as an institution, should, even at great sacrifice, be kept in the sacred realm of religious ordinances. The Methodist Church must ere long frame a law with reference to divorce that saves us from the indefiniteness of our present legislation. If God has set the solitary in families, we should earnestly endeavor to take care of the gem.

Our Christian Sabbath claims that same protection. As an institution it has been of inconceivable benefit. To destroy its sacredness, at the behest of convenience or pleasure, is a vast blunder. Too often our Saviour's word, "The Sabbath was made for man, and not man for the sabbath" is tortured out of its meaning. Man is defined in terms of chemistry; the arguments of flesh then prevail. Our instruction should finish the quotation—"The Son of man is Lord also of the sabbath." That restores the Day's Owner to his calendar rights. It maintains not only the resting place between the weeks of working, but the dominion of the Redeemer over his redemptive Day. My feeling that Voltaire was correct when he affirmed that men must destroy Christianity's Day ere they destroy Christianity's power has given to my preaching a more vigorous emphasis on the sacredness of the Christian Sabbath.

V

My ministry has strengthened the early conviction about the devotion of work itself. When, several years ago, someone asked what was the prevailing sin in ministerial life, my reply was, "Extemporaneousness!" This opinion was not a harsh one. Even maturity may know the doubtful joy of students when a holiday arrives! Many of us do not achieve the power of sustained study. We surrender our habit of reading. False economy tempts us to curtail purchases that feed the intellectual life. We may "uneducate" ourselves in an endeavor to educate our children. This temptation comes in the middle years.

311

The stretched rope sags at the center. There is "a destruction that wasteth at noonday." A return to a Conference with whose personnel one was familiar years ago sometimes compels this question: Why have not the early promises of these men been realized?

The frequent explanation is that industry has departed. Not all of us can adopt Mr. Wesley's saying that he has bade leisure a farewell. Our founder was a denial of the idea that constructive work ceases at sixty. For twenty-eight years beyond that age he read books, made sermons, wrote tracts, traveled widely, and achieved steady gains in influence over the empire and the world. There are many examples to prove that the years beyond seventy may be grandly productive, if men pay the price of producing. The minister has no close overseer; only a cultivated devotion can keep him at his tasks. Henry Drummond's interpretation of the "yoke" and "rest" passage may apply to "work." The yoke that is only half worn is not only a galling thing; it is a weakening thing. The unhappiest men in the ministry are those who have lost the devotion that records itself in toil.

Personally, I was belated in reading biography. One of the important lessons gained in perusing the lives of Christian leaders lies at this point: Paul, Augustine, Luther, Calvin, Wesley, Edwards, Dwight, Muhlenberg, Asbury were toilers. The men who have made the Church of Christ powerful have been for the large part men who wrote, and wrote, and wrote. The Prophecies and the Epistles were pioneers of the literature of the Kingdom. The habit of the pen is not only a taskmaster that commands to industry; it is a guard against carelessness, and the agent of a considered propaganda. I have a tremor when I recall how I almost succumbed to extemporaneousness. My first sermons were laboriously written— and as laboriously committed to memory. Called upon suddenly to speak at a convention, I was compelled either to proceed without definite preparation, or to appear at a disadvantage before a rural audience that had no liking for manuscript. Surprised by the discovery that I seemed to talk more effectively when there was no written page in the background, I soon found myself using a dangerously extempore method. Yet when called upon for larger occasions, I invariably chose one of the sedulously prepared sermons of my earliest ministry.

I quickly saw the point. Back to my desk I hastened. For several years memorizing a manuscript made a frightful toil. But I persisted until the process of printing the penned page on my mind became a virtual absorption. Thus for more than half a century I have trained myself as a writer. When I review the Methodist records I note the products of my pen. In the *Discipline*, I have rewritten the Episcopal Address and the Historical Statement, composed considerable sections of The Plan of Union, and revised slightly The Declaration of Union itself. My own sentences make many sections of legislation, while reams of interpretation and volumes of alleged inspiration greet me in minutes and journals. All this has been due, not at all to any superior mind, but solely to the fact that the pen has educated me, and has given me so many hours of agony and ecstasy.

I have often pushed myself to industry by an ethical motive. I have known the spiritual motive to fail because it became falsely mystical. One of my young ministerial friends declared that reliance upon the toil of the pen indicated a distrust of the Holy Spirit! This leads to the scarcely reverent idea that the divine power may be converted into a labor-saving device. Certainly God is far less likely to bless costless utterances than he is to bless the expensive labors that have been mingled with prayers. There is pressure in the conviction that when we

343

are careless in our preparation we are not good men. Extemporaneousness may spell the loss of character. We are followers of One who said, "I must work."

VI

I have caught signs that some of my ministerial partners were disturbed by an address that I delivered on "Ministerial Balance." It was prepared for the guidance of preachers in the regular pastoral ministry rather than for specialists. I still believe that certain men may with gentle charity be called monomaniacs or duomaniacs. Often their obsession relates to a thing that is good in itself. I have been asked to remove men because they laid undue stress upon worship—in an effort to live up to a new Gothic edifice; because they ferociously overdid preaching on Prohibition; because they used the doctrine of Christian Perfection as a club rather than as a handclasp; because they were like a pastor of whom the committee complained to me, "He has so much to say about the new birth that nobody in our town would consent to be born again."

These are but samples of an unbalanced ministry. The first World War led many to an unsymmetrical work. We well-nigh lost for the Church one generation of young people. In the colossal struggle that now engages the planet our pulpits are wiser. There is more conviction about the righteousness of our cause; but the obsession is less and less angry. More attention is given to spiritual preparation for the world's peace. The Delaware Conference rendered a wonderful service. Inasmuch as at the final tables of negotiation we must deal with some of the stubborn and wicked characters who have deluged the world in a crimson flood, we can foresee that the framing of a peace pleasing to the warlike will be no jaunty work. Since war, save in such instances as our struggle from 1861 to 1865, or in the more recent Spanish tragedy, is between or among nations, American sentiment turns strongly toward an international tribunal endowed with an adequate force. The recent volume prepared jointly by Herbert Hoover and Hugh Gibson has the right conclusion. Our people must not jeer at a League of Nations which we decline to join. Until the parallel of courts that settle disputes among individuals and communities by police powers, when necessary, is followed by the nations, war will be a recurring disaster. The Christian dream is that someday we shall find solutions at the Cross. The problem is how to make the redemptive processes work with those who will not meet the Redeemer at Calvary.

VII

With me there has been a return to features of the Wesleyan movement. It has affected the use of some old-fashioned phrases that were brought into the warm and spontaneous ritual of experience. Robert Collyer, the Methodist who passed over into Unitarianism, was never able to evade the old vocabulary. His parishioners smiled when the white-haired minister fell back upon the spiritual lexicon of his youth. So do we have an "assurance" that grows more assured as we have the longer experience. In a way we surpass logic. The syllogism has its rights, but it is not the final judge. We know a lily and a rose, a stream and a mountain, a blue sky and a golden sunset, because we experience them. We know mathematical formulas by the like test. We come more and more to believe that our spiritual faculties own that same law—we have "the witness in ourselves."

Within the region of character we find a similar credential. Glad that the old controversy between Calvinism and Arminianism does not make turmoil, we still rejoice in Robertson's great sermon, "Obedience the Organ of Spiritual Knowledge." We become aware of our freedom

315

when we break the spell of a wrong determinism by doing things under a recognized moral imperative. We shake our souls loose from evil chains. We discover what free will can do in the inner life, finding in God a power that disposes our dispositions instead of allowing our dispositions to dispose us. We do not yield to Henri Frederic Amiel's confessed weakness, "Because an act is essentially voluntary, therefore I act as little as possible." Freedom becomes joy rather than fear. We no longer plead family traits as an excuse for meanness, or Adam's sin as a wholesale alibi. We adopt Ralph Waldo Emerson's philosophy when he affirmed that our dust is so near to grandeur that the emancipated youth may reply to the voice of duty by saying, "I can." We remove the dogma from the forum of debate and make it a doctrine that moves in the rooms of life. The Christian is saved from the curse of an unaided conceit that boasts, "I can do all things," because he humbly adds, "through Christ which strengtheneth me."

That power of experience bears upon the evangelistic life. It adds intensity to our appeal. The Church is now concerned over its Sunday-school statistics. The downward curve again appalls us. The splendid men who have specialized in "religious education" are chastened by the records. They are being convinced by sad revelations that the young soldier of Christ must be recruited as well as trained. In the other forms of evangelism, too, the ancient phrase comes with its call. Our fathers spoke of "a burden for souls." What genius pushed that piercing thing into our liturgy? Harry Emerson Fosdick was one of the first to point out that liberalism was weakened by the lack of an outstanding passion. If our faith is what we declare it to be—"the power of God unto salvation to every one that believeth"—then it is certain that an unevangelistic Church must become a tragedy. We cannot redeem the world without a Redeemer. If Protestantism lowers her gospel

336

to the level of an abstract ethic, her candlestick will sputter into darkness, and the world will flee to another Altar.

VIII

Near the end of his ministry John Watson, known as Ian Maclaren, said that if he were living his ministry over again he would give his people more consolation. Whatever critics may say about the original documents, the word of Christ in the Nazareth synagogue sounds like him: "He hath sent me to heal the brokenhearted." In these periods of stress I have seen clearly that the Church is the depository of comfort, and the minister its agent. The preacher presides over the one altar to which the sorrowing may flee. His work may not have the skill of the modern psychiatrist, but he is in charge of a Clinic. Grief travels to this door— especially the final grief. Parents and children seldom become so skeptical as to deny themselves the offices of the Church in the funeral hour. Good ministers will testify that their sense of mission is revived when they perceive how imperative are their presence and their work when death invades homes. The Saviour ever waits to seek Mary and Martha when Lazarus dies.

This clamorous world may conceal from us another world. I am disturbed when I hear a preacher indulge in a flippant contrast about being more interested "in good tenements on earth than in many mansions in heavens." Why set in opposition things that belong in one Gospel? It is simply dreadful to drop the eternal motive. A gospel for this world only is a tiny fragment, if Jesus spoke truly. Gibbon was right when he declared that one of the reasons for the spread of our faith was its glorious dogmatism about the eternal life.

I am not willing to have this advocacy discounted because it is urged by one beyond seventy-five years of age. I have no fear of death itself. My long-cherished faith has removed that terror from my heart. Even the prospective grief of parting from beloved children and fond friends has an offset in the prospective joy of meeting again "those who have gone before." They are very many—so many that occasionally I wonder if my native country has not been transferred to a celestial territory!

I accept for myself the anticipated farewells of the believing poets: the "couch" of rest, mentioned by Bryant; the "pilot," foreseen by Tennyson; the waiting "breast" of love, anticipated by Browning; and the "humble door," and the "music of the new and happy song," preheard by Whittier. The list of life's griefs is ample. I have become acquainted with the varied forms of sorrow. Yet these experiences have been transformed into evidences. There is a testimony in them. One hour we speak with those who have never failed us. Their affection held amid all difficulties. Feet never wearied on the errands of love. Hands never ceased their caressing service. Eyes never lost their fond gaze. Be they mothers, fathers, wives, children, they have written dear chapters of sacrifice on our hearts. The next hour there is no reply from them to our word or clasp of endearment. Men may say that what loved us to the end was a chemical compound, or atoms and molecules that automatically flashed into consciousness, or a complex machine whose cogs and wheels assumed a pseudo spirituality and deceived us into the sense of souls. But when the Saviour comes into our midst we catch the word of immortal hope, "Let not your heart be troubled: . . . . I go to prepare a place for you." It is wonderful to believe in a Saviour who has love and power adequate for the making of a heaven.

Thus sitting amid evening shadows that are happy and peaceful, and delighting in the service that God may yet assign, I write this will and testament of my heart.

And I will meet you in the morning.

INDEX

Abbott, Lyman, 164, 211, 304
Abolitionists, 18, 266, 269
Adams, Brooks, 120
Adams, William H., 104
Addresses by the author, significant, 48, 60, 145, 231, 234, 239, 290, 298
Ainsworth, Bishop W. N., 274, 284
Albion, James F., 77
Allen, George W., 31
Allen, Ray, 224
American University, 128, 129
Amiel, Henri Frederic, 316
Anderson, Bishop William F., 192
Anderson, William K., 219
Andover Review, 35, 166
Andover Seminary, 36, 168-69
Andrew, Bishop J. O., 190, 267-68 301
Andrews, Bishop Edward G., 185
Annual Conferences, 190, 230, 266, 285, 286; Baltimore, 267; Central Illinois, 125; Central New York, 37; Delaware, 314; Idaho, 110; Illinois, 125; Indiana, 41, 108; Iowa (now Iowa-Des Moines), 16, 30, 45, 162, 212; Maine, 213; New England, 27, 38, 75, 119, 266; New Hampshire, 41; North-East Ohio, 41; Northwest Indiana, 85; Oregon, 187; Southern Illinois, 124; West Virginia, 16, 30, 134; foreign-speaking, 125
Appointments, pastoral, 193-200. *See also* Bishops; Episcopacy
Arnold, Edwin, 32, 33
Arnold, Matthew, 29
Arthur, Chester A., 136
Asbury, Francis, 6, 20, 51, 106, 107, 120, 126, 131, 187, 218, 234, 235, 291, 293, 312

Augustine, 43, 131, 312
"Aunt Ellen," 56-57
Austin, Cyrus B., 29
Autobiography, reasons for title of this, 1-2; purpose in writing, 3-8 *passim;* character of, 4-5

Bacon, Charles E., 85, 108
Bailey, William M., 83
Bain, Sir A. Ernest, 235
Balzac, Honoré de, 116
Banks, Louis Albert, 120
Baptists, 16, 17, 18, 119, 233
Barnaby, Charles H., 104
Barth, Karl, 44
Bartholow, Otho F., 41
Barton, James O., brother-in-law, 202
Barton, William E., 307
Bashford, Bishop James Whitford, 84, 91, 108, 186, 188
Baumer, Charles, 62
Beach, Bettina (Mrs. Francis M. Hughes), daughter-in-law, 260
Bebout, Gladys (Mrs. Holt Hughes), daughter-in-law, 260
Beecher, Henry Ward, 136, 211
Bennett, Jonathan, great-uncle, 14, 155
Bennett, Lewis, son of Jonathan, 14
Beveridge, A. J., 39, 91, 95, 100, 149
Biblical criticism, 5, 35-38, 163-70
Bickley, Bishop George H., 188
Bieger, Martin V., 87, 88, 104
Birney, Bishop Lauress J., 120
Bishops, Board of, 36, 41, 184, 189, 217, 224, 230, 279; meetings, 190-91; problems, 193-200; revision of Ritual, 219-20
Bishops, Methodist, 183-200; known

319

by author, 184-86; home life of,
187-89. *See also* Episcopacy
Blackstock, Ira Burton, 104
Blaine, James G., 132, 136
Blake, Bishop Edgar, 284
Blakeney, James B., 134
Blanchard, William M., 90, 91, 105
Bolt, Nils, 233
Boreman, Arthur I., 132, 133
Boston: in *1889*, 31; Tremont Temple, 32, 70; Hope Chapel, 40-41,
64-66; Old South Congregational
Church, 41, 64, 66; Chamber of
Commerce, 67; Common, 79-80,
122; Methodist Social Union, 81;
author's episcopal administration
in, 118-22; Home Market Club,
145; Trinity Church, 184
Boston Herald, 142-43
Boston University, 34, 35, 67, 71, 81,
120; School of Theology, 26, 30,
36, 39, 42, 43, 64, 81, 84, 121-22,
165, 233; faculty, 33-38
Bovard, Freeman D., 110, 114
Bowne, Borden P., 42-44, 148, 163-64
Bradford, Gamaliel, 163, 164
Briggs, M. C., 112
Bristol, Bishop Frank M., 186
Brock, Thomas S., 296
Brodbeck, William Nast, 120
Brooks, Phillips, 7, 31, 32, 40, 64, 68,
184, 211, 241, 242
Broomfield, Bishop John C., 278,
282, 283
Brown, H. B., 96
Brown, Bishop Wallace E., 278
Brown, Wilbur V., 90
Brown, William Adams, 225, 307
Brownell, Henry B., 31
Bryan, Elmer L., 95
Bryan, W. F., 296
Bryan, William Jennings, 147-49
Buell, Edith, 34
Buell, Marcus D., 34, 35
Bunin, Ivan, 111
Burchard, Samuel Dickinson, 136
Burgess, William R., 229
Burt, Bishop William, 186
Butler, William, 67

Cadman, S. Parkes, 245-46
320

Caldwell, Adelbert F., 93
Caldwell, Charles, 208
Calhoun, John C., 277
California: Northern, 111, 113, 114,
124; Southern, 113, 114, 124, 202
Campbell, Marvin, 92
Candler, Bishop W. A., 154, 185, 287
Cannon, Bishop James, 287
Cape May Declaration (1876), 272
Carnegie, Andrew, 92, 139
Carnegie Foundation, 96, 98, 139-40
Cartwright, Peter, 267
Catholics, Roman, 78, 133, 142-43,
189-90, 191, 310
Central Jurisdiction, 285
Chadbourne, George S., 134
Chandler, John G., 82, 83
Cherrington, Ernest H., 130, 283
Chester, William F., 82
Chicago, 122-27
Child labor amendment, 176
Children: ideas of religion, 57; the
author's 68, 71, 72, 110, 125, 223,
225, 244-45, 256, 259-62
Christian Advocate: California, 114;
Nashville, 273; Pittsburgh, 271;
Richmond, 268; Southwestern, 281
Christians (denomination), 78
Christie, Arthur C., 129
Church of England, 107, 307
Circus, Robinson, 23
"Cityitis," 126
Clark, Lucius C., 129
Clark, William R., 67
Clarke, William Newton, 33
Clay, Henry, 277
Cleveland, Grover, 136
Coffin, Henry Sloane, 225
Coke, Bishop Thomas, 187, 230, 291,
293
Cokesbury College, 129, 218
College: constituencies of the denominational, 89-90; selection of
teachers, 90; finances, 91; administration, 94, 98; preaching, 99
Collyer, Robert, 315
Conference Courses of Study, 219
Congregationalists, 74-76, 78, 119,
120, 169, 307
Conklin, Clara, 29
Controversies: antislavery, 153-56;

INDEX

"holiness," 157-63; liberalism, 163-70; social relations, 170-82

Converse, Elisha S., 80

Cook, Joseph, 32

Cooke, William P., 72

Coolidge, Calvin, 131, 142-45, 152

Crane, Charles A., 120

Cranston, Bishop Earl, 133, 139, 186, 192, 290, 293, 294

Criticizing, 52

Crook, Robert, 230

Crooks, George R., 6

Crowe, John M., 30

Crummey, D. C., 113

Crummey, John D., 113

Curtis, Olin A., 33, 39, 42

Dana, J. D., 164

Darlington, Bishop U. V. W., 296

Darwin, Charles, 163-64

Davage, Matthew S., 285

Davies, Madeline Baker Sharp, 30

Davies, Sir William Howell, 235

Dean, Charles L., 82

Decell, Bishop J. Lloyd, 283

Degen, Henry D., 72

Delaware Conference, 314

Delta Tau Delta, 30, 151

Deneen, Charles S., 151, 152

Denman, Harry, 287

Denny, Bishop Collins, 274, 275, 287

Denver, University of, 63

De Pauw, Newland T., 104

De Pauw, Washington C., 85-86

De Pauw School, 117

De Pauw University, 84, 103, 108, 139, 149, 150, 151, 184, 204, 261; author as president, 6, 42, 85, 87-94; trustees, 84, 87, 92, 104, 105; finances, 85-86, 87, 91-92; alumni record, 87; students, 87, 93, 101, 109; faculty, 90-91, 93

Dille, Elbert R., 110, 114

Dimmitt, Lewis Fred, 109

Disciples (denomination), 18

Discipline, The, 1, 219, 313

Divorce, 310-11

Dixon, Arthur, 231

Dixon, Edwin C., 41

Dixon, George W., 123

Dixon, William W., 123

Dolliver, Jonathan P., 134-35, 274

Dougherty, Hugh, 104

Douglass, George C., 295

Downey, David G., 219, 230, 274

Doyle, Laura Holt, aunt, 15

Drummond, Henry, 164, 312

Dublin, Ireland, Conference, 229-32

Dunbar, Paul Laurence, 304

Dunham, William H., 126

Dunn, "Father," 196

Durbin, Winfield T., 94, 149

Eaton, George F., 134

Ebbert, Frank Baker, brother-in-law, 178

Ebbert, Dr. and Mrs. Jonathan Baker, parents-in-law, 67, 249

Education, Board of: Indiana State, 94; Methodist, 217-19

Eiselen, Frederick C., 126

Eliot, Charles William, 94, 96-99

Elliott, Charles, 264, 267

Ellis, Thomas D., 275, 284, 286

Emerson, Ralph Waldo, 316

England: Methodist Conference at Leeds (1930), 225, 232, 235-47; fraternal relations with, 238-44; author's address, excerpts, 239-42

Enyart, Arthur D., 34

Episcopacy, Methodist, 106-31, 183-200; character of, 106-7, 183, 192; election of author to, 108, 209; unity, 190; administrative problems, 193-200. *See also* Bishops

Episcopal Address, 171-73, 221

Episcopalians, 119, 184, 224, 307

Estes, Lud M., 287

Evangelism, importance of, 175. *See also* Preaching, evangelistic

Evolution, 148, 163-64

Ewart Circuit, Iowa, 208, 213

Experience, witness of, 315-17

Fairbanks, Charles W., 150, 274

Fall River, Mass., Union Church, 121

Fellowship, Christian life as a, 305

Fifer, Orien W., 247, 296

Finland, Conference, 225-26, 233

Fisher, Bishop Frederick B., 188

Fitzgerald, Bishop James N., 187

321

INDEX

Hoss, Bishop E. E., 185, 273

Howe, Julia Ward, 78

Howe, Samuel G., 78

Hughes, derivation of name, 19

Hughes, Anna Louise (Mrs. Mayo H. Soley), daughter, 225, 244-45, 259, 260-62

Hughes, Blakeney, nephew, 214

Hughes, Caroline Robinson (Mrs. Walter Simpson Harban), daughter, 225, 244-45, 259, 260

Hughes, Ebbert Magee, son, 109, 259, 260

Hughes, Edwin Holt: call to the ministry, 1-2; use of ritual, 1, 122, 124; loyalty to early convictions, 2, 4, 5, 306; career a succession of surprises, 5-6; why this autobiography, 6-10; family background, 11-24, 232, 265, 292; boyhood recollections, 11-12, 15, 16, 18, 20, 22, 23, 24, 177, 201, 204, 205, 215, 232, 265, 271, 292; birth, 22; contacts with famous men, 42-44, 96-99, 100-3, 132-52, 184-86; first sermon, 45, 47-48; first pastoral appointment, 5, 48-62; marriage, 67, 249; children, 68, 71, 72, 110, 125, 223, 225, 244-45, 256, 259-62; death of first child, 68, 259; educational service to Indiana, 89, 93, 94, 95; as college preacher, 96, 99-100; as lecturer, 99-100; addresses Commonwealth Club, San Francisco, 112-13; addresses Home Market Club, Boston, 145; controversial issues, 153-82; anniversary letter to Bishop McConnell, 180-82; brothers and sisters, 201-16; elected bishop, 107-8, 209-10; revision of Ritual and Hymnal, 219-20; in European war camps (1917-19), 221-22; holds Conferences in Norway and Finland, 225-28, 233; fraternal delegate to Irish and English Conferences, 225, 229-47; poem to Mrs. Hughes, 252; grandchildren, 260, 262; contribution to Unification, 263-302; reflections, 303-18

————, Education: early schooling, 25; West Virginia University, 26; Ohio Wesleyan, 26-30, 39; Grinnell, 29; Boston University School of Theology, 30; meeting expenses, 30, 31, 46, 66; seminary years, 30-44, 64-66, 249; graduate study, 42-44

————, Pastorates: Madison, Iowa, 5, 48-62; Marengo, Iowa, 62; Tiffin, Ohio, 63; Hope Chapel, Boston, 40-41, 64-66; Newton Centre, Mass., 66-73; Malden, Mass., Centre Church, 73-83

————, College administration: DePauw University, election as president, 6, 85; inauguration, 42, 91; problems and achievements, 88-94; Boston University, 35; American University, 129

————, Episcopacy: attitude toward, 108; elected bishop, 108, 209; service in San Francisco, 109-18; in Boston, 118-22; in Chicago, 122-27; in Washington, 127-31; retirement, 197

————, Foremost activities: education, 88-94, 217-19; evangelism, 175, 316; Methodist union, 263-302; social reforms, 173, 176, 177-79, 223, 304

Hughes, Effa (Mrs. James O. Barton), sister, 202-3

Hughes, Elizabeth, great-grandmother, 11

Hughes, Esther, niece, 214

Hughes, Francis Montgomery, son, 225, 244-45, 259, 260, 262

Hughes, Francis Tincher, grandfather, 11-12, 18

Hughes, Harriet Wheeler (Mrs. Matthew S.), sister-in-law, 214

Hughes, Holt, son, 109, 259, 260, 262; *Croix de Guerre*, 223, 258; ordination, 253, 254-58

Hughes, Hugh Price, 173

Hughes, Isabel (Mrs. William H. Remy), daughter, 259, 260

Hughes, Isabel Ebbert, wife, 67, 109, 223, 225, 226, 229, 235, 237, 238, 244, 245, 248-59, 262; memo-